Diary Fiction

WRITING AS ACTION

Diary Fiction

WRITING AS ACTION

H. Porter Abbott

Cornell University Press

ITHACA AND LONDON

First published 1984 by Cornell University Press.
Published in the United Kingdom by
Cornell University Press Ltd., London.

International Standard Book Number 0-8014-1713-9
Library of Congress Catalog Card Number 84-7111
Printed in the United States of America
*Librarians: Library of Congress cataloging information
appears on the last page of the book.*

*The paper in this book is acid-free and meets the guidelines
for permanence and durability of the Committee on Production
Guidelines for Book Longevity of the Council on Library Resources.*

FOR MY FATHER AND MOTHER,
HORACE AND BARBARA ABBOTT

Contents

Preface   9

1. Functions of the Diary Strategy   15
   The Diary Novel/Diary Fiction
   Mimetic Functions: The Illusion of the Real
   Thematic Functions: Isolation and Self-Reflection
   Temporal Functions: Immediacy, Suspense, and Timelessness

2. The Special Reflexive Function of the Diary Strategy   38

3. The Expressive Text and Textual Self-Concealment   55
   Goethe and Werther
   Lermontov's *A Hero of Our Time*

4. Textual Rescue: The *Portuguese Letters*   72

5. Textual Healing   83
   Richardson and the Puritan Diary
   The Organic Elegy: Tennyson's Verse Diary

6. Textual Madness: *The Golden Notebook*   107

7. Textual Salvation   125
   Bernanos's *Diary of a Country Priest*
   Mauriac's *Vipers' Tangle*

8. Toward the Textual Object: Sartre's *Nausea*   137

9. The Writer's Laboratory: Saul Bellow and the Return to Character   158

10. The Writer's Laboratory: Samuel Beckett and the Death of the Book   183

A Bibliography of Diary Fiction   207
Index   223

I would like to note here Heine's remark to the effect that sincere autobiographies are almost impossible and that a man is bound to lie about himself. In his view, Rousseau must have lied about himself deliberately and out of sheer vanity in his *Confessions*. I'm sure Heine is right. I realize that it is sometimes possible to pin full-fledged crimes on ourselves out of vanity. I can see that, all right. But Heine was passing judgment on a man confessing publicly. Now, in my case, I'm writing this just for myself, for even if I do address myself to imaginary readers, I do it only because it makes it easier for me to write. It's just a matter of form, nothing else, for as I said before, I'll never have any readers.

I don't want to let considerations of literary composition get in my way. I won't bother with planning and arranging; I'll note down whatever comes to my mind.

Now, of course, you may feel you've caught me and ask me why, if I really don't expect to have any readers, I bother to record all these explanations about writing without a plan, jotting down whatever comes to mind, and so on. What's the point of all these excuses and apologies then?

My answer is—well, that's the way it is.

—Dostoevsky, *Notes from Underground*

Preface

Roy Pascal argued that writing the story of one's life is itself an act in that story "and like every significant new act it alters in some degree the shape of [one's] life, it leaves [one] different."[1] Whether Pascal is right that such an act necessarily alters the writer, rather than, say, confirming the writer in his or her ways, his fundamental insight is correct. It would seem, moreover, that any writing in the first person (not simply the writing of one's life) is action of the kind Pascal describes, action that exerts an influence on the writer. The unique advantage of fiction in the diary mode is its capacity to expose this ordinarily unnoticed reflexive action by giving the writing itself a role in the plot. So important is this phenomenon, for the study of both narrative and the representation of the self, that I have devoted to it the central chapters of this book (2 through 8). They follow a general survey of diary fiction in Chapter 1 and precede two final chapters in which the book's principal concern is extended to the reflexive advantages of diary fiction for the developing artist—specifically, for Saul Bellow and Samuel Beckett.

Diary fiction, as I use the term, includes single-writer epistolary fiction, and since (as the Underground Man would point out) letters are not the same thing as diaries, I should defend my conjoining of them before the reader gets under way. Technically, letters require an *addressee* and a diary does not. The genuineness of the diary, as a record of inner life, has often been pegged to the absence

[1]Roy Pascal, *Design and Truth in Autobiography* (Cambridge: Harvard University Press, 1960), 183.

9

of an addressee. Diarists are supposed to write only for themselves; they have no one to impress, no one to perform for, and thus can be quite simply themselves. But the existence or nonexistence of an addressee is an issue that can quickly become more academic than real. For example, if a fictive diary is addressed to someone, as Eveline's is in André Gide's *School for Wives*, is it disqualified as a genuine diary novel? If it is, then are novels disqualified in which the diarist addresses her remarks to a reader she has made up, as is not uncommon? There is really no end to this. Fictive diarists commonly address their remarks to someone—friend, lover, God, the diary itself. Even the hackneyed commonplace "the diarist writes only for himself" contains the glimmering of an addressee in that self objectified sufficiently to be written for.

This is just one more reason why the study of diary fiction has for so long been an appendage to the study of the epistolary novel. The letter strategy and the diary strategy are so similar that what can be said analytically about the one is frequently transferable to the other. Such transference is abundantly observable in three excellent analytical studies of the epistolary mode in fiction: the third chapter of Jean Rousset's *Forme et signification* (1964), the second chapter of François Jost's *Essais de littérature comparée, II* (1968), and, most recently, Janet Gurkin Altman's *Epistolarity* (1982). Conversely, in the only book (as of this writing) on diary fiction, Valerie Raoul's *The French Fictional Journal* (1980), one can find insights applicable to epistolary fiction. Raoul defines her subject by concentrating on the complex relations between the codes of the journal and those of fiction, but in the process she makes a number of points that carry over intact to the field of fiction cast in letters. This same interchangeability will also be quite clear in my own general remarks in Chapter 1 on the functions of the diary strategy.

The difference, then, between a study of epistolary fiction and a study of diary fiction derives not from a strict semantic distinction, "letter" versus "diary," but from a difference in focus or emphasis. The crucial issue is not the existence or nonexistence of an addressee but the degree to which the addressee is given an independent life and an active textual role in the work. After a certain point the illusion of a hermetic seal is broken, and we have a *Briefwechselroman*, or correspondence novel. This is the true countercategory to diary fiction: a book that features a drama of literary exchange, the interplay of independent texts and intelligences. In contrast, the role of William, the addressee of *The Sorrows of Young Werther*, is not substantially different from that of the silent friend, real or invented, whom fictive diarists frequently address. As he is unchanging, represented for us entirely through Werther's words, he is easily conceived as Werther's other self, the solid rational self that Werther seeks to override. In this light, he is much like those imaginary rational "gentlemen" the Underground Man would address in his notes almost a century later.

The term "diary" evokes an intensity of privacy, cloistering, isolation, that the term "letter" does not. From our point of view, the strategic decision that the author makes is not the decision to have periodic entries in letter form or in diary form, but the decision to create cumulatively the effect of a consciousness thrown back on its own resources, abetted only by its pen. This effect is enabled by a proportional suppression of other writing, writing by narrators or correspondents. Cloistering both the writer and the text in this way creates the conditions for the kind of reflexive drama that is the main burden of this volume.

In writing this book, I owe most to my students at the University of California, Santa Barbara, who have helped me sharpen my ideas over the years it has taken to set them down, not to mention that inestimable period of time in which we pursued those ideas together simply as a pleasure. I am also glad to acknowledge the efforts of two keen and indefatigable research librarians, Betty Gadol and Lieselotte Fajardo, as well as the entire staff of the UCSB Library's Interlibrary Loan Office, who cheerfully processed my requests week after week for several years. A place of honor, too, belongs to two of the world's great typists, Louisa Dennis and Kristina Nash, who prepared successive versions of the manuscript. To the Academic Senate of the University of California, Santa Barbara, go thanks for a General Research Grant to help in conducting computer searches and preparing the manuscript. And to those who read the manuscript in whole or in part, who criticized and encouraged, my warm gratitude: David Gordon, Anita Abbott, Stuart Atkins, Edgar Bowers, David Cooper, Ruth Haber, Vivian Mercier, Leonard Michaels, Jon Pearce, and Everett Zimmerman. As in all endeavors of this kind, there are more people to thank than I can name, but I would like, finally, to take special notice of that first reader for Cornell University Press whose ability to see my project at once from the inside and the outside contributed much to its final shape.

Parts of Chapters 3, 4, 5, 7, and 8 have been revised from my article "Letters to the Self," *PMLA* 95 (January 1980), by permission of the Modern Language Association of America. A version of Chapter 1 appeared as "Diary Fiction" in *Orbis Litterarum* 37 (1982), copyright © 1982 by Munksgaard International Publishers Ltd., Copenhagen, Denmark, and a version of Chapter 9 appeared as "Saul Bellow and the 'Lost Cause' of Character" in *Novel: A Forum on Fiction* 13 (Spring 1980); both are used by permission of the publishers. Part of Chapter 10 has been revised from my article "A Grammar for Being Elsewhere" in *Journal of Modern Literature* 6 (February 1977) and is used by permission. Another part of Chapter 10 has been revised from my chapter "The Harpooned Notebook: *Malone Dies* and the Conventions of Intercalated Narrative" in *Samuel Beckett: Humanistic Perspectives*, edited by Morris Beja, S. E. Gontarski, and Pierre Astier, copyright © 1983 by Ohio State University Press, all rights reserved; I am grateful to the editors and publishers for permission to use these materials.

H. Porter Abbott

Santa Barbara, California

Diary Fiction

WRITING AS ACTION

1

Functions of the
Diary Strategy

The Diary Novel/Diary Fiction

For the sake of clarity, we can make a distinction between the diary novel and diary fiction: the former is a genre, or literary kind; the latter is fiction cast in diary form. The genre then, is the subset: all diary novels are diary fiction, but not all works of diary fiction are diary novels. The diary novel requires a loose confederation of repeatable elements that accompany the device of the diary; diary fiction requires simply the device itself. The diary novel has been around long enough and makes up a high enough percentage of diary fiction for it to be recognizable. Its collection of expectations has become a generic language that an author can use and a critic describe. Its parts can be marshaled under four headings of fictive equipment: the setting, the action, the writer, and the writing.

The setting: where is the diarist? In the male version (the version most frequently imitated) he is seated at a desk. On the desk there is ink, pen, and paper. The desk is in a room. The room contains at least two things: a window with a view and a mirror. It is a shabby room in a shabby house. The house is in a city.

The action: what does the diarist do? He writes. He paces the room. He gazes out of the window and meditates upon those passing below. At least once in the course of his entries, he looks in the mirror and describes what he sees there. He walks the city streets. He falls in love, or fails to. He falls ill. There is a good chance he will die. If he dies, there is a good chance he will die by his own hand.

The writer: what is he like? He is intelligent. He is sensitive. He is acutely introverted and self-conscious. He is alienated. He has no gift for social life. He is either in love or obsessed with the fact that he is not. He is poor. He is powerless. He is young, in his twenties or early thirties. He is alone. He is prone to melodrama. He is doomed.

The writing: how does the diarist write? Intermittently. His style is unregulated. It ranges from the purple to the colloquial. It is marked by false starts and abrupt stops, by blanks, and by logorrhea. It speaks in the present of present emotions. It is as self-conscious as its author, anxiously reflecting upon the words by which it manifests itself.

In the female version, the major differences are that the writer is usually married; she is oppressed by the indifference, the insensitivity, or the love of her husband (or lover); she is a victim of the stereotyping imposed on her by virtue of her gender; her powerlessness is a function of her social condition as a woman; her sense of identity is more tenuous; she is less melodramatic.

There is, of course, no fixed necessity for any one of these elements. Their ratio and coloration vary according to historical period and geographical location. Before 1830, the male diarist tends to be more passionate; after 1830, more cerebral. The understated despair of the Scandinavian male diarist contrasts with his frenetic and impulsive Russian counterpart. Finer details could be added to the inventory above (the diary is found and read by someone else, it is damaged, the diarist falls asleep on it, a page is torn out), but what I have isolated is by and large the diary novel.

Among the handful of studies on diary fiction to date, there is a general tendency to treat the subject generically—to seek the contours of the diary novel.[1] These studies are good, and few are

---

[1]Studies specifically concerned with the question of genre are H. Porter Abbott, "Diary Fiction," *Orbis Litterarum* 37(1982), 12–31; Lyn Barstis, "The Modern Diary Novel: Heir of the Journal Intime" (Ph.D. diss., University of Illinois, 1974); Juliet Kincaid, "The Novel as Journal: A Generic Study" (Ph.D. diss.,Ohio State University, 1977); Lorna Martens, "The Diary Novel and Contemporary Fiction: Studies in Max Frisch, Michel Butor, and Doris Lessing" (Ph.D. diss., Yale University, 1976); Gerald Prince, "The Diary Novel: Notes for the Definition of a Sub-Genre," *Neophilologus* 59 (Oct. 1975), 477–481; and Valerie Raoul, *The French Fictional Journal: Fictional Narcissism/Narcissistic Fiction* (Toronto: University of Toronto Press, 1980). Other studes of diary fiction or the use of the diary in fiction are H. Porter Abbott, "Letters to the Self: The Cloistered Writer in Nonretrospective Fiction," *PMLA* 95

as conventional in their conception of genre as I have just been. But what I wish to do in this book is to put the whole question of the diary novel on a subsidiary plane and turn to the broader field of diary fiction. To conceive our subject in this way is to redirect attention to a presentational strategy rather than to a repeatable constellation of literary elements or to a single necessary function or buried speech act. It is to stress the diversity of effect available to a device. It is to recognize that the diary strategy—or more precisely, the strategy of casting one's fiction as a nonretrospective document authored by a single fictive agent—is historically coextensive with the novel (a "genre" that is itself something of a categorical embarrassment). It is to allow us to see the diary as an author, planning a work, may well be able to see it: that is, as exploitable equipment that may be adopted to serve one or several functions (witness, for example, the variety in the work of Gide alone). It is to allow us, finally, to obviate the common (though not inevitable) weakness of genre study, its tendency to elevate the general, or generalizable, over the discrete: to endow genre with a purely abstract existence, a life of its own at the expense of the original and distinctive effects of particular art.

The importance of the diary novel is not at all at dispute. In this century, the male version of the genre has become so recognizable as to be easily parodied. Sartre, Bellow, and Beckett all made the diary novel serve their originality. Later in this book, when I discuss

---

(Jan. 1980), 23–41; Peter Brang, "Uber die Tagebuchfiktion in der russischen Literatur," in *Typologia Litterarum, Festschrift für Max Wehrli* ed. Stefan Sonderegger, Alois M. Haas, Harald Burger (Zurich: Atlantis, 1969), 443–466; Dorrit Cohn, *Transparent Minds: Narrative Modes for Presenting Consciousness in Fiction* (Princeton: Princeton University Press, 1978), 208–216; James P. Pusack, *German Monologic Fiction in the Eighteenth Century* (Ph.D. diss., Indiana University, 1977); Bertil Romberg, *Studies in the Narrative Technique of the First-Person Novel* (Stockholm: Almqvist and Wilsell, 1962), 43–46; and Jean Rousset, "La monodie épistolaire: Crébillon fils," *Etudes littéraires* (1968), 167–174. One can also find pertinent remarks on the subject in Janet Gurkin Altman, *Epistolarity: Approaches to a Form* (Columbus: Ohio State University Press, 1982); Maurice Blanchot, "Recherches sur le journal intime," *La nouvelle nouvelle revue française* 3 (1955), 683–691; Gérard Genette, "Discours du récit," *Figures III* (Paris: Editions du Seuil, 1972), 67–267, trans. Jane E. Lewin, *Narrative Discourse: An Essay in Method* (Ithaca: Cornell University Press, 1980); Edith Kern, *Existential Thought and Fictional Technique: Kierkegaard, Sartre, Beckett* (New Haven: Yale University Press, 1970); Fritz Neubert, "Zur Problematik der französischen Journaux Intimes," *Neuere Sprachen* 6 (1956), 318–394; Jean Rousset, "Une forme littéraire: Le roman par lettres," in his *Forme et signification: Essais sur les structures littéraires de Corneille à Claudel* (Paris: Librairie José Corti, 1964), 65–103.

these three authors, I shall return to the diary novel and make it a secondary theme, but the principal focus throughout will be the diary's potential as a literary strategy. In this chapter, I shall lay out diary fiction as a field. I have chosen to organize the field not historically but according to the three functional capacities—mimetic, thematic, and temporal—that distinguish the diary as a literary document. This approach will permit me to demonstrate, along the way, an irreducible diversity of effect, not only through the differences of these functions but within the functions themselves.

Mimetic Functions: The Illusion of the Real

From the start, the diary method of narration has been functionally linked to that collection of conventions that Ian Watt called "formal realism."[2] Like the devices of letters, "true narratives," and confessions, the diary was, in the eighteenth century, employed to give the illusion of a literary found object, something that people write but that is not supposed to be art. Although the first complete novel cast in the form of a diary did not appear until 1777 (*Chant de Schwarzbourg ou, les aventures du jeune d'Olban* by Ramond de Charbonnière)[3], it was common practice before that to interject diaries or fragments of diaries into the narrative to augment the sense of interior reality. Well before 1777 we can also find the letter-journal strategy, or "échange unilatéral,"[4] notably in the work of Crébillon fils and Mme Riccoboni (*Pamela* qualifies), which is so close in effect to the diary strategy that we can safely consider it a version of the same thing.[5] In purporting to give the truth of a real, not an invented, consciousness, the diary strategy favors a conception of the real as the artless, and thus in a familiar paradox

---

[2]Ian Watt, *The Rise of the Novel* (Berkeley: University of California Press, 1962), 32–34.

[3]In most studies this is the consistently cited first instance; however, the anonymous *Pamela in High Life, or Virtue Rewarded* (London: Mary Kingman, 1741), though addressed as a letter to her parents, is technically a daily journal, referred to as such by Pamela, and kept faithfully from the beginning of her novel to the end. Four-fifths of the original *Pamela* (1740) and two-thirds of Mrs. Francis Sheridan's *Memoirs of Miss Sidney Biddulph* (1761) similarly qualify as "letter journals."

[4]Rousset, *Forme et signification*, 78.

[5]For my defense of this procedure see the Preface.

it has become a formal attribute of the absence of form. Belford, Richardson's fictive editorial agent in *Clarissa*, stresses this virtue of the form: Clarissa is, he says, "writing of and in the midst of *present* distresses! How *much more* lively and affecting, for that reason, must her style be, her mind tortured by the pangs of uncertainty (the events then hidden in the womb of fate), *than* the dry narrative, unanimated style of a person relating difficulties and dangers surmounted; the relater perfectly at ease; and if himself unmoved by his own story, not likely greatly to affect the reader."[6]

In the preface to his fictive letter journal, Sénancour adjures us to regard his book not as a work ("ouvrage") but as "the feelings, the opinions, the unfettered and inaccurate dreams of a man often alone, who wrote in private and not for his bookseller."[7] One hundred and twenty years later, Gide's Eveline in *School for Wives* establishes the same kind of contract when she narrates even those things about which "I should keep silent had I not promised myself to be sincere in these pages."[8]

It is important to stress, however, that the sense of reality that the diary can foster is of two kinds. The artless spontaneity of the internal, nonretrospective record is one. The other is the document itself, which, as a *document*, claims to be real. In other words, this is the sort of document that people who are not professional writers actually write. As such, it is a kind of realistic absolute or terminal point. For, though novelists have gone beyond the diary strategy in their efforts to portray the reality of internal shapelessness, they have done so by employing narrative devices—monologue, interior monologue—that are necessarily fictive.

The illusion of reality in the document itself has been attended over the years by at least two recurrent details (minor components of the genre of the diary novel) that are basically the exigencies of a strategy, the means of buttressing the illusion of the real. One of these details is the reason invoked to account for the diary's publication. Frequently the convention employed is the "editor's note"

[6]Samuel Richardson, *Clarissa, or the History of a Young Lady* (1747–1748; reprint, London: Dent, 1932), 4:81.
[7]Etienne Pivert de Sénancour, *Obermann*, ed. G. Michaut (Paris: Droz, 1931), 1:i,v, my translation.
[8]André Gide, *School for Wives, Robert, Geneviève*, trans. Dorothy Bussy (New York: Knopf, 1950), 80.

that explains with greater or less plausibility why so private a document would have wound up in the hands of the public. The editor refers to the diarist's untimely passing, to the discovery of these pages in a desk drawer or in a briefcase in an attic. They are published in the hope that they may clear up some confusion about the deceased, now perhaps famous. Or they are published because the editor discovers in them an importance and literary value of which the diarist, it is emphasized, was not aware. In short, we are encouraged to stifle whatever minimal suspicion we may have had that what we are about to read was designed for a public. In Mikhail Lermontov's *A Hero of Our Time*, the editor of Pechorin's diary stresses the superiority of that document to Rousseau's *Confessions*, which had been read to several intimates before being committed to the public. Such concern accounts for the inordinate frequency of the boring entry—the entry that has nothing to do with anything, a pure irrelevancy that would never find its way into a work of art.

The other essential recurrent detail is the account of why the diary exists in the first place. This detail is generally left to the diarist himself, who relates somewhere in the course of his entries the reasons for making them. Again, the comment is designed in part to disavow the artistic, or public, intention, and as such it requires delicate handling. By asserting too emphatically that he writes simply for himself he appears to protest too much. Therefore, at times some other job is found for which the diary is a necessary tool. The diarist of *The Red Rock Wilderness*, for example, is at work on a biography: "I hadn't intended for anyone to see it [the diary]. I wrote it for the record, and to help me with Clausen's biography, and for practice putting words on paper."[9] Another expedient is simply to have the keeping of the diary part of the rules. The diarist is in jail (Maxim Gorky, "Karamora"; Max Frisch, *I'm Not Stiller*) or taking a rest-cure (John Updike, *A Month of Sundays*); he is given paper and asked to fill it, either for legal or therapeutic reasons.[10]

Such a recurrent problem, which is susceptible to so many dif-

---

[9]Elspeth Huxley, *The Red Rock Wilderness* (London: Chatto and Windus, 1957), 205.

[10]In Beckett's *Molloy* (technically not diary fiction) this convention is pointedly absent. In this way, Beckett expresses the gratuitousness of the text and the mysterious compulsion to write that the author shares with his creature.

ferent solutions, is also subject to a fine modulation of mimetic ends. It is interesting, for example, to note how a detail like this, which arose primarily in response to a demand for *sincerity* in the diarist, was modified to meet an increasing interest in the *authenticity* (to draw on the distinction argued by Lionel Trilling[11]) of the text as an expression of the diarist's character. The following, for example, seems innocent enough: "I scarcely know why I should have written all this, except that the history of things interests me, and I find it is even a greater pleasure to write it than to read it." Yet in the context of the Henry James story in which it occurs ("The Impressions of a Cousin"),[12] its casualness is too pointed. Disclaiming motives in such a way and in such a fictive world makes the motive for writing the diary of special importance. If Catherine Condit believes she is merely writing "the history of things," we know that it is a history in which she becomes steadily more involved. That there may be a motive controlling this document, cutting into its factual accuracy, of which the fictive writer has little conscious understanding becomes one of the central interests of the document. As readers, we no longer ask our diarist to give a wholly sincere account of her feelings. We ask instead that we be allowed to see the truth of those feelings through the mixture of sincerity and self-deception that governs her text. It is this readiness in the modern reader to find layers of that sort that makes Gide's heroine in *School for Wives* appear so charmingly anachronistic when she makes her resolution to tell all.

Thus, though the illusion of genuine revelation has stuck with the diary form, it has done so in part by a ready adaptation of conventions designed for the expression of a different version of the real. As is often the case with an evolving fictional strategy, the range of adaptation has been wide. Max Frisch, for example, takes James's layering to the point of featuring a patently dishonest diarist. In *I'm Not Stiller*, Stiller flatly declares that he is not Stiller and fills his diary with rich fabrications of a life he never lived. But the lies he tells are expressive in many ways and in none so much as in the urgency they reveal of the diarist's desire to escape himself.

[11]Lionel Trilling, *Sincerity and Authenticity* (Cambridge: Harvard University Press, 1972).
[12]*The Complete Tales of Henry James*, ed. Leon Edel (London: Hart-Davis, 1963), 5:179.

Functions of the Diary Strategy

When Humbert Humbert includes excerpts from his diary to bring us in close to the early day-to-day experience of Lolita, he introduces another form of sabotage, though the effect is somewhat similar. Before he sets the entries in front of us, Humbert deliberately essays to destroy precisely the illusion the diary is supposed to create:

> Exhibit number two is a pocket diary bound in black imitation leather, with a golden year, 1947, *en escalier*, in its upper left-hand corner. I speak of this neat product of the Blank Blank Co., Blankton, Mass., as if it were really before me. Actually, it was destroyed five years ago and what we examine now (by courtesy of a photographic memory) is but its brief materialization, a puny unfledged phoenix.[13]

The effect of such apparent "play" is the revelation of authentic emotional depth. Humbert's effort to turn the whole business into a game, to give the illusion of freedom by mocking the conventions of formal realism, itself expresses what a slave he is to memory and desire. Yet, because Stiller and Humbert are basically sane, and thus consciously manipulating their texts, it is possible to argue that such accounts derive their effect from our double awareness of the account itself and what we know would be a "sincere" rendering. But take one more step and we are in the record of a mad diarist where, because of his mental disjunction from himself, sincerity becomes an irrelevancy, and we are immersed in a realm of pure emotive authenticity: "This is a day of great jubilation. Spain has a king. They've found him. *I* am the king."[14]

Another, qualitatively different, departure from sincerity can be found in "Quidam's Diary," the first two-thirds of Kierkegaard's *Guilty/Not Guilty*. In his "Advertisement" for the work, Frater Taciturnus describes how the diary was found in a steel box recovered from the bottom of a lake. He had accompanied a naturalist one day, a specialist in submarine plants who was pulling specimens out of the lake with an apparatus. Frater Taciturnus, trying his hand at it, snags the box:

[13]Vladimir Nabokov, *Lolita* (New York: Berkeley, 1966), 39–40.
[14]Nikolai Gogol, *The Diary of a Madman*, trans. Andrew MacAndrew (New York: Signet, 1960), 21. For other examples, see Maupassant's "A Madman" and "The Horla," Paul Bowles's "If I Should Open My Mouth," Charlotte Perkins Gilman's "The Yellow Wallpaper," and Elaine Kraf's *The Princess of 72nd Street*.

When I wanted to pull it up I encountered so much resistance that I was almost afraid of proving the weaker of the two. I pulled again, then up rose a bubble from the depths, it lasted an instant, then burst— and then I succeeded. I had the strangest feeling, and yet I did not have the remotest notion what sort of a find it was I had made. Now when I reflect upon it I know all. I understand it, I understand that it was a sigh from below, a sigh *de profundis*, . . . a sigh from the shy and secluded lake from which I had wrested its secret.[15]

This passage is playfully emblematic. Kierkegaard uses a standard convention of formal realism to establish his work's status as invented art. In so doing he does not completely undermine the realistic immediacy that he clearly wanted to generate by his use of the diary form; but by establishing at the start the diary's fictitious existence, he encourages a distance appropriate to this fragment of a larger philosophical project. The same sort of adjustment of our response—though with differences both in means and effect— was achieved much more recently (1950) by Martin A. Hansen, also a Dane and in many ways influenced by Kierkegaard. In Hansen's diary novel—significantly entitled *The Liar (Lögneren)*—the diarist, Johannes Vig (rhymes with *svig*, that is, "fraud"), confesses in the last pages that the whole notebook was composed, with the exception of the first entry, a year after the events described. Vig tells us that he engaged in the deception, "to make it real for you, to give it vitality."[16] But by choosing to confess this, at a stroke he reduces the work's "reality." So again, as in Kierkegaard, the author "tunes" our response to his work. The difference is that in this case it is the fictive diarist himself who exposes his deception, not, as in Kierkegaard, an editor (who is himself obviously specious). In Hansen's work, then, both the deception and the decision to confess it are part of the characterization of the diarist himself.

This should give some indication not only of the constant association of realistic ends with the diary in fiction but also of the variety of individually distinctive effect with which authors have adapted this association to their own purposes.

[15]Sören Kierkegaard, *Stages on Life's Way*, trans. Walter Lowrie (Princeton: Princeton University Press, 1945), 182.

[16]Martin A. Hansen, *The Liar*, trans. John Jepson Egglishaw (New York: Twayne, 1969), 193.

Thematic Functions: Isolation and Self-Reflection

One of the great expressive advantages of the diary lies in its confinement of the reader to the internal world of a single ego. The diarist is preeminently alone. This confinement, or the sense of it, is immediately reduced with the intrusion of a participant addressee as in correspondence fiction. In diary fiction, one is encouraged by the form itself to let go of the perspective of the other. We are restricted to a document that emanates from *inside* the story. We sit at and read what the diarist describes himself as sitting at, writing, and often, as we are, reading himself. Again, I speak not of an inevitable effect of the form, but of an available one—an effect, moreover, that can be made a part of the explicit thematic content of the fiction by the simple expedient of having the diarist speak of it.

The principal convention that has evolved to buttress the theme of isolation in diary fiction is, quite simply, the room in which the diarist writes. There is, of course, a certain practical inevitability involved here. Diaries are commonly composed in rooms. To the extent that they are composed elsewhere, a strain can be placed on the illusion of reality. The room is the natural place. Thus, the expressive quality of the room emerges only through the diarist's references to it. What it looks like and where it is can be employed to compound or qualify the writer's isolation. In *A Month of Sundays*, for example, John Updike triply seals the Reverend Marshfield in a room, in a sanatorium, and in the middle of Arizona. Martin A. Hansen effects another triple seal by locating his diarist's room in an isolated house on a little island that is icebound through most of the narrative. As for the prison cell (Victor Hugo, *Last Day of a Condemned Man*; Gorky, "Karamora"; Frisch, *I'm Not Stiller*; Jarl Hemmer, *A Man and His Conscience*), its expressive effect would appear hard to avoid. *Robinson Crusoe*, among nineteenth-century fictional diarists especially, is almost required reading. Alone on his island, keeping his own diary, Crusoe is the emblem of the diarist's moated self.

In the mode of the diary itself, aloneness is, as it were, continually and empirically verifiable in the aspect of staggered composition. In normal retrospective narrative, the author may highlight the circumstances of composition at the outset, but typically this focus gives way to absorption in the tale, which is so much the art of traditional narration. The interrupted composition of the diary brings us continually back to a new beginning in the present. Each entry, as it begins, returns us to the moment of composition and in so doing returns us to that point of temporary withdrawal, outside the action, necessary for the putting down of the words on paper. The effect is, in general, little more than subliminal. But it need not be. The narrator has great latitude here and in many ways can reinforce both the concluding and resuming of his text as reminders of his present isolation. In dystopia, this return to the page can put a continual stress not only on the isolation but on the entrapment of the moral intelligence that writes. George P. Elliott's horrific tale, "The NRACP," gives fresh reminders of this entrapment by the letter writer's references to the fact that he is writing in invisible ink.

One of the most philosophically tortuous (and torturous) thematic resources of the diary mode, as I shall discuss almost everywhere in the body of this study, is its availability to projects of self-perception. In diary fiction of any psychological pretension, the diarist is usually concerned, with greater or less intensity, to see himself through the agency of his diary. It can be a task roughly equivalent to levitation, involving as it does the difficulty of the subject's being its own object. A standard piece of equipment is the mirror (usually somewhere in the diarist's room). Its presence is predictable—though, it is worth noting, predictable in art, not reality. One of the telling differences between fictional diaries and even the most claustrophobic nonfictional *journaux intimes* of the nineteenth century is that the fictive diarist is directed at least once by his author to look into this symbolic instrument (without determined searching, I can locate instances in Lermontov, Turgenev, Rilke, Bernanos, Sartre, Gide [twice], Mauriac, Zamyatin, Beauvoir, Updike, and Bellow).[17]

One of the very painful developments of this theme is Simone de Beauvoir's *The Woman Destroyed* (*La femme rompue*), the third novella in the trilogy of the same title. The diary in this work is written at that point in Monique's life when, her children out of the roost and her husband abandoning her for his lover, she is

---

[17]On this difference between fictional and nonfictional diaries, see Barstis, 179.

forced to determine who she is with her own unassisted subjectivity. Her psychiatrist has encouraged her to take up writing a diary in order, she says, to "reconstruct my identity."[18] She is advised, in effect, to use it as a mirror. Yet in losing her husband, Monique has lost a mirror she had come to depend on without realizing it: "I used to see myself so clearly through his eyes—too flattering a picture, perhaps, but one in which I recognized myself. Now I ask myself, *Whom does he see?*" (181–182). So deeply ingrained is this dependency on the perspective of the other that in writing her diary mirror she holds it up to every face but her own, trying to reconstitute her identity through the subjectivity of anyone but herself. Therefore it is the expressions on her husband's face that crush her. In effect, they reflect her nonexistence. Likewise, the discovery of her husband's systematic lying is an erosion of her "self" in that it reveals the unreliability of the very instrument through which she had viewed that self. Nowhere in her diary can she find what she truly is. Pathetically, she takes samples of her handwriting to a graphologist. The final implication in this book is that Monique has no real identity at all. The small inadequate message she gets from the outside world is like that of the graphologist: she has "poise, cheerfulness, frankness and a lively care for others" (201). But all that emerges in the diary that could be called the essential Monique is fear—more specifically, fear of nonexistence. Her identity is her fear of having no identity.

I have gone into Beauvoir's novella not simply to exemplify a theme but also to emphasize how thoroughly the diary mode can be bound into it when that theme is the book's principal idea. But, as I stressed in treating the subject of realism, I should stress in this case, too, the variety to which the diary strategy is susceptible. At the other extreme from diary fiction like *The Woman Destroyed* or Hjalmar Söderberg's *Doctor Glas* or Sartre's *Nausea*, in which the diary is a mirror of internal nothingness, are those works that follow a precedent common in real diaries (Samuel Pepys, W.N.P. Barbellion, Julian Green), finding in the diary so strong and intimate a revelation that the diary is virtually identifiable with the self:

[18]Simone de Beauvoir, *The Woman Destroyed*, trans. Patrick O'Brian (New York: Putnam's, 1979), 240.

I keep it all to myself—myself being this little book. I grew tired of myself some months ago, and locked myself up in a desk.[19]

This time I shall be written. I am the impression that will transform itself.[20]

These stammerings betray me, but no matter....Let this become a piece of superb cartography. Let me be laid out here in relief, to be pored over by professional students of the soul's geology.[21]

A third variation can be seen in such works as Alberto Moravia's *The Lie (L'attenzione)* and Frisch's *I'm Not Stiller*, in which the diary, because of its lying and misrepresentation, becomes a lens through which the artist can catch glimpses of his unrepresentable self:

At times I have the feeling that one emerges from what has been written as a snake emerges from its skin. That's it; you cannot write yourself down, you can only cast your skin. . . . The more exactly one succeeds in expressing oneself, the more clearly appears the inexpressible force, that is to say the reality, that oppresses and moves the writer. We possess language in order to become mute. He who is silent hasn't even an inkling who he is not.[22]

Temporal Functions: Immediacy, Suspense, and Timelessness

As I mentioned earlier, there is a danger to credibility when the author removes the diarist from the room and sets him or her down somewhere else to write. When the travelers in *A Journey to the Center of the Earth* set sail by raft on a subterranean sea, Verne has Harry, his heretofore retrospective narrator, switch to his diary (the ship's log) principally to record, as they happen, a three-hour fight to the death between an ichthyosaurus and a plesiosaurus and

---

[19]James, "The Impressions of a Cousin," 117.
[20]Rainer Maria Rilke, *Journal of My Other Self*, trans. John Linton (New York: Norton, 1930), 50.
[21]Lawrence Durrell, *The Black Book* (New York: Dutton, 1960), 191.
[22]Max Frisch, *I'm Not Stiller*, trans. Michael Bullock (New York: Vintage, 1958), 290–291.

a five-day storm of hurricane strength. Drenched, lashed to the mast, Harry manages somehow to make periodic entries: "I have just come out of a long fainting fit. ... Are we still upon the sea? Yes, and being carried along with incredible velocity."[23] Verne characteristically took risks with credibility but, even for him, this is a great one, and the fact that he took it shows the depth of appeal of what is probably the most popular, if not the oldest, function of nonretrospective narrative.

There is really a combination of two distinguishable kinds of appeal in this example, and as they can exist quite separately, it would be best to take them up separately. The first is the effect of immediacy: that is, the illusion of being there, of no gap in time between the event and the rendering of it. This is one of the frequently cited virtues of nonretrospective writing, yet it requires at least one important critical distinction. If, when one speaks of the immediacy of the effect, one is speaking of presence at an action in the story—as we have rendered in this example—one is speaking of a relatively rare occurrence. Sartre noted this in describing the temporal effect of most epistolary fiction: "As to the event itself, although it is recent, it is already rethought and explained: the letter always supposes a lag between the fact (which belongs to a recent past) and its recital, which is given subsequently and in a moment of leisure."[24] In fact, it is precisely the annihilation of that lag that can lead, in a novel with any pretense to realism, to disastrous consequences, such as the disaster that Verne skirts or fails to skirt (depending on one's receptivity) in the example above. The confusions of mode in Edgar Allan Poe's "MS Found in a Bottle" derive in part from the author's having chosen the diary strategy. Unlike *A Journey to the Center of the Earth*, Poe's tale may be either fantasy or allegory, but the fact that Poe had the document "written" and the fact that he solved the practical problem of its survival by stowing it in a bottle, were in effect recognitions of practical problems that allegorists and fantasists need not recognize. He invites the realistic response and thus, when the time of action and the time of writing converge, invites the dangers of unintended comedy.

[23] Jules Verne, *A Journey to the Center of the Earth*, trans. anon. (New York: Dodd, Mead, 1959), 162.
[24] Jean-Paul Sartre, *What is Literature?* trans. Bernard Frechtman (New York: Harper, 1965), 132.

How can one possibly continue to write on a ship descending a maelstrom? Where did the narrator find the bottle and cork, not to mention the time, to package his now rather lengthy document?

So, if immediacy is a genuine advantage of the diary strategy, and more broadly of nonretrospective writing, it is rarely featured (understandably) as the immediate rendition of an external action in progress. And though one can find frequent instances of proximate immediacy (the writer, fresh from the event, recording it with greater passion and less perspective than could be afforded in time), the principal advantage of diary fiction on this score is the *immediacy of the writing itself*, however variable its distance from the action (the recorded events, some of which may be far back in time). This is the appeal that Richardson caught in his phrase "writing to the moment." Nonretrospective procedure, with its potential for heightening our awareness of the process of writing and with the possibilities it affords of allowing an alteration of the narrator's point of view *over the course of narration*, can convert the narration itself into a kind of action. Gérard Genette, in his discussion of "narration intercalée," speaks of the hero's possible division into two heroes, the one narrated and the other narrating: "The Cécile of yesterday, very near and already far off, is seen and spoken of by the Cécile of today. We have here two successive heroines, (only) the second of whom is (also) the narrator and gives her point of view, the point of view—displaced just enough to create dissonance—of the immediate *post-event* future."[25] As noted above, I see no need to stress, as Genette does, proximity in time (in James's "The Diary of a Man of Fifty," for one example, the "two heroes" are separated by a gap of twenty-five years), but the interesting possibility that Genette's analysis affords is that of doubling not simply the hero, but the event. Thus, as we read, we are made simultaneously aware of two events, the event recorded and the event of recording. Moreover, where the heroes, recorded and recording, are not at bottom two heroes but one complex one, the two events can be different to the point of irreconcilability.

In speaking of the strategic advantage of immediacy in the diary format, then, one is speaking of an immediate event, an event in progress, which is the writing itself. In the phrasing of Jean Rousset,

[25]Genette, *Narrative Discourse*, 218.

"the event is the words themselves and the effect produced by means of these words; it is the way in which they are said, then read and interpreted."[26] The drama in this event is a function of the tensions in the mind that produces it—crises of honesty, deception, passion, as that mind reflects not only on itself (the hero in the recorded event) but on everyone and everything else. Thus, a seeming paradox of the immediacy of the diary is that it depends on events of another time, usually past, to be realized. The range is great: from the intensity of Pamela's rendition of Mr. B's latest attempt on her virtue to highly subtle nuances of selective perception and distortion—the "dissonance" between the past event and the written version of it referred to by Genette.

If the past, and commonly the recent past, is a vital factor in the special effects of the diary strategy, even more distinctive is the role of the future. Among the strategies of formal realism, it is the nonretrospective ones that preeminently emphasize the future by virtue of the illusion that during the course of the narration itself, the future has not yet happened. We are dealing here, of course, with suspense—an ancient property of tales—but suspense brought into the telling. The "present" of the narration is, in this regard, to quote again from Jean Rousset, a "true present": "Author and character live from day to day an open destiny of which the final end is unknown to them; they know their past, they are ignorant of their future; their present is a true present, a life in progress, a wish or an expectation, a hope or a fear concentrated on the still unformed tomorrow."[27] This consideration brings us back to the example from Verne with which we started, for suspense is the obvious second effect he sought when he switched to the diary strategy. Will the raft be destroyed by beast or storm? Even though the account as a whole is retrospective—so we know that Harry survives—the suspension of disbelief is augmented at this critical point by introducing a technique of intercalated narrative. One can find the same kind of switch in strategies, only this time to letters, in Schiller's *Der Geisterscher* in which a certain edge of suspense is added through delaying the post. Essentially what we are discussing

[26]Rousset, *Forme et signification*, 74, my translation.
[27]Rousset, *Forme et signification*, 70.

ward the future—gives way in the Werther diary to its opposite, a destruction of time (again, abetted by the diary mode) through the immersion in feelings of the moment. The form, in short, becomes more static; the novel becomes less of a story and more of a portrait.

The main adjustment I would want to make in Martens's analysis is to eliminate the equation of a complexity of feeling with an increased "complexity of character."[32] In the Werther novel, it is not character that displaces action but feeling. The subtleties and nuances of mood, not character, displace the excitement of coming events. This adjustment is important because it goes to the heart of what is basically a difference in world view between two literary traditions. Henry James, for example, who had few peers in the realm of characterological nuance, could observe that plot and character are two aspects of the same thing. Indeed, in one of his fictive journals, "The Diary of a Man of Fifty," James accentuates plot to a degree beyond his own norm. Briefly, the fifty-year-old diarist meets a man half his age who has fallen in love with the daughter of a woman the diarist had fallen in love with twenty-five years before. He becomes a spectator at what appears to be a rerun of his own story. As events unfold, suspense mounts not only to see what will happen but to see how closely what happens repeats what happened in the past. As the denouement approaches, the importance of plot is accentuated by the diarist's own terminology. "Let him," he says of his young friend, "finish the story in his own way as I finished mine. It is the same story, but why, a quarter of a century later, should it have the same *dénouement*? Let him make his own *dénouement*."[33] The denouement in the second story does turn out to be different, and the difference forces our diarist, who had been judging the second story by the first, to revise his judgment of the first by the second. In the process, he is forced to revise his view of his own character as it is expressed in the plot of the first. In James's view, then, as in Richardson's, plot is inseparable from character because action is inseparable from character.

[32]Martens, 76. Her distinction between a stress on suspense in the Pamela novel and a stress on character in the Werther novel echoes a distinction originally argued by Ian Watt—"a principle of considerable significance for the novel form in general: namely, that the importance of the plot is in inverse proportion to that of character" (*The Rise of the Novel* [Berkeley: University of California Press, 1962], 279).

[33]*The Complete Tales of Henry James*, ed. Leon Edel (London: Hart-David, 1962), 4:415.

So the Werther novel would appear to have evolved from a strain distinct from that which produced *Pamela* and its imitators. The short, lyrical, nonretrospective novel is primarily a European development. Though a number were indeed translated into English with no little popular success, the original English product tended to reflect what Matthew Arnold called the English gift for the moral and practical life (a gift inherited by James). Its emphasis on the responsibility of the ego brought in its wake an emphasis on education, choice, and consequence. This accounts, certainly in part, for why English novels tend not only to be plotted but to be long. Conversely, a world view that stresses the helplessness of the ego in the world of external events relocates human significance and freedom in an internal world of feeling. Thus, it is not an interest in character, per se, which produces the static, vertical quality of such post-Werther novels as those of Charles Nodier and Ugo Foscolo, but a disbelief in the freedom of the subject as an acting being. Impotent in the world of action, incapable of altering the course of an inexorable fate—"une fatalité tout-puissant—" the only freedom that the subject can exercise is the expressive freedom achieved in his diary. Plot, correlatively, loses the importance it has in a less fatalistic literary culture. Not that plot disappears, but it is a short step from the plotted tragedies of Racine to the *Portuguese Letters* (1669), which had the virtue of having displaced the plot to focus attention on what the readership was absorbed by: the effect of the plot (now past) on the suffering consciousness. The Portuguese nun herself admits that this is where her own attention lies (as she says to her lover: "You were less dear to me than my passion"[34]). It is the *Portuguese Letters* and its numerous imitations that lead through the letter-journal novels of Crébillon fils and Mme Riccoboni to the efflorescence of the Werther novel at the turn of the century.

This basic difference is what causes a reversal of temporal function in the diary structure. Suspense, which is an aggravation of the experience of time, is replaced by the experience of timelessness, because the feelings of the subject have become emancipated from the action. They have become their own end. The diary struc-

---

[34]Gabriel-Joseph de Lavergne de Guilleragues, *Lettres portugaises, valintins et autres oeuvres*, ed. F. Deloffre and J. Rougeot (Paris: Garnier, 1962), 62, my translation.

ture, now breaking down time into a nonlinear collection of effusions, assists the novel in approaching the condition of the associative meditation or prose lyric. The epitome of this may well be Gide's *Les cahiers d'André Walter* (1891), his adolescent first novel and a late nineteenth-century recrudescence of the Werther novel. In it, Gide explicitly displaces character itself as a subject of interest for the feeling of love alone ("to study our love, rather than some vain character who declaims about such things"[35]).

Another useful aspect of Martens's study is her demonstration of how the Werther novel evolves during the course of the nineteenth century into what could be called the Amiel novel, typified by the diary novels of such authors as Edouard Rod, Arne Garborg, Hugues Le Roux, and Jean Lorrain.[36] In these novels, the diarist, following the lead of major nineteenth-century keepers of journaux intimes (particularly Henri Amiel), suffers from essentially the opposite condition of the Werther diarist. Where the earlier diarist suffered from the frustration of too great a passion, the Amiel diarist suffers from a deficiency of passion. Nonetheless, the point I have just made for the Werther novel holds for the Amiel novel as well. For all the radical differences between the two kinds—the one passionate, absorbed in feeling; the other arid, intellectual, plagued by crippling self-scrutiny—they share a fundamentally deterministic fatalism, and it is this similarity that maintains in the fin-de-siècle mode the static, unsuspenseful quality of its predecessor. Perhaps the best example of this difference with a similarity is Hjalmar Söderberg's 1905 novel, *Doctor Glas*. In this diary of "the shadow who wished to become a man," Söderberg accentuates the distance of his novel from such muscular Christian plots as those of Dostoevsky by introducing the shadow of a plot. The climax comes, casually, on a hot summer day, when Glas offers his victim a poison pill while the two of them are chatting. The victim is entirely unsuspecting; he believes it is for his heart. He dies a moment later, is buried, and *nothing* comes of it. Earlier, as he plans the murder, Glas underscores the gulf between his project and Raskolnikov's when he notes, "But if he refuses to take the pill?

---

[35]André Gide, *Les cahiers et les póesies d'André Walter* (1891; reprint, Paris: Gallimard, 1952), 27, my translation.
[36]Martens, 86–110.

. . . Well, I can't help it, the matter must drop. After all, I can't kill him with an axe."[37]

To sum up this final point, diary structure in fiction can be used in the service of opposite temporal objectives, suspense or timelessness. But the aggravation or annihilation of time depends not on the degree to which the novel focuses on character but on the assumptions about freedom and character that are behind the novel. In the Werther novel, feeling, and in the Amiel novel, anxiety, can be seen as instrumentally disengaged from action. Thus they become objects of interest in themselves; diary fragments catch them in different facets. Plot, of course, can exist in such novels, just as it can exist in the plays of Racine, but in a diary novel, with its opportunities for the expression of interior, private life, the option of displacing plot is often taken, for what plot there is takes place in a world that levels the human with the nonhuman. In a novel like *Doctor Glas*, acts are not even acts but utterly insignificant events in an embracing determinism: "I felt my 'action' to be a link in a chain, a wave in a greater movement; a chain and a movement which had had their beginning long before my first thought, long before the day when my father first looked with desire upon my mother. I felt the law of *necessity*: felt it bodily, as a shiver passing through marrow and bone. I felt no guilt. There is no guilt" (123).

As always, we must conclude with what must be by now a familiar caveat: the danger is in neatness. When, for example, determinism is completely dissolved—when, that is, freedom is extended everywhere so that it is the condition of all things and all acts in an entirely *un*determined universe—then diary structure can lend itself to the same static effect we have been discussing, for in such a universe, all things and all acts have an equality that the apparent jumble of a diary can imitate. The novel that springs to mind is Sartre's *Nausea*, in which the diary obviously contributes to that end.[38]

[37]Hjalmar Söderberg, *Doctor Glas*, trans. Paul Britten Austin (New York: Universal, 1969), 94.

[38]The example generates one more complication. In Sartre, the perception of freedom is accompanied by the inevitability of choosing, and therefore, in the novel, Roquentin's education draws him to a climactic decision. So Sartre is working both sides of the street, here as elsewhere, formally as philosophically. Simone de Beauvoir reports that during the course of the novel's composition they both felt the need to counter an even greater formlessness than can be found in the finished

I have focused on three aspects of fiction—mimetic, thematic, and temporal—in which one can isolate functions served by the distinctive characteristics of diary structure itself. The *actual* functions to which a diary can be put in fiction are nearly infinite. Writers can accomplish almost anything in a diary that they can accomplish in narrative by virtue of the fact that fictional diarists are readily convertible into narrators. I have therefore stuck to definitive features of the form we are dealing with—its documentary character, its privacy, its nonretrospective structure—to isolate the distinctive contribution it can make and thus the distinctive appeal it makes to authors planning their work.[39]

Equally important, no one of these functions is necessarily, or even predictably, served in any particular work. It is for this reason more than any other that it would be a mistake to consider what I have been calling diary fiction a genre. This caution should be reinforced by what I hope also has been amply demonstrated—the sheer variety of ways in which authors, using the diary structure, have met functions within one functional category. So, as the diary novel (the literary kind) gradually emerged, it took shape within the richer and more diverse life of diary fiction. If we resist the impulse to reduce the latter, we can keep our eye on the flexibility of the diary as a device—on its *disponibilité*—and in the process on the particular achievement of the author who bends it to his or her purposes.

---

novel: "I insisted that Sartre should give Roquentin's discovery some fictional depth, and infuse his narrative with a little of that suspense which we enjoyed in detective novels. He agreed" (*The Prime of Life*, trans. Peter Green [New York: 1962], 89–90).

[39]It is perhaps arguable that I have slighted the diary's congeniality to the unsystematic collection of *pensées* or meditations. It is true that a good deal of unsystematic thinking can go on in diary fiction, particularly in those patterned on the *journal intime*. But I do not see anything in the form that specifically invites it. There are novels that are entirely a collection of meditations cast in the form of a diary or letter journal—Sénancour's *Obermann*, Gissing's *The Private Papers of Henry Rycroft*—but only by the loosest of definitions can they be called novels. In both works, not only is plot absent but narrative has been reduced to the merest servant of meditation. In fact, there is some question whether either is fiction. Both would appear to be generically closer to the *Essais* of Montaigne.

2

The Special Reflexive Function
of the Diary Strategy

So far we have dealt with *general* functions of the diary strategy. They are general in the sense that they are commonly found in diary fiction. They are also general in the sense that they can be achieved by means other than the diary strategy. Suspense, for example, can be gained by a variety of techniques. It is not found only in diary fiction. Is there, then, a *special* function of the diary strategy, one that can be served only by the diary strategy? There is at least one, and to it the central portion of this book is devoted.

Dotting the history of diary fiction are cases in which the narrator's diary not only tells a tale but plays a demonstrable role in determining the outcome of that tale. I do not mean by this such devices as the fortuitously discovered manuscript—papers introduced at the right point to unravel the mystery. The kind of text I am referring to plays its role in the tale because of the *way* in which it is written. By its rendering of events, it can move its own fictive creator to insight or maintain him in blindness and thus influence the course of events that follow. It is a reflexive text—not simply in the sense of a self-reflecting or self-conscious text, but in the sense that the text exerts an effective influence on its writer.[1] It

---

[1]"Reflexive," "self-reflexive," "self-conscious," "self-designating," "metafictional"—these are the terms most commonly used in discussions of literary reflexivity. Depending on who one reads, these terms are not necessarily interchangeable, but with varying shades of discrimination they are all applied to the general phenomenon of literature that features its textual condition (formal, fictional, technological, or artistic) as a part of its content. For a taste of the diversity that has characterized recent work in the field, see Robert Alter, *Partial Magic: The Novel as a Self-Conscious*

may be objected that the influence of which I speak is an influence endowed the text by its creator, that basically it is the diarist's energy that we are dealing with. My physics is poor; but I know that when some one pushes a pendulum, it is the kinetic energy of the pendulum itself that he or she experiences when it returns. This is the quality I want to stress—the reciprocal participating role of the text in the tale of its fictive author.

However common this special reflexive condition may be to the *actual* pursuit of writing, it is clearly demonstrable only in diary fiction or in that strain of epistolary fiction confined to the letters of one correspondent, which we have included in our definition of diary fiction. There are two practical reasons for this. First, such narratives being chronologically intercalated instead of retrospective (as one finds in most first- or third-person narrative), much of the writing antedates not simply the conclusion but in many cases the major events of the tale. Second, such narratives being written instead of voiced or thought (as one finds in monologue or interior monologue), they become independent documentary objects capable of exerting an influence on their creators. Given these two conditions, the writing itself can assist or impede change in the writer and thus help to determine the outcome of the tale—even as it renders that tale.

Though this dynamic engagement of the telling in the tale is demonstrable only in "intercalated single-narrator" (i.e., diary) fiction, and in a subset at that, its importance exceeds its narrative type. In such texts, the authors (the real authors) examine their craft. They do so in such a way as to examine the vital function of their chosen medium in the life (or better, the living) of the one who uses it. Diary fiction, by its nature, keeps the whole subject of verbal representation in focus. It is no accident, then, that such texts have tended to be works of more than ordinary literary significance.

Genre (Berkeley: University of California Press, 1975); Michael Boyd, *The Reflexive Novel: Fiction as Critique* (Lewisburg: Bucknell University Press, 1983); John Fletcher and Malcolm Bradbury, "The Introverted Novel," in *Modernism*, ed. Malcolm Bradbury and James McFarlane (Harmondsworth: Penguin, 1976), 394–415; Bruce F. Kawin, *The Mind of the Novel: Reflexive Fiction and the Ineffable* (Princeton: Princeton University Press, 1982); Steven G. Kellman, *The Self-Begetting Novel* (New York: Columbia University Press, 1980); and Robert E. Scholes, *Fabulation and Metafiction* (Urbana: University of Illinois Press, 1980), 103–138.

To clarify our subject, let me describe a representative fiction. The plot is roughly that of Chastity overthrown by the Sensual Beast. Chastity in this case is a writer recently successful in her first book of stories. The Beast is a sculptor who specializes in welding and neon. The seduction takes place on an Edwardian estate in New England where artists are invited each year to work in quiet seclusion. The book as a whole is rendered through the diary of the writer (a chapter a day).

A symptom of her unnatural constraint, her self-imposed innocence both as a writer and as a woman, has been the diarist's two-year friendship with a painter (now also at the estate)—a friendship with "all the overtones of a love affair" but without a hint of sexual desire. These people feel an intense loyalty to each other, and each reinforces by encouragement the other's artistic narrowness and respectability. They maintain their "conservatism" by a reiterated expression of scorn for the more sensational popular alternatives to their kind of art ("gluing angora fur on radiators"). Yet the painter's coolness on the subject of love and loving puzzles the writer. She ponders this side of his character and early in her diary produces an explanation that appears to be satisfactory: her friend has been emotionally traumatized by an alcoholic and sexually insatiable wife. Knowing about his wife, she writes, "explains a lot—so much that I probably should have guessed it before." Among other things, it explains his "odd lack of sympathy with people's love affairs . . . his tendency to rather downgrade that side of things."[2] Five days later, however, it is suggested to her that her friend is homosexual. The suggestion comes as a shock, and she wrestles with it in her diary. If her friend is homosexual, then he would explain his wife more than his wife would explain him. He might even, for that matter, explain the diarist herself. By turns she records the evidence for his homosexuality and resists it with what she takes to be her loyalty; but as the facts fall into place, so, finally, do the implications. If he is homosexual, then either he "has been silently and consciously misleading me for two years, or I have been silently and unconsciously misleading myself" (98). Both hypotheses would appear to be the case. As she writes in her

[2]Alison Lurie, *Real People* (New York: Avon, 1969), 40.

diary, our narrator shows a capacity to go against the strong current of her will to mislead herself. What happens, then, at this point in the diary is that crucial aspects of the story are rewritten before our eyes. The text corrects itself. In other words, our enlightenment about both of these people roughly keeps pace with the enlightenment of our narrator.

So far, what I have described is not unique to nonretrospective narrative, though it may be more common in it than in other modes. One can think of basically retrospective narratives, particularly from this century (Ford Madox Ford's *The Good Soldier*, William Faulkner's *Absalom, Absalom!*, Thomas Mann's *Doctor Faustus*), in which narrators gradually clarify or deepen the confusion of their stories by a process of repeated cancellation and correction. What is different about the narrative situation that I am describing is that the story is still in progress during the course of the narration. Therefore, how the narrator corrects (or fails to correct) her story can actually play a part in how her story will continue.

To return to our example, what happens immediately after her debate with herself in her diary is that the diarist, "still upset" about her friend, goes off to the races with the sculptor we mentioned at the outset—that good-looking animal for whom she feels an amused condescension. To her great surprise, she winds up sleeping with him that night. During the whole seduction, she is confused about who she is and why she is doing what she does. She comments several times on how she seems a stranger to herself, but this stranger is essentially a continuation of the stranger who began to emerge in the meditation in her diary that immediately preceded the whole evening. Moreover, whoever the stranger is, it is clear that she enjoys making love to the sculptor. The seducer has an accomplice in the seduced. In context, then, her retelling of the story of her "love affair" with the painter has prepared her for her sexual affair with the sculptor—prepared her, and may well have led her to it. The text, in other words, has played the role of a live agent in the story.

Lurie's *Real People* provides a good, paradigmatic example of the special reflexive function of the diary strategy because it allows us to isolate many of the issues, essential and tangential, that we will be returning to in this study. To begin with, Lurie's novel shows very clearly how such a text joins writing and plot. As I mentioned above, this quality makes it essential that there be a fiction of writing at the very least. Other intimate modes that feature self-reflection— monologue, interior monologue, retrospective meditation—lack the commitment of a text.[3] In stream of consciousness, the reflected self is perpetually subject to a quick dissolve, but a text is a record. By having her protagonist reflect on herself in writing, Lurie examines the dynamic moral character that writing itself can have. Much of the dramatic tension of this tale comes from the possibility of its being *written* in one way or another. The possibilities of choice, then, a traditional core fascination of plot, are extended into the text itself. The text in this way becomes a part of the action. Overt acts in the "external" sequence of the plot can be born in the text. Conversely, acts can fail to occur, and it is in the text that they can be stifled.

To return to our example, the day after the seduction, our diarist goes back to her journal in an effort to restore her old image of herself. This requires rendering the night before as "an accident, a momentary aberration." The sculptor has invited her to stop by his studio again that evening, but her comment in her diary is "Of course I'm not going. I hope this time he'll get the message, and I won't have to be rude." She then reinforces this textual act by attempting to convert the tale of her seduction into a ghost story, changing or blurring the characters and events; but the tale does not come off, and two hours later she is forced to admit to her diary that she has been abusing her craft:

> There was something in the original ideas, but then I changed the people to types, and the precipitating incident from a seduction to news of a death. Which is of course more conventional for a ghost story, less apt to surprise or offend anyone—and also isn't what I want to write about. I'm tired of ghosts—whether they're real "spirits" or just spiritualized versions of myself and the people I know. [125]

One can note in passing that the alteration of the key event to "news of a death" indicates the intensity of fear that leads her to

---

[3]Some novels come very close to diary form but still lack this crucial element. See, for example, Barbusse's *L'enfer* (discussed briefly in Chapter 8), Malraux's *Les conquérants*, Lagerkvist's *The Dwarf*, Caroline Blackwood's *The Stepdaughter*.

try to bury the incident. At the same time, it gives an indication of the courage it takes *not* to accept the ghost story. Unable to sleep, she goes for a walk and winds up again making love with the sculptor. There is no real clarification yet in her mind about her motives. She had gone off to his studio with the intention of telling him that she "was never going to his studio again." But the point to stress is that her ability to read her ghost story critically had helped to keep her awake in the first place. Canceling her story in the diary is the emergent act that culminates in sleeping again with her lover.

The passage as a whole shows that the diarist, through the agency of her writing, can effect an evolution as a human being or, through the same agency, impede or prevent it. The passage also shows how thin the line can be between the creative and the critical. What I have been calling the writer's textual acts are versions of herself that she can test as she makes them. She does not always test them, and when she does not the text becomes a kind of cushion, part of the equipment of her inertia. But when the writer works side by side with the critic, the interest mounts. She hones a new image of herself as, by consequence, she hones a new, more mature craft. Her art will still be a form of distortion, as all successful art is an alteration of the real particulars that inspire it, but now she will alter "by addition, not by subtraction as I've been doing" (155). By the end of the novel, she has broken with her friend the painter and is setting out be a bolder, more honest writer than the one who arrived at the estate nine days before.

So far I have been stressing the writing side of that fusion of writing and plot that characterizes this special version of reflexivity. It is worth turning for a moment to the other element in this fusion, plot. One of the broadly accepted conditions of the diary, or at least the journal intime, is that it is necessarily without shape and by consequence almost entirely without plot. As James said of the first person, it is "a form foredoomed to looseness."[4] This is what so upsets Hermann, that curious mixture of the demonic and the foolish who narrates Nabokov's *Despair*. With the unraveling of his

[4]Henry James, "Preface to *The Ambassadors*" in *The Art of the Novel* (New York: Scribners, 1909), 320.

perfect crime comes the unraveling of his plot. In dismay, he watches his elegant retrospective narrative deteriorate into a diary—"The lowest form of literature."[5] What Hermann the aesthete loathes is more commonly taken to be one of the diary's defining virtues: "A diary which has a consistent pattern is a literary work and no diary at all."[6] Or in the words of George Sand, "To keep a diary is to renounce the future. It is to live in the present. . . . It is to drink one's ocean drop by drop for fear of swimming across."[7] It is, in short, to get as close as possible to a purely contingent reality.

The author of the fictional reflexive diary loves to play off the surprise of an emergent plot against the conventional expectation of discontinuity in diaries.[8] It is this plot, moreover, emerging in the text, that so sharply distinguishes the special reflexive text from the stretch of diary fiction that traverses the nineteenth century from Sénancour and Nodier to Söderberg and Rod (*La course à la mort*). In texts like these, which are basically dominated by a deterministic vision, the kinetic relationship between the text and the world of "external" acts is severed, because in such a vision the will of the writer operates, if it does so at all, independently of the enlightenment that may be registered in the text.[9] The reflexive diary, in contrast, is so plotted as to make *the will of the writer in its*

[5]Vladimir Nabokov, *Despair* (New York: Capricorn Books, 1970), 218.

[6]William Matthews, *British Diaries: An Annotated Bibliography of British Diaries Written between 1442 and 1942* (Berkeley: University of California Press, 1950), x.

[7]George Sand, *Journal intime (posthume)*, ed. Aurore Sand (Paris: Calmann-Lévy, 1926), 41, my translation.

[8]As I have already noted, the augmentation of suspense is one of the oldest and most consistent functions of the diary mode in fiction. Its pedigree in this regard may possibly be suggested in Frank Kermode's speculations on the codex, the Greek precursor of the paged book: "The codex, originally perhaps the memorandum-books of the Hellenistic businessman, became the vehicle for a new kind of narrative, reflecting new views on the divine and human arrangement of time. In its way the novel perpetuates that archaic confidence in the figural relation of the new event to the old, in continuities of sense ever to be renewed and reestablished, and in the expectation, however qualified, that the end must cast its potent shadow over all that preceded it" (*The Genesis of Secrecy: On the Interpretation of Narrative* [Cambridge: Harvard University Press, 1979], 89).

[9]This statement needs qualification, for there is a gray area here between enlightenment and overt acts. Certain implicitly fatalistic texts (the *Lettres portugaises*, for example) contain dramas very similar to the one we have been describing, but in them the writer is personally helpless to effect any major alteration in the course of events that control her destiny. They are suspenseful dramas nonetheless because at stake is an enlightenment that can result in either acceptance or rejection of the world as it is. Such enlightenment in turn has the potential of leading to acts, however slight, like the sending or burning of a letter to a lover.

freedom the central mystery and point of focus. Time and again one finds in these texts the possibility of a "true plot" (actualized or suppressed), which at once grows out of and expresses the self that the writer both discovers and creates in her writing.

Another salient characteristic of this kind of text is the way, generally, it modifies the theme of solitude. It does so primarily by undercutting the solipsism that so frequently attends the diary mode in fiction. As I have already noted, the experience of isolation is an unavoidable component of the diary, if only for the mere practical necessity of the diarist's being alone somewhere in order to write. As it is a continually interrupted document, we are continually reminded of that isolation. For this reason, as I showed in Chapter 1, the mode has been used to evoke some of the more harrowing fictional experiences of solitude. Saturated by the condition of isolation, the reflexive diary is no exception to this "rule." Their solitude is a continual refrain among the keepers of such texts, particularly as they seek in the variable mirrors of their diaries some genuine image of themselves. In spite of this, however, a condition of the drama in these reflexive works (that plot I stressed above) is acknowledgment of the objective world—that world that carries on independently of the writer's consciousness. Though these works may present studies of solipsism, they are themselves not, finally, solipsistic. Another way to put this is that they are about the improvement of subjectivity—or the possibility of its improvement. Indeed, much of the dramatic tension derives from how the external world impinges on the diarist's consciousness, how these impingements are represented in the diary, and the consequences of those representations. The whole process suggests that the hermeneutic circle is neither closed nor vicious.

In *Real People*, the idea that her friend is homosexual comes not from the diarist herself but from the sculptor. Once the idea has entered her consciousness, the test is how she works with it in her diary, how this in turn leads to adjustments in her view of herself, and how, finally, these adjustments assist in altering her behavior toward both men. The reciprocity of external and internal can get rather intricate. Her future lover, for example, goes right to the heart of her "chastity" when he comments (well before they sleep together) on a trick of her speech: "You know something? Janet has an imaginary friend named Wun. An Oriental. She's always telling us his opinions. 'Wun prefers the kind of art Wun is brought up on. Wun is *responsible*, after all' " (75). It hurts, and Janet is forced to recognize how in the style of her speech itself she is not *"responsible*, after all." Continually, she has disclaimed personal responsibility for her views by attributing them to the anonymous and general "one." Turning back to the text of her diaries, we find especially in the early entries numerous references to her Oriental friend ("At Illyria one becomes one's real self, the person one would be in a decent world" [17]). Alerted by someone other than herself, someone who hears her, she turns now to her written style and scrutinizes it as she scrutinizes herself: "I just read over my new story, in imagination changing One to I throughout. A tedious character appeared, sententious, supersensitive—" (76). Over the course of the diary itself, she gradually effects a change in style. The change is not dramatic, but by the end One, at least, has departed; I speaks for herself. In achieving this, Janet has done the work, but she performs that work as part of a dialectic that includes not only herself and the text but also the world beyond them both.

A counterexample to put beside Janet's diary would be the diary of Updike's Reverend Marshfield (*A Month of Sundays*), who has been confined, not to a writer's colony, but to an institution in Arizona designed as a sanatorium for troubled or wayward clerics. The Reverend Marshfield's trouble has been his inability to keep from fornicating with his parishioners. Part of the cure is the careful maintenance of a diary (an entry a day), and it is Marshfield's diary that we read. The difference between Janet and the Reverend is that while Janet changes, the Reverend remains the same. He not only remains the same, but he converts an austere and frigid head nurse to his point of view. Suspecting that she is reading his diary, he uses it as an instrument of seduction. Hours before his scheduled departure, success crowns his efforts. As a final twist, it is strongly suggested that the vital key to Nurse Prynne's heart is the Reverend's "profession," recorded in his diary, of a rediscovered faith.

The same basic conception of a maieutic, or therapeutic, diary lies behind both Lurie's adaptation and Updike's elaborately ironic travesty. That the device can be quite plausibly introduced as an institutionalized part of a sanatorium cure shows to what extent this conception of the diary has become popularized. As a popular idea, it rests on two assumptions. One is that the true self is necessarily the hidden self, difficult of access, requiring special tools for its excavation. The other is that the diary is just such a tool because, writing as he often does with emotional immediacy, unconstrained by a concern for an audience beyond himself, the diarist is allowed to uncover the contours of his buried self. "When we read a diary, we are not merely looking over a man's shoulder. We are looking into his inmost mind, his hidden heart: here everything is forthright and without subterfuge. . . . everything is spontaneous, unpremeditated, and completely convincing."[10]

Most studies of the nonfictional diary, until recently, have implicitly or explicitly endorsed the view that the "genuine" diary is really a nonliterary form in the sense that it is unpremeditated and free of artifice.[11] But, as Robert Fothergill effectively demonstrates in his study of the English diary, the formal equivalent of spontaneity is neither a guarantee of self-knowledge nor a preventative against self-deception.[12] In diary fiction, the same holds true. In *Real People*, as I argued, there is the constant possibility of the drama's having a very different outcome, assisted by the same document in which Janet achieves her insights. Gide provides a helpful figure here. In *The Counterfeiters*, the fictional diarist, Edouard, describes his diary as a "pocket-mirror."[13] The analogy is a good one because it allows us to formulate a double-question: does the diarist catch herself in her mirror or does she use it to put on her makeup? That a writer can in all sincerity perform the latter operation while she believes she is performing the former is hard to deny. It is the very mystique of the diary—its illusion of sincerity—that can make it a particularly treacherous form.

[10]Louis Untermeyer, Introduction to *A Treasury of the World's Great Diaries*, ed. Philip Dunaway and Mel Evans (New York: Doubleday, 1957), v.

[11]William Matthews, *British Diaries*, vii–x; Kate O'Brien, *English Diaries and Journals* (London: William Collins, 1943); Arthur Ponsonby, *British Diarists* (London: Ernest Benn, 1930). See also Alain Girard, *Le journal intime* (Paris: Presses universitaires de France, 1963).

[12]Robert Fothergill, *Private Chronicles* (London: Oxford University Press, 1974), 38–63.

[13]"I cannot feel that anything that happens to me has any real existence until I see it reflected here" (André Gide, *The Counterfeiters*, trans. Dorothy Bussy [New York: Random House, 1973], 157).

The Special Reflexive Function of the Diary Strategy

Two basic kinds of kinetic relationship, then, can predominate between fictive diarists and their diaries. These, in turn, yield two basic kinds of plot. The diarist can, as in Lurie's novel, engage her text in such a way that she changes. Or the diarist can, as in Updike's novel, engage his text in such a way that he remains the same.

The phenomenon we are going to explore in the central chapters of this book ought to be kept conceptually clear of the idea, frequently encountered in the literary discourse of the last twenty years, that all texts may be seen as participating in the drama of their own creation: that is, that all texts are in some immediate way self-creating. I shall return to this argument toward the end of my chapter on Sartre's *Nausea*. At this point, it is appropriate to stress that the special reflexive diary, as it is found typically in Lurie's novel, requires an acceptance of the principle of referentiality. More specifically, it requires that we conceive a fictive world of place, character, and action (a writers' colony, a sculptor, a seduction) separate from the text. Even though all we know about that world comes from the text, we are required to keep the two separate. So we say that the text *refers* to the fictional world (just as we maintain a confidence that that fictional world, by different rules, refers to the external world we share with the author). Only by assuming this basic distinction can we go on and speak meaningfully of the unique character of these reflexive texts as, in another way, *not* separate from the world to which they refer, for it is the very quality of their referentiality that participates like an agent or a character in the world to which they refer.

We must maintain the principle of reference if we are to empathize to any degree of earnestness with the drama in which such texts participate. We have to believe that there is a world there that the diarist, together with her text, can either obscure or clarify. If, however, we assume that no such separation is possible, then we cannot hope to have any standard of obscurity or of clarity. With such an assumption, it becomes pointless to speak of an improvement of vision; the "fictional world" is at the mercy of the text and is made or unmade entirely as the text commands. Texts governed by such an artistic assumption do have their own kind of drama, but it is the kaleidoscopic drama of the moment-to-moment creation and recreation of worlds. What this means for us, in this study, is that despite their veneer of modernity, these special reflexive texts are embedded in the traditional mimetic assumptions of the novel.

As I mentioned earlier, the reflexive diary closes the gap between the creative and the critical. It is a drama of both writing and reading. Insofar as reading is a part of this drama, the text puts a light on the whole field of interpretation. In that light, the writer and his or her intentions stand out as principal concerns. Paul Ricoeur's highly original effort to resolve the hermeneutic dispute between strict intentionalists and relativistic structuralists invoked (as I do) the idea of an energetic encounter with the text, but one in which both the author and the text's "ostensive references" are dispensed with. According to Ricoeur, the act of reading sends us forward into "new modes of being": "not the intention of another subject, presumably hidden behind the text, but the project of a world, the pro-position of a mode of being in the world that the text opens up in front of itself by means of its non-ostensive references."[14] His remarks throw into sharp relief the interpretive situation they can*not* accommodate: when the text is your own and the ostensive reference is yourself. In such an interpretive situation, particularly as it overlaps the moment of writing (reading yourself as you write), we also have an "energetic encounter," but one in which the intention behind the text is necessarily the absorbing object of attention. Such an act of writing/reading is simultaneously to say who I am and to ask Who am I? The self disclosed *behind* the text is the *project* of the text.

This active reflexive relation may well be the universal condition of first-person writing. If so, it is commonly veiled. Most writing is governed by an illusion of transparency. "The writer commonly believes himself," as Samuel Johnson said. By joining writing and action, the reflexive diary removes the veil. It exposes a drama of interpretation, blended or fused with a drama of creation. Writing the text, the self seeks (or projects) the intending self behind that same text. In the process, assumptions about the world—assumptions to which the intending self is attached—come into focus or remain screened from view. Only by coming into focus do they

[14]Paul Ricoeur, *Interpretation Theory: Discourse and the Surplus of Meaning* (Fort Worth: Texas Christian University Press, 1976), 94.

lead, finally, to Ricoeur's "new modes of being." Only by seeing behind her writing her old intending self and the world it assumed is Janet enabled to create her new self.

In these reflexive texts in which writing is demonstrably part of the action, the *craft* of representation plays such an active part in the tale that it would seem hard to deny a special urgency of vocational interest on the part of the work's (real) author. Small wonder that so many of the protagonists of such texts are themselves either writers or artists. It is an unavoidable percentage. Diary fiction not only mirrors the author's own situation (writing alone in a room), but, more important, its unique conditions can make it a kind of laboratory in which the real author examines the behavior of his or her medium in the course of day-to-day living. "Laboratory" may perhaps be misleading, since, like most art, these texts are finished, polished, edited, whole, and fictive. The text's own drama of composition is hidden from the reader and is only in rare cases made public by the diligence of scholars. What we read instead is an imitation of a drama of composition. The real author is implicated at one remove. She gives us a story in which this craft she practices alone and out of sight is made visible as a moment-to-moment kind of action complete with consequences and moral implications, inextricable from the process of living.

When the fictive diarist is also a writer (professional or aspiring), the network of analogies is, as it were, squared. The vocation of Lurie's heroine is that of a writer of stories. By consequence, the diary she writes is not only an investigation of the truth about herself, but also a place in which she can investigate the lack of truth in her stories. As its contents are confidential, she can conduct in it a private examination of her public art. As she proceeds, it becomes clear that the inadequacy she finds in her public art is no more or less than the failure of her life in private. Practically, her problem as a writer is that she has been stalled since the publication of her first book of stories. Everything she writes seems to repeat what she has already written. Vaguely, she feels that this repetitive narrowness is a form of dishonesty—a constriction of her art to what will not hurt or offend the people she knows. As her diary progresses, however, it gradually becomes clear that the one she has been protecting from hurt or offense is herself. I have already discussed how the special reflexive diary closes the gap between writing and living (how acts are born or suppressed in the text); as a writer's diary, it can also close the gap between public art and private life. The crisis of Janet's art is a crisis of her life; its falsehood is the falsehood of her image of herself.

The epigraph for *Real People* comes from the letters of Charlotte Brontë: "Come what will, I cannot, when I write, think always of myself and of what is elegant and charming in femininity; it is not on those terms, or with such ideas, I ever took pen in hand: and if it is only on such terms my writing will be tolerated, I shall pass away from the public, and trouble it no more." A hundred years later, Lurie through her fictive agent is fighting the same fight, in effect declaring by her epigraph that she will not be that decorous and decorative nonbeing, the lady novelist. But, as Janet's intimate record shows, the threat of the type lies within as well as without— in her own desires as well as those of the literary marketplace. As the diarist struggles to train her critical eye on herself, she continues to run another course in her art, converting her experiences into "entertaining" ghost stories:

> I read my ghost story over again this morning, and I didn't like it. It seemed both trivial and pretentious; a thin, silly tale, elaborately overtold. Every sentence was like an awful parody of my work, artificially composed to deserve, in the worst sense, all the adjectives they used on the jacket of *At Home*:
>
> > charming
> > feminine
> > witty
> > sensitive
> > subtle
> > original
>
> I'm reminded of the "certain kind of woman" in the Peck & Peck ads, who has such charming, feminine, witty, etc., tastes, but always dresses with dowdy conventionality. One knows that her clothes tell the real truth, and her advertised enthusiasm for dandelions and French poetry is sheer affectation. [58]

As she struggles against the stereotype, we see at the same time the strong internal appeal that it has: the lady novelist threatens no one, including herself. She is a form of makeup. During that first evening with the sculptor, the lady novelist works overtime, busily converting the facts of her situation into "the sort of unconventional adventure Janet Belle Smith often has" (102). Listening to this man's loud radio, drinking out of his dirty glasses, "I still thought I was collecting an interesting anecdote, and overlooked these sordid details—rather I looked them over, in case they should come in handy when telling the story later, or writing about it" (106). It is only when she actually makes love to her "seducer" that the lady novelist takes flight, and Janet the private person is forced to recognize that "whoever I was" is having a hand in making the scene turn out the way it does.

Though Janet exposes the falsity of her art through the honest scrutiny of her diary, the struggle for truth in the diary, as noted above, can end either in failure or success. By extension, the falsity of Janet's art—its insidious "charm"—not only afflicts the ghost stories she writes offstage but infects the diary itself. Well past the middle of the book, her entries often read like letters from camp, composed by a dutiful prodigy. She is busy collecting anecdotes, and, from time to time, she even collects passages of her own writing: "A warm, windy night. Down below the roof garden I can hear cars whirring past on the thruway, or like gusts of wind. Gusts of wind like cars whirring past? (SAVE THIS)" (43). It is all a part of the same urge that leads her to say "one" instead of "I," the urge *not* to be herself. Her diary, therefore, is as apt an instrument as her stories for avoidance, constriction, falsehood.

In its lies together with its truth, what such a diary offers the storyteller is what her best stories offer the public: authentic revelation. It is an *available* revelation that the diarist may or may not recognize, but the lies are an important part of the diary's embracing authenticity. Alberto Moravia developed this paradox in his diary novel, *The Lie*. Moravia's diarist is a novelist who has turned to the diary because the novel he has written, like Janet's stories, is infected by the artificiality of his life: "like a subtle poison which has become blended with the soil and which passes through the roots of a tree into its most intimate fibers—artificiality had penetrated, from the things I had tried to depict, into the very words I had used to depict them."[15] He decides to keep a diary that as

---

[15] Alberto Moravia, *The Lie*, trans. anonymously (New York: Dell, 1967), 34.

an honest record would provide the basis for an honest novel. Once this honest record is complete, his plan is to extract from it the material for a novel. But as the novel proceeds, Francesco finds that he (like Janet) is continually shading the truth, altering facts, in short, novelizing. Unlike Janet, Francesco is unembarrassed by his lies. He accepts them as part of the larger authenticity of his diary. Instead of scorning or rejecting them, he lets them stand in order to expose and analyze them in the entries that follow. He takes the lies as expressions of the truth about himself. Exposing their falsehood is followed by the question Why these particular distortions of the facts? Answering the question exposes the truth of his motives. His lies, like Janet's, serve the truth in a record that as a whole achieves authenticity. In contrast to Janet, Francesco learns to accommodate the distortions of his fictionalizing by making them a part of a dialectical rhythm that includes the scrutiny of their falsehood. While Janet, at the end of her diary, sets out to write better than she has, Francesco, at the end of his, concludes that he has written his novel.

What both *Real People* and *The Lie* suggest, then, through the foregrounding of an artist's struggle with his or her art is another kind of reflexivity to which the diary mode can lend itself. It is related to the special kind of reflexivity I have been discussing, yet it is different. Whereas in the one, writing is part of a dialectic with action in the world, in the other, writing is part of a dialectic with art. The diary experience in the latter has the capacity to generate a new departure in craft (or, conversely, to prevent its coming into being). Though the real author is out of sight, she is nonetheless implicated—Alison behind Janet—experimenting with her art in what amounts to a kind of laboratory. I cannot strongly argue that Lurie's next novel, *The War between the Tates* (1974), is an artistic advance that grew directly out of her diary fiction. I can, however, make the case that both Saul Bellow and Samuel Beckett capitalized on the diary strategy at a critical point in their careers to generate a fundamentally new departure in their art. I have saved the discussion of their work and this aesthetic reflexivity of the diary mode for the last two chapters. Still, throughout the book such reflexivity will remain on the edge of our concern—particularly in our discussions of Goethe, Tennyson, Lessing, and Sartre.

Real People and *The Lie* are only two of a proliferation of twentieth-century diary fictions that feature a professional writer as a diarist.[16] This proliferation is no historical accident but part of a broader twentieth-century inclination to make the difficulties of mimesis a subject of mimesis: that foreshortening of perspective described with partial insight by Ortega y Gasset as "the dehumanization of art." It is the same inclination that has led to the production of large, formally precarious works like Gide's *The Counterfeiters* and Lawrence Durrell's *Alexandria Quartet*, which are not, properly speaking, diary novels but which make extensive use of the diary as they explore the relations of art and life.

It is tempting to generalize from this historical phenomenon to that of the special reflexive diary, with which we will be centrally concerned in this study—the spread of the one accompanied by the spread of the other. The temptation should be resisted. Though these modern experiments capitalize on the epistemological flexibility afforded by the diary, its traditional difference from art, few of them are demonstrably reflexive in the way defined here. The dynamic movement of special reflexivity involves not only the scrutiny of a text but the active engagement of that text in the tale it tells, and this sharply reduces the field. Reduces and broadens it at the same time, for while it reduces the number of examples, it spreads them out over the last three hundred years. These texts are not the exclusive property of any particular literary epoch. Their recurrence is a logical extension of an old insight, the insight that writing and behavior can be inseparable aspects of the same event.

[16]Clyde Brion Davis, "*The Great American Novel* . . ."; Lawrence Durrell, *The Black Book*; Jean-Jacques Gautier, *Cher Untel*; George Gissing, *The Private Papers of Henry Ryecroft*; Reinhard Goering, *Jung Schuk*; Ferdynand Goetel, *Z Dnia na Dzien (From Day to Day)*; Julien Gracq, *Un beau ténébreux*; Malcolm Lowry, "Through the Panama"; James Merrill, *The (Diblos) Notebook*; Howard Nemerov, *Journal of the Fictive Life*; Raymond Queneau, *Les oeuvres complètes de Sally Mara*; Rainer Maria Rilke, *Die Aufzeichnungen des Malte Laurids Brigge*; Françoise Sagan, *Des bleus à l'âme*; Jean-Paul Sartre, *La nausée*; Upton Sinclair, *The Journal of Arthur Stirling*; Yevgeni Zamyatin, *My (We)*.

3

The Expressive Text and
Textual Self-Concealment

> To charge those favorable representations, which men give of
> their own minds, with the guilt of hypocritical falsehood, would
> shew more severity than knowledge. The Writer commonly believes
> himself.
>
> —Samuel Johnson, "Life of Pope"

Goethe and Werther

In Chapter 1 we discussed in passing the short, lyrical, predom-
inantly European strain of diary fiction with its reduced emphasis
on plot and its complementary stress on feeling. Behind this strain
of fiction (and a good deal of other writing beginning roughly in
the second half of the seventeenth century) is the assumption that
writing can be sincere or purely expressive. The expressive text is
assumed to be transparent. Through it, the emotion of the writer
becomes that of the reader. In such texts expression itself is often
its own end, because such texts are so frequently accompanied by
a fatalistic view of life. Powerless to alter his or her destiny, the
letter writer or diarist turns to a belief in textual transparency to
achieve the only available freedom: the expression of his or her
true emotional being. In the introductory letter to Crébillon fils'
remarkable *Lettres de la Marquise* (1732), the anonymous "editor"
pleads for tolerance and in the process puts her finger on the
reigning world view of the expressive text: "I would have been
pleased to discover in these letters more signs of virtue; but the
marquise was in love: this was the original calamity, and out of it

all the rest was to some degree inevitable."[1] Thanks to her society and her marriage, her feeling nature and that of the count, there is no other sequence for the marquise but love, betrayal, and an early grave. But thanks to her pen and the transparency of her letters, she can achieve a textual liberation. It was an emotional triumph in which her readers were happy to participate.

When the belief in an expressive text governs not fiction but autobiography, the consequences can be severe. It would appear certain, for example, that the mystique of the expressive text lies behind the terrible pathos of Jean Jacques Rousseau's *Confessions*. In his relations with society, Rousseau was in a situation not distant from that of a jealous lover. His *Confessions*, written in isolation, compiled in stages over a period of five years, have as such the qualities of an intimate journal or series of letters to a lover, designed to set the record straight. But though Rousseau believed he was writing an entirely expressive text, he was also composing the kind of reflexive text we discussed in Chapter 2, a text that in Rousseau's case exerted its own control over its writer. In setting out to write his life story, Rousseau committed himself at the outset to a particular version of himself. It was a textual commitment, but precisely because it was written *down* it was inflexible. Though writing, for Rousseau, lay at a dangerous remove from the authenticity of immediate speech, and transparency was a technical impossibility, he nonetheless aimed, in the words of Jacques Derrida, at "the greatest symbolic reappropriation of presence."[2] As Rousseau labored to remind us, his text is a faithful one. To the honest reader, it communicates expressive truth. Rousseau may get the facts wrong, but his essence—that is, his emotional character—shines through. Therefore, once that self has been committed to the text, there is no longer any room for revision. The text functions to conceal as well as reveal. The whole darkening second half of his *Confessions*, the elaboration of gnostic fantasies, the projection of his own doubts about himself into the acts and words of his "enemies," can be seen in this light as an effort to preserve his text: to preserve it as he would himself.

---

[1]Claude Prosper Jolyot de Crébillon, *Lettres de la Marquise de M*** au Comte de R**** (1732; reprint, Lausanne: Guilde du livre, 1965), 27, my translation.
[2]Jacques Derrida, *Of Grammatology*, trans. G. C. Spivak (Baltimore: Johns Hopkins University Press, 1976), 143.

If there is something of hyperbole in this characterization of Rousseau—a man held hostage by his text—the effect of exaggeration can be mitigated to some degree by imagining the relationship of author and text were the *Confessions* expressly delivered to the public not as the actual truth but as fiction. At a stroke, Rousseau would have liberated himself—more exactly, would have created the possibility of liberation—from the inhuman burden of sincerity with which he had weighed down his fictional counterpart. We can only speculate about this, of course, but I raise the possibility because I want to turn now to Goethe, who appears to have capitalized on precisely this power of fictional liberation. In dealing with *The Sorrows of Young Werther*, I want to concentrate not so much on the text itself as on the relationship of author and text. We are fortunate in this regard because we have not only the text (composed in 1772, published in 1774) but an account of its composition in Goethe's own autobiography, *Poetry and Truth* (*Dichtung und Wahrheit*, 1814). Examining the two together can show how a novel that *contained* the popular ideal of the expressive text and that powerfully moved so many of its readers to accept it simply as such, was in the eyes of its creator a more complex reflexive text. Thus, the sincerity that was for the general reader a matter of the heart, was for the author a matter of the text as well. And the fatalism that was so firmly wedded to the expressive tradition, was in the authorial view seriously qualified by an awareness of the hero's textual control.

Several reasons account for the great impact of Goethe's novel. To begin with, Werther had great appeal as a type, in particular his sincerity and his gift for passionate expression. His appeal was so great that it overrode the general capacity of readers to maintain critical distance. Critical distance, of course, was itself, in the ethos of Werther, a deadly or at least deadening quality, allied with common sense and the gray stability of bourgeois life. Critical distance was the gift of his rival, Albert, and it was fatal to the full and immediate expression of his feelings of the moment. Therefore, in the internal aesthetic of the letters, there are conditions for the public acceptance of powerful acts of self-projection, almost entirely unscathed by irony or critical self-awareness.

The form of Werther's novel—a chronologically arranged collection of his letters—also strongly encouraged the popular acceptance of the hero on his own terms. Not only do the letters tell the story of his sensibility, they are themselves the expression of it. By adopting the single letter-writer mode, excluding the letters of Werther's more reasonable correspondent and avoiding any censoriousness in the voice through which he recounts Werther's final days, Goethe intensified Werther's claim on the whole mind of his reader. Werther is in charge of the world, as it were, and as such enjoys great rhetorical authority.

Another cause of Werther's extraordinary persuasiveness was that in inventing the letters Goethe allowed his hero to claim a good part of his own mind as well. The author told Eckermann that *Werther* was "one of those creatures which I nourished, like the pelican, with the blood of my heart. In it there is so much that sprang from the depths of my own being, and enough of my feelings and thoughts to furnish the material for a novel in ten such little volumes."[3] The circumstances of its origin are well known, and were well enough known by Goethe's readers to cause that continual series of questions concerning the real identities of his fictional characters that was to plague Goethe throughout his life. Yet, in a real sense, he wrote not only in a "state of mind" like Werther's but *as* Werther. He produced the book, as he himself attests in his autobiography, "almost unconsciously, like a somnambulist."[4] He records how, before he began the novel, or even consciously intended to write it, he had developed the habit of carrying on imaginary conversations with absent acquaintances. As he points out, these conversations were closely akin to the particularly solipsistic, self-reinforcing kind of correspondence that Werther engages in:

> How nearly such a mental dialogue is akin to a written correspondence is plain enough: only in the latter one sees returned the confidence one has bestowed; while in the former, one creates for one's self a confidence which is new, ever-changing and unreturned. When, therefore, he had to describe that disgust which men, without being driven by necessity, feel for life, the author necessarily hit at once upon the plan of giving his sentiments in letters. . . . for no one feels immediately

[3] J. P. Eckermann, *Conversations with Goethe*, trans. Gisela C. O'Brien (New York: Ungar, 1964), 22.
[4] *The Autobiography of Johann Wolfgang von Goethe*, trans. John Oxenford (New York: Horizon Press, 1969), 217.

opposed to a written effusion, whether it be joyful or gloomy: while an answer containing opposite reasons gives the lonely one an opportunity to confirm himself in his whims,—an occasion to grow still more obdurate.[5]

So important to Goethe was the force of such "written effusions" that he used it, so to speak, on himself as he composed the novel and then sustained it, as I have noted, by excluding from the book any other narrative voice (correspondent, "editor") whose words might undermine the effect of these effusions. Only after the book had already been introduced into a cultural milieu so susceptible to the power of those effusions that readers began not only to adopt Werther's dress but also to take their lives, did Goethe in dismay add the epigraph to the second printing: "Be a man, do not follow me." So strong was the effect of the book that Goethe told Eckermann he himself had read it only once and feared rereading it, lest it arouse in him again the dangerous state that produced it.

Although Goethe had submitted himself to Werther's influence in writing the novel and feared rereading it because of that influence, the book's main effect on him was the opposite of its effect on its audience, "for by this composition, more than by any other, I had freed myself from that stormy element, upon which, through my own fault and that of others, through a mode of life both accidental and chosen, through obstinacy and pliability, I had been driven about in the most violent manner. I felt, as if after a general confession, once more happy and free, and justified in beginning a new life."[6] The disparity between his own and others' responses to his work confirmed Goethe in his despair of exerting any control over his readers through preliminary remarks or editorial comments: "an author may preface as elaborately as he will, the public will go on making precisely those demands which he has endeavoured to avoid."[7]

The whole situation and Goethe's interpretation of it might be taken as evidence for the view that a text's meaning derives solely

---

[5]Goethe, *Autobiography*, 205–206. Stuart Atkins has shown how Goethe in addition trained, as it were, for the writing of his novel in writing his own letters: "The Apprentice Novelist: Goethe's Letters, 1765–1767," *Modern Language Quarterly* 10 (1949), 290–306.

[6]Goethe, *Autobiography*, 217–218.

[7]Goethe, *Autobiography*, 224.

The Expressive Text and Textual Self-Concealment

or broadly from the mental set brought to it by its reader. The readers of *Werther*, having been saturated by a variety of fatalistic expressive texts—the literature of melancholy, English graveyard poetry, an epic (*Fingal*) in which life is conceived as a continual frustration of one's passionate hopes—would find in *Werther*, as they would even in Shakespeare, confirmation of their own dark view of life. Yet Goethe had laughed himself out of the idea of suicide well before composing *Werther*, and though he had inhabited the soul of his character in order to compose the letters, he had nevertheless been allowed in the process to rise above that soul's point of view and its valuation of its experiences. He achieved a "bird's-eye view" and with it a final purgation of the sufferings represented in Werther. He went on, not to commit suicide, but, as he says, to lead a new life and to write works of a spiritual variety quite beyond the gifted youth he depicted in his early novel.

Whatever the variety of response his text may have generated, it is clear that for Goethe all responses are not equal. The phrase "bird's-eye view," which I quoted above, is taken from a passage in which he describes the proper effect of "true poetry":

> True poetry announces itself thus, that, as a worldly gospel, it can by internal cheerfulness and external comfort free us from the earthly burdens which press upon us. Like an air-balloon, it lifts us, together with the ballast which is attached to us, into higher regions, and lets the confused labyrinths of the earth lie developed before us in a bird's-eye view. The most lively, as well as the most serious, works have the same aim of moderating both pleasure and pain by felicitous intellectual form.[8]

As Goethe found to his dismay, however, the "intellectual form" of a work is no proof against the habits of its readers, particularly if those habits are as strong as those of Goethe's generation. In part because of his own immersion in the spirit of Werther during the composition of the book, his readers accepted the work as essentially that of the lesser artist—that is, of Werther. The power of his momentary effusions held sway in their minds over the retrospective contemplation of the whole—the creation of its greater artist. In short, they did not recognize that the work was repre-

[8]Goethe, *Autobiography*, 209.

sentational (*dargestellt*) but assumed instead, generalizing from the melancholy poetry of which they were so fond, that it was didactic (*didaktisch*).

For the author of *Werther*, the depiction of a certain type of sensibility was also the depiction of a certain type of self-representation. And it is this manner of self-representation that sustains and abets the limitations of character that lead Werther to suicide. Werther reads himself as his readers read him. He is not of that species of diarist or letter writer who engages in close, honest self-scrutiny or who, because of his freedom from restraint in composing, wins his way to a discovery of his true character; rather, he uses that freedom to project a fixed particular self. Through his letters he shores up his identity against alteration or growth, taking for his ideal the impulsiveness of the children he loves so much. He is, in writing as in conversation, the constant advocate of his feelings of the moment. It is this quality that allows him on July 1 to lecture Herr Schmidt for giving way to his moodiness and infecting others with it and on August 12 to lecture Albert, with even greater passion, on the impossibility of controlling one's moods. It allows him to find in a madman a noble representation of his own plight and to find in a flooded river an image of eternal nature in conformity with the deluge of his own hopes. And it is what allows him at the end to compose his suicide and his final letter in such a way as to ensure the torment of the woman he claims to love.

If we recall, for a moment, Lurie's novel, we can see how markedly Goethe's stands in contrast. Where the former's artist grows, the latter's does not. Janet, turning her critical eye not only on herself but on the prose through which her immaturity is sustained, alters both herself and her prose. Werther, in contrast, maintains a constant unity of identity between himself and his writing. In fact, so completely does he employ his letters to seal himself off from critical self-perception that one might be tempted to put them in another category than that of *Real People* on the ground that the conflict of self-perception and willed blindness that is allowed to emerge in Janet's diary is never really allowed in the letters of young Werther. This is why I have concentrated on the etiology of *Werther*. By understanding the positive kinetic role that this text played in

Goethe's life, we see the negative kinetic role the same text plays in the life of its fictional hero. The profound difference, then, between Goethe's work and so many of the works out of which it grew is that Goethe's does not accept the principle of spontaneous expression on its own terms. Through Werther's letters, Goethe revaluates the popular aesthetic of the effusion by giving it a role in the tale—specifically, as an agent by which Werther resists the possibilities of self-perception and growth.

We spoke of the irony of the book's reception—the fact that its readership responded to it according to Werther's, not Goethe's, aesthetic. The irony extends into the literary subgenre it founded—what has come to be called the "Werther novel." It is instructive in this regard to compare Charles Nodier's comments in middle age on the Werther novel of his youth, *The Painter of Salzburg* (1803), with Goethe's. The reflections are quite similar, particularly in recalling the activity of writing the story from inside: "My hero is twenty years old; he is a painter; he is a poet; he is a GERMAN. He is exactly the man with whom I identified myself at that age."[9] Yet where Goethe recalls the cathartic character of the writing and the development of a "bird's-eye view" (after his own involvement in an affair similar to that of Werther), Nodier recalls with a certain indulgent condescension the "malheurs" prepared for, even forseen, by the twenty-two-year-old author. With its "no doubt false" language, he adds, the novel nevertheless could not have been written otherwise. It is, in short, an expressive text featuring a language of unquestioned sincerity. No alternative perception to that of its diarist is even implied (the perception of characters, for example, like *Werther's* Lotte and Albert). All the people in this book are equally excessive in their passion, equally noble for it, and equally the victims of "an all-powerful fate."

Another work that can fruitfully be put beside *Werther*, to highlight both *Werther's* complexity of effect and its "representational" character, is Ugo Foscolo's *The Last Letters of Jacopo Ortis*. Composed a year before *The Painter of Salzburg*, it reflects an even stronger influence of *Werther*, an influence that extends into major details of the plot. Yet the work is written in essentially the spirit in which

[9]*Oeuvres de Charles Nodier* (1832; reprint, Geneva: Slatkine, 1968), 2:10–11, my translation.

so many readers took Goethe's work—a spirit that Goethe would call "didactic." It is composed almost entirely of Jacopo's letters to his intimate friend Lorenzo. The protagonist's love, Teresa, is betrothed to the orderly and passionless Odoardo. Jacopo, like Werther, leaves for a while, attempts to stay away, fails, returns, and eventually commits suicide. His suicide note, like Werther's, is written by stages, and the account of his burial (with no priest in attendance) is delivered in the same perfunctory way. But there is little to indicate that the novel does not fully endorse the passionate pessimism of its letter writer. Crucial to this difference in effect are differences in plot and supporting characters. Teresa, for example, not only loves Jacopo but fully shows that she does. She is forced by political and economic necessity to marry someone she loathes. Because she is not a free agent, unlike Lotte, and because her betrothed, unlike Albert, is not sympathetic, there is little to counterbalance the ideal of passionate immediacy expressed so often in Jacopo's letters.

One can see, then, in the vogue of the Werther novel itself to what degree *Werther* stands alone, islanded, a critical reassessment of the sentimental tradition out of which it came and back into which it was immediately absorbed. In the tradition, the text is held as a constant, an agent of conveying, not influencing, emotion and narrative. Seeing *Werther* in this context allows us to underscore Goethe's achievement in producing a reflexive diary novel and to understand the rarity of its occurrence. It is art of major difficulty because it expresses art in transition, art turning back on itself, examining itself in terms of its consequences in life. I want now to turn to a novel, which, for all its differences from *Werther*, emerges from basically the same sentimental/expressive tradition and represents the same kind of rare and difficult achievement.

Lermontov's *A Hero of Our Time*

A Hero of Our Time (1840) was published two generations after *Werther*. It owes much to Goethe but more still to Byron, and the latter's *Childe Harold* is a good work to keep in mind as we look at Lermontov's novel, not simply because of the Byronic qualities of Lermontov's hero, but conversely because *Childe Harold* is not intended, as *A Hero of Our Time* is, to be an exposure of self-deception. As an endorsement of the authority of spontaneous utterance, it stands in relation to *A Hero of Our Time* in much the same way as the poetry of passionate immediacy stood in relation to *Werther*. It is the latest relevant version of the expressive text.[10]

As a psychological study of its central character, Pechorin, *A Hero of Our Time* is a nest of Chinese boxes, the innermost box being the chapter entitled "Princess Mary." To get to it, the reader passes through a series of stories that give varying outside views of the hero. Lermontov originally planned to have Pechorin compose his journal with publication in mind—a kind of Russian *Childe Harold*. But as the book materialized, Lermontov hit on the strategy that would allow him to enhance the effect of authentic revelation: he made Pechorin's document a genuine journal intime, intended solely for Pechorin's eyes, then capitalized on a valid element in Pechorin's character (his Byronic indifference) to allow the diary to fall into the hands of the traveler who publishes selections from it in tandem with two Pechorin stories he has picked up in his journeys. In the completed book, the stories precede the diary and serve to whet our interest in its author—especially because, like Byron, one of Pechorin's striking features is his quality of impenetrable mystery. So the diary is served up as a rare glimpse behind the facade, a privileged view uncontaminated by any attempt on its author's part to perform for a public. It combines the assumptions of the expressive text with the motive of internal exploration characteristic of nineteenth-century journaux intimes. In this regard, our traveler compares it favorably with the *Confessions* of Rousseau, which "have already the defect of his having read them to his friends."[11] We are thus delivered into the heart of the novel's subject. The document is accorded the standard romantic guarantee of its virtues as a literary record: its "editor" informs us that "while reading over these notes, I became convinced of the sincerity of this man who so mercilessly exhibited his own failings and vices" (63).

Briefly, the "Princess Mary" section concerns a lovers' triangle that

---

[10]Byron rarely, if ever, allowed his heroes to unmask themselves through their own words. When it came to unmasking the Byronic hero, he performed the operation (notably in *Don Juan*) through an alteration of his own voice.

[11]Mikhail Lermontov, *A Hero of Our Time*, trans. Vladimir and Dmitri Nabokov (New York: Doubleday, 1958), 64.

culminates in a duel. The third member of the triangle is Gruzhnitski, a hapless character who, in his humble soldier's coat, poses
as a Byronic mystery and who courts the Princess in his inept and
sentimental fashion. It is Pechorin, however, who wins her heart—
thanks to his coldness, his arrogance, his indifference, his good
looks, and his altogether more impressive air of mystery—and his
success is what occasions the challenge. Gruzhnitski in effect stumbles into the duel. He is managed throughout by his unscrupulous
second, a captain of dragoons, who plots with Gruzhnitski to have
Pechorin's gun loaded with a blank. Pechorin overhears their
scheme, so that when the hour of the duel has arrived and Gruzhnitski has already fired, Pechorin stops the action, loads his gun, and
kills his opponent.

There is something quite fitting in having Pechorin, the hero of
his time, eliminate a low imitation of what he stands for. Gruzhnitski
is a shallow character, transparent, the opposite of a mystery, who
makes the fatal mistake of pretending to be one. The pretense
enters him in Pechorin's bad book before any thought of the duel
and even before the development of the lovers' triangle. Though
our "editor" introduces Pechorin's journal with a version of the
maxim "tout comprendre, c'est tout pardonner," it is *incompréhen-
sibilité* that is the key element in the Byronic hero's appeal, the
source of much power and the cause of a good deal of forgiveness,
at least in the hearts of women. Gruzhnitski, whose "object is to
become a hero of a novel," "a being not made for this world and
doomed to suffer in secret," mocks the prestige of Pechorin's office.
The mode of vanity Gruzhnitski represents may well be a self-
revelatory threat to his executioner and may well account for the
disparity between the reader's sense of Gruzhnitski's smallness and
the heat that he generates in Pechorin. It is Pechorin who, in the
eyes of the Princess, is "the hero of a novel of the latest fashion"
(95), and the Princess should be an authority, for she has read
Byron in the original English.

I stress the importance of Byronic mystery because it bears directly on the structural character of Pechorin's diary that we are
concerned with. Pechorin is a mystery not only to others but to
himself. Why he behaves the way he does—why, particularly, he
toys with the heart of a girl he does not love and allows himself to
become the executioner of his silly double—he does not under-

stand. His diary, then, is both our privileged glimpse into the interior and his own means of self-exploration. Because he is a fearless self-observer, used, as he says, to being frank with himself in everything, the form generally fulfills its function well. The editor is right; Pechorin can be quite merciless in his self-scrutiny. It is a trait that puts him well above a number of his Byronic predecessors, including Byron's Oriental heroes, and that contributes to the originality of his book. Yet Lermontov's genius lay also in his ability to show Pechorin's powers of self-concealment, exercised in the same document that serves for self-exploration. This can be demonstrated in two passages covering the hours immediately after the duel.

Riding back alone, Pechorin spots his rival's bloodstained body below the cliff from which it fell when Gruzhnitski was shot. Pechorin notes that involuntarily he shut his eyes and also that "a stone lay on [his] heart. The sun seemed ... without luster; its rays did not warm [him]" (171). When he arrives home he discovers two letters, one from his "pal" Werner informing him that the death of Gruzhnitski has been successfully arranged to look like an accident so that "you can sleep in peace ... if you can" (172). The second is from an old love of his who has been visiting the same watering place. It tells Pechorin that her love for him has been discovered by her husband, that she has lost everything for him, that she will always love him, and that at that very moment the coach is being readied which will carry her out of his life forever. Nothing that we have read so far anticipates Pechorin's reaction to this second letter. He jumps on his horse and races "like a madman" to intercept her coach. He never makes it. Instead, in his violence, he rides his horse to death. With the merciless candor for which his editor justly praises him, he describes what follows:

Worn out by the agitation of the day and by insomnia, I fell on the wet grass and began crying like a child.

And for a long time, I lay motionless and cried bitterly, not attempting to hold back the tears and sobs. I thought my chest would burst; all my firmness, all my coolness vanished like smoke; my soul wilted, my reason was mute and if, at that moment, anyone had seen me, he would have turned away in contempt. [175]

66

Throughout, Pechorin has featured himself as a man beyond such emotional displays—an enigma capable of arousing great passions of love or hatred in others but doomed himself to a continual series of withdrawals from intimacy. His attachment to his old flame is a disturbing ache, but one that nevertheless permits this man of candor to affirm that he has never been dominated in love. His sudden tearful collapse, then, comes with the force of a revelation, and coming as it does immediately after the duel, it is hard to avoid seeing his actions in that affair, as he himself acknowledges, as an immediate cause. He explains that he was "worn out by the agitation of the day." The phrasing is broad, but his actions suggest another, more specific motive: the desire to be forgiven. The bad child weeps for forgiveness. So painful are the implications of his behavior that he momentarily includes his other self in the scene and records his observation: had anyone "seen me, he would have turned away in contempt." Even more revealing are the reflections he then goes on to make on what he has recorded with such admirable candor:

> Yet it pleases me that I am capable of weeping. It may have been due, however, to upset nerves, to a sleepless night, to a couple of minutes spent facing the muzzle of a pistol, and to an empty stomach.
>
> Everything is for the best! That new torment produced in me, to use military parlance, a fortunate diversion. Tears are wholesome, and then, probably, if I had not gone for that ride, and had not been compelled to walk ten miles home, that night, too, sleep would not have come to close my eyes. [176]

His casual tone and lighthanded treatment of the episode are a way of restoring a certain image of himself. In a sense, he is now putting on his makeup, for he has reached a point in his self-exposure beyond which he cannot go. He has already exposed the usual Byronic sins, and in certain cases, with admirable ruthlessness, he has exposed them as shallow and unglamorous. But when it comes to recognizing his guilt, craving forgiveness, weeping for the kind of love a mother gives her child, he has reached his limits in composing a journal of self-exploration. In short, he allows the form to reverse its function.

There is much for him to regret. He has humiliated the Princess and broken her health, while throughout the Gruzhnitski affair he has acted as choreographer. Though his love of controlling the destinies of lesser people is a vice he will admit to on occasion ("To be always on the lookout, to intercept every glance, to catch the meaning of every word, to guess intentions, to thwart plots, to pretend to be fooled, and suddenly, with one push, to upset the entire enormous and elaborate structure of cunning and scheming—that is what I call life" [136]), he must reinforce his defenses when he is enduring the emotional consequences of his choreography. The nonretrospective, wholly private form in which he writes lends itself readily to the task.

When Werner comes to take his leave of Pechorin the day after the duel, Pechorin remains "cold as a stone," refusing even to shake his hand, for Werner, in his note of the preceding day, has had the temerity to suggest that Pechorin's conscience might be bothering him ("so you can sleep in peace . . . if you can"). Pechorin comments:

> That's the human being for you! They are all like that: they know beforehand all the bad sides of an action. They help you, they advise you, they even approve of it, perceiving the impossibility of a different course—and afterwards they wash their hands of it, and turn away indignantly from him who had the courage to take upon himself the entire burden of responsibility. They are all like that, even the kindest, even the most intelligent ones. [177]

The central idea here is "the impossibility of a different course." Fate is the personal myth that Pechorin invokes to protect himself from his conscience, which is telling him that this has been no predestined comedy but a comedy he has helped to write.[12] By treating his fear of humiliation and his craving for revenge as fixed determinants, Pechorin avoids recognizing what he knows to have been the case: that throughout this comedy he had numerous opportunities to rewrite the play. In these two passages, then—his reflections on his wild ride and his reflections on Werner—Pechorin uses his diary in much the same way he uses his mirror. Two hours before the duel he looks at his reflection: "a dull pallor was spread

---

[12]This reading of Pechorin's character is supported by John Mersereau, Jr., in his analysis of "The Fatalist," the novel's last chapter, in *Mikhail Lermontov* (Carbondale: Southern Illinois University Press, 1962), 132–143.

over my face, which bore the traces of painful insomnia; but the eyes, although surrounded by brown shadows, glittered proudly and inflexibly. I was satisfied with myself" (160).

One of the central revelations of this novel is the grave consequences of Pechorin's relationship with his diary. At two o'clock in the morning before the duel, he meditates on the mystery of his life ("why did I live, for what purpose was I born?") and concludes with one of his most characteristic wishes: "One keeps expecting something new ... Absurd and vexatious!" (159). The account of the duel and its aftermath is entered a month and a half later, and when he has brought it to a close, Pechorin recurs to precisely the same desire: "Will there not appear there, glimpsed on the pale line separating the blue main from the grey cloudlets, the longed-for sail, at first like the wing of a sea gull, but gradually separating itself from the foam of the breakers and, at a smooth clip, nearing the desolate quay?" (180–181). What has preserved the cycle is Pechorin's own management of his diary. His breakdown after the duel creates the possibility of change. It is genuinely "something new." In recording it forty days later, the possibility is revived; but in his reflections on his collapse, Pechorin collaborates with what he is fond of calling "Fate," and the "new torment" is entombed as "a fortunate diversion."

Another way of putting this is to say that Pechorin's capital vice is his failure to write as well as Lermontov. In the introduction to the novel, Lermontov describes his principal character as a "portrait composed of all the vices of our generation in the fullness of their development" (2). What keeps these vices intact is Pechorin's failure to reflect appropriately on the autobiographical details he records. To call this his capital vice is no extravagance, for the book is very much about writing. This is the "wicked irony" of its title: the hero of our time is the hero of our fiction. The low mimesis of this hero is Gruzhnitski; yet Pechorin is not so distant a cousin of his victim. Despite his sophistication, the fixity of type invades his own character ("the eyes, although surrounded by brown shadows, glittered proudly and inflexibly"). The presumption of personal mystery that is ridiculed in Gruzhnitski is also exposed as one of the limits of Pechorin's own character.

This is not to deny the complexity of both Pechorin and his story, nor to deny the host of qualities—not the least of which is an impressive power of self-perception—that raise him above most of the other people in the book. It is to say, rather, that the limits of his literary powers are what maintain his status as the kind of hero one finds in "novels"—the Byronic heroes of authors who cannot write as well as Lermontov. At the same time, Lermontov's power to disengage us from the current valuation of heroes helps make the book more than a novel of fashion.

As a reflexive text, *A Hero of Our Time*, like *Werther*, is a case of art in transition. It is art, in other words, that both contains and transcends the art out of which it grows. This is, of course, an arguable distinction of any original art—one that has been given renewed emphasis in contemporary deconstructive criticism. The accomplishment of the reflexive *diary*, however, is to give the *written* character of the old art an active role in the new. In doing so, it adds a special depth to the originality of the work by uniting, in a dramatic way, its levels of thought and action. It accomplishes this by recombining what in the Western, Cartesian tradition we have tended to keep separate. We are shown how the written words of the *intimiste*—the abstract representations of his private mind—are an inseparable part of his living behavior.

In these two examples of the special reflexive text, I have been stressing the diary's negative agency in the lives of the writers. As Rousseau appears to have done, Werther and Pechorin have exploited the "spontaneous" modes in which they write to the end of preserving a textual version of themselves. "Exploit" is a hard, and reductive, word; and as I have emphasized, both of these narrators are gifted and are meant to be sympathetic. That said, it is still something like the exploitation of written language that is going on here. Cloistered as they are, working within the moment and without the whole pattern of their lives in view, they yield to the temptation to create in what they write the image of themselves they wish to see. In doing so, Werther and Pechorin prevent revelations about themselves that could lead to major alterations in the way they live. However attractive they are, however moving in their sensibility and gifted in spontaneous utterance, they are (unlike Lurie's protagonist) narrower, less philosophically mature writers than their creators.

Putting Werther and Pechorin side by side enables one to gain a sharper insight into the relations of sincerity and authenticity. Lionel Trilling, in his seminal study of that subject, suggests a historical movement from an emphasis on sincerity to an emphasis on authenticity. The present study in contrast suggests a closer contemporaneity of sincerity and authenticity. It is possible to see, through these examples, how the high valuation of sincerity in the culture and in its popular art coexisted with, indeed served, the pursuit of authentic artistic representation in the two exceptional works discussed here. We have seen how in both cases the reflexive text comes out of and revaluates the popular art and also, in the case of Werther, how that achievement is immediately reabsorbed by the literature of sincere spontaneity. The cultural and artistic strains lie side by side. One does not give way to the other but feeds it and feeds upon it.

In his remarks on authenticity, Trilling also develops its possible relationship to another cultural development: the erosion of confidence in narrative history.[13] I have argued, however, that the text that most capitalizes on the diary's or letter's breaking up of time is the expressive text, the text of tragic sincerity that features an emotional "now." The reflexive text, in contrast, combines this emotional appeal with a drama in progress, a drama in which the stakes are self-knowledge and the capacity to change. If the method is not that of conventional narrative, the reflexive diary nonetheless maintains attention on the traditional driving interest of plot. What is different is that we have been drawn inside. Instead of reading a narrative that has been delivered to us as something finished, we are allowed to observe it in the making. And, crucially, it is the very making of the narrative that can influence how it continues. Shades of Scheherazade. The fate of the narrator depends on how she narrates.

[13]"But now the narrative past, like the divine Beginner for whom it was for a time a surrogate, has lost its authenticating power. Far from being an authenticating agent, indeed, it has become the very type of inauthenticity. *Here* and *now* may be unpleasant, but at least they are authentic in being really here and now, and not susceptible to explanation in some shadowy *there* and *then*" (Lionel Trilling, *Sincerity and Authenticity* [Cambridge: Harvard University Press, 1972], 139).

4

Textual Rescue:
The *Portuguese Letters*

Our next work is a more complex reflexive diary than the two just discussed. It is also the earliest example of this special kind of reflexivity I have been able to find. The *Portuguese Letters (Lettres portugaises)*, five in all, appeared anonymously in French in 1669. A note to the reader explained that they were translated from Portuguese originals, all of them lost, but it is almost certain that they were composed by a minor literary figure, the future French ambassador to Constantinople, Gabriel-Joseph de Lavergne de Guilleragues (1628–1685). His creation, Mariane, writes from her convent to the French officer who has loved and left her. The five letters chart the course of her passion after his departure. Their popularity was extraordinary, and for the rest of the century and well into the next they were pirated, imitated, and translated. Portuguese "originals" appeared, as did the letters of the French officer—reputed to be a fat dull fellow, weighty evidence that love is blind—and more letters by Mariane. As one scholar has noted, the slim volume virtually created its own suburb of literary culture:

> The letters were printed in every conceivable order and were read as avidly one way as the other. Their success was so great that it tempted writers and booksellers alike, and from their mutual emulation arose a new literary genre, that of the "Portugaises." The word "Portugaise" became generic and was applied not only to imitations . . . but also to every kind of correspondence in which passion was laid bare.[1]

[1]Charles E. Kany, *The Beginnings of the Epistolary Novel in France, Italy, and Spain* (Berkeley: University of California Press, 1937), 116.

Guilleragues did not, by at least 1700 years, invent the epistolary fiction. Its ancestry is classical, and during the sixteenth and seventeenth centuries it flourished in the romance languages and English, particularly in the literature of *l'amour-passion*. Guilleragues's generic originality lay in the mutation he effected in the art of letters, most notably in psychological intensity. As several scholars have convincingly argued, Guilleragues achieved this by crossing the style and passionate movement of tragic *tirade* with the epistolary mode. Yet even here, Ovid's *Heroides* and its seventeenth-century imitations form a highly suggestive precedent (the *Portuguese Letters* themselves were transcribed into verse and were compared favorably to the *Heroides*). Guilleragues helped to revolutionize the epistolary genre not simply in the intensity of language but also in the hermetic containment he achieved by making his heroine a nun, confined to her cell, and by suppressing her cavalier's replies, cold as they are supposed to be. Thus, Guilleragues compounded his own effacement as author with a further effacement of all characters other than Mariane. The effect is that of a subjectivity thrown back almost entirely on its own resources.

Thanks to this strategic isolation of the writer, the text has recurred from time to time as a major exhibit in the ancient controversy between the advocates of *art* and the advocates of *génie*. Is it the product of an artist's patience and craft or is it found art, the natural effect of passion?[2] I mention this conflict not so much to review the merits of the two sides as to point out that it directly parallels a conflict that Mariane (let us accept her fictional status) experiences during the course of her letter writing. The poles of this conflict could be expressed thus: Am I nature's innocent child whose words spring directly from the torments of my love for this man (génie), or is there a form of calculation operating here, something more complex of which I am not wholly aware and which exploits this occasion for my own ends (art)?

---

[2]When, in the early nineteenth century, a real Portuguese nun, Mariana Alcoforado, was discovered to have been in her convent during the probable time of composition, partisans of innate and untrained creativity—of which that century had its fair share—carried the field, and to this day most libraries keep the volume in the Portuguese literature section, catalogued under "Alcoforado, Mariana." It was not until Deloffre and Rougeot published their edition of the *Lettres* in 1962 that the debate was conclusively decided in favor of art, primarily through a wealth of excellent internal observations.

Postulating the conflict is not to deny that there is a level of simplicity in the nun's love—that she has, or at least had, a genuine, outgoing love for the cavalier. But she is no patient Griselda, and the complexity of her departure from that type stems primarily from the fact that she is engaged in creating, or at least in preserving, a special idea of herself: engaged in something like art. This complexity of the nun, added to her confinement (her lack of anything *but* her pen), gives her text its reflexive energy. It focuses all her attention on writing itself, causing that writing in turn to play its own reciprocal part in her tale. It is a faint tale, as tales go, with a very constricted field of action, but it is nonetheless a genuine drama, with a genuine plot, in which the opponents are insight and self-preservation and in which the external world, shadowy and distant as it may be, plays its part as well. As we shall see, it is the intrusion of a letter from her cavalier that leads the nun to a strenuous effort to renegotiate her textual life in Letter 5.

There is a buried syllogism in these letters and it goes like this: (1) All great love is greatly to be loved, (2) I love greatly, (3) therefore I am greatly to be loved. As Mariane struggles to win back her lover, she also struggles to maintain the truth of the syllogism. When, with the arrival of the cavalier's letter, the syllogism appears doomed, she seeks to rescue it by disengaging its third clause from her lover (that is, to change the sense from "I am greatly to be loved by you" to "I am greatly to be loved, period"). She does not decisively win or lose this struggle for the syllogism. But in struggling for it at all she is engaged in an *art* of self-preservation. This in turn generates a parallel struggle: the struggle to keep full awareness of this object from her consciousness. Such a clear understanding of her motives would diminish her self-conception; her love would appear too much a form of egotism, too little a spontaneous devotion to her lover. In this light, her nunship is again an important supporting feature of the work, for she carries over into her love two often conflicting moods of the devout—a craving for glory through self-sacrifice and a horror of self-aggrandizement.

She never lets her lover forget that she is a nun. As she says, nuns may not offer the most exciting prospects, but they can give the most unalloyed devotion—"nothing keeps them from thinking incessantly of their passion."[3] Even in her abandonment, moreover, there are advantages in being a nun rather than her lover's French mistress. Were she his French mistress she would be getting a second-rate love because his heart must belong to a nun in Portugal (why? because the nun loves him greatly and therefore is greatly to be loved): "better to suffer as I do than to enjoy the dull pleasures of your French mistresses. I do not envy your indifference; I pity you. I defy you to forget me. I flatter myself that I have affected you so deeply that all your pleasures must be imperfect without me; while I am happier because I have more to occupy me" (44–45).

In both these passages Mariane's consciousness of herself as a lover bears a strong resemblance to what in religious terms would be called spiritual pride. Note that she says nuns think incessantly, not of their lover ("à leur amant"), but of their passion ("à leur passion"). And though the second passage, "better to suffer as I do ... " is formulated as a way of making the best of the worst, the formula recurs so often that it gives evidence of a positive desire for martyrdom: "make me suffer still greater torments," "treat me severely!" ("faites-moi souffrir encore plus de maux"[42], "traitez-moi sévèrement!"[49]). How else can she prove the intensity of her devotion? In one particularly abandoned passage, she yearns for her own public repudiation of all other idols: "Let everyone know; I would not keep it a secret. I am thrilled at having done what I have for you against all decorum. My only honor and religion are to love you all my life"(45). Her extravagance is the enthusiasm of a convert, and at moments she hints a vague awareness that the enthusiasm is of more importance than the object that inspires it: "I strongly feel that my remorse is not sincere, that I would willingly have risked far greater dangers for love of you, and that I take a fatal pleasure in having gambled my life and my honor"(49).

And could it be—as she asks in Letter 5, more in hope at the moment than chagrin—that her lover is less dear to her than her passion ("que vous m'étiez moins chère que ma passion"[62])? Com-

---

[3]Gabriel-Joseph de Lavergne de Guilleragues, *Lettres portugaises, Valintins et autre oeuvres*, ed. F. Deloffre and J. Rougeot (Paris: Garnier, 1962), 65; translations from this work are my own.

mon as the condition may be, it is nonetheless a paradox—and with painful implications if one looks at it closely. Yet at times she does catch glimpses of it, even becoming aware of the corollary function of her letters: the pocket mirror in which she applies her makeup. "Does my despair, then, exist only in my letters?"(49). At the end of the fourth letter, when the lieutenant who is to take it to the cavalier tells her he must go, she lets him leave and continues to write. "Let him go. I write more for myself than for you; all I seek is consolation"(58). The solace she derives from her letters lies in a form of self-reassurance. Though I may not be greatly loved by you, still I find myself greatly loving and therefore greatly to be loved.

If this attitude can be called the spiritual pride of a lover, it can also be seen as Mariane's attempt to free her self-conception from dependency on her cavalier—to displace him, that is, from the third clause of the syllogism. One of the features that makes the letters as moving as they are is that this attempt coexists, side by side, with her efforts to maintain the syllogism in its original form. I love you greatly, therefore you ought greatly to love me. Look at the evidence; look at these *letters*: "Before you engage in a passionate affair, consider well the extremity of my sorrows, the confusion of my hopes, the range of my passions, the extravagance of my letters, my trust, my despair, my desire, my jealousy" (56–57). Letter 5— which in its main intention at least is a letter of rejection, expressing Mariane's confirmed hatred of her lover, announcing the return of his letters, and threatening vengeance should he come back— opens by referring to itself as the logical effect of the syllogism's corollary: (1) Only great love is greatly to be loved, (2) you do not greatly love me, (3) therefore I cannot greatly love you. "I hope to convince you, by this letter's change in wording and manner, that you have finally persuaded me that you no longer love me, and that, accordingly, I should no longer love you" (61).

Yet even in her determination to be firm, she softens the terms of the syllogism as she applies them to their situation. Not "You *do not* love me," but "You *have persuaded me* that you do not"; not "I *cannot* love you," but "I *should not*." Many touches in the letter show that her heart is not so fully resolved as her mind, including the pathetic note on which it concludes ("must I give you a complete account of all my feelings?"[69]), and it becomes clear that the one she is really trying to convince "by this letter's change in wording and manner" is herself. She is recomposing her features in her mirror.

One source of her pain is that the reflection that has worked so well for her has left her lover unmoved. Indeed, the immediate cause of the fifth letter is his latest letter in which he has proposed friendship, a proposal the effects of which are far worse than a proposal of undying enmity. He has broken a universal law. Very well, she says, I will not pretend to deal logically with you—"I do not intend to prove by rational argument that you ought to love me; that would be a feeble method"—but then, with the implicit power of the syllogism behind her words, goes on: "I have used much better ones that have failed"(65). The better methods have been her passionate letters, which his latest letter proves he has read, but read unmoved ("they have not aroused the slightest feeling in your heart, and yet you have read them" [63]). By the last pages of the letter, she makes it clear that she now knows that as far as love between men and women is concerned she has adopted the wrong syllogism. "To be loved requires artifice; one must cunningly seek out ways to arouse passion, for love alone cannot inspire love"(67). She comes close to the sober cynicism of La Rochefoucauld: No great love is greatly loved; I have greatly loved you; therefore you must not have greatly loved me.

It is her lover's latest letter, this intrusion of fact from the external world, that has severely undermined what has been a sustained effort in imaginative construction. Though she had been asking repeatedly for some testimony of his true feelings, now that she has it, she is furious that he sent it. "I detest your candor. Did I ask you for the truth? Could you not leave me to my love? All you had to do was stop writing; I had no wish to be enlightened"(63). Her motives are mixed as she writes this, and her sarcasm is meant to cut both her lover and herself. Yet, however ironic in part, she expresses a genuine, though necessarily fleeting recognition that in writing she has been engaging in self-creation. "Do not trouble the state I am preparing for myself" ("Ne troublez pas l'état que je me prépare" [63]). Don't write any more; you have done enough damage already. "Do not rob me of my incertitude" ("N'ôtez point de mon incertitude" [63]). Give me room.

Though, thanks to his letter, a new syllogism must emerge for the love between men and women, it is still a version of the old syllogism that governs her efforts in the fifth letter. If the laws of mundane love allowed her lover to move without being moved, she may still inspire admiration in her own eyes and those of eternity (where great love is still greatly lovable). She reconstructs: I was responsible for my suffering because I loved too sincerely ("avec trop bonne foi"). You were responsible for my suffering because you calculated. "Since you had conceived this plot, there was nothing you would not have done to carry it out; you were even ready to love me, had it been necessary; but you knew in advance that you could succeed in your enterprise without passion"(67). You were even ready to fall in love if need be—even passion (as it turned out it was not necessary) was part of your scheme. In short you were a monster of art, but as for me, "I was young, I was unsuspecting, ... I had never heard the flattery that you constantly used"(68). I was a child of génie.

Readers have tended to see the fifth letter as calmer and more resolved than the others. Some have found in it the emotional purgation of tragedy's fifth act (Spitzer, Deloffre).[4] Still others have gone on to find in it a romantic transcendence in which Mariane transmutes her physical love into an ideal love and thus wins independence from her lover (Rilke, Dronke, Highman).[5] Though my own interpretation is closer to the latter, it differs in several essentials. As I read the *Letters*, Mariane is engaged throughout in a sustained act of idealization, both of her love and of herself as a lover. Her fifth letter, however, is an emergency operation. Its changes in tone are a consequence of the shattering effect her lover's most recent letter has had on her project. Instead of purging her soul, her last letter leaves several conflicts still in progress: her desire to repudiate her lover once and for all, and her desire to

---

[4]Leo Spitzer, "Les *Lettres portugaises*," *Romanische Forschungen* 65 (1954), 94–135.
[5]"For centuries now, women have undertaken the entire task of love.... And from among them, under the stress of endless need, have gone forth those valiant lovers, who, while they called him, rose above their man; who grew beyond him when he did not return, like Gaspara Stampa or like the Portuguese nun, who never desisted until their torture was transmuted into an austere, icy, splendour which nothing could confine" (Rainer Maria Rilke, *The Journal of My Other Self*, trans. John Linton [New York: Norton, 1930], 127–128). See also E. P. Dronke, "Héloise and Mariane: Some Considerations," *Romanische Forschungen* 72 (1960), 223–256; and David E. Highman, "*Lettres portugaises*: Passion in Search of Survival," *Modern Language Quarterly* 33(1972), 370–381.

have him back; her desire to be left free to invent her life and the necessity of hiding that motive; her desire to find in her love alone a sufficient source of self-esteem and the necessity of masking the implications of sterility and egocentrism inherent in such an enterprise. The nun loves her lover simply, I believe, but she also loves herself, or wants to, and from that motive arises much of the complexity of her tone and phrasing. If the French *art* is too strong a word for what she does, she nonetheless, in her spontaneous way, uses her pocket mirror to touch up again and again certain intolerable facts of her life.

From our point of view in this study, the nun's performance has a psychological density that exceeds that of the two fictional writers we examined in the last chapter. She was endowed by her creator with a considerable courage of insight that adds markedly to the complication of her text. At the molecular level of her prose, one finds evidence of her struggle everywhere. Moreover, she is not, like Werther and Pechorin, a romantic hero at large in the human community. Because she is instead a nun, confined to her convent, with little power to help or hurt anyone beyond herself, the moral character of her performance is less distinct than its continual pathos. She is clearly intended to be seen as a Racinian sensibility contending nobly with her plight.

The year 1669 may be one of the neglected dates in the history of fiction. It saw not only the publication of the *Portuguese Letters* but also the publication of Edme Boursault's *Lettres de respect, d'obligation et d'amour*, more commonly known as the *Lettres de Babet*.[6] Boursault's distinction is to have doubled the letter writers so that what one reads is a coherent and unified correspondence. Like the *Portuguese Letters*, the *Lettres de Babet* was immediately imitated, pirated, and travestied. Put them beside each other, and you have the seeds of the two major developments of epistolary fiction during the next two hundred years. Boursault's work grows into the com-

---

[6]Boursault's *Lettres de respect* may have originally appeared in 1668. We should also note here a third work from 1667, the Abbé d'Aubignac's *Le roman de lettres ou Nouveau Roman composé de lettres et billets*. Between them, Aubignac, Boursault, and Guilleragues established a new departure from the general run of letter manuals, found collections and imitations of the *Heroides* that Yves Giraud calls "the prehistory of the letter novel" (*Bibliographie du roman épistolaire en France des origines à 1842* [Fribourg: Editions universitaires Fribourg Suisse, 1977], 7).

plex symphonic correspondence novels for which the eighteenth century is noted both in quantity and quality. Guilleragues's work gives birth to the more claustrophobic minor strain, overshadowed (in historical retrospect, at least) by the much longer and more richly plotted correspondence novels, yet kept alive by such writers as Crébillon fils, Mme Graffigny, Mrs. Sheridan, and Mme Riccoboni until it blossomed out in *Werther*. With the subsequent development of the diary novel, it has survived the passing of the correspondence novel and is still around today.

It would, of course, be foolish to try to argue for some generic purity in this distinction. Like most literary distinctions, it defines two poles between which a variety of imitation and experiment ranges. The *Portuguese Letters* was quickly appropriated by the correspondence form (Mariane's letters were published in several editions with replies from her cavalier), just as the correspondence novel appropriated degrees of cloistering and self-communion. But what the *Portuguese Letters* represents is a strategy that in the main goes counter to the effects of sharing and communion with another, which are so much a part of correspondence fiction. Of course, Mariane is writing *to* someone, but her isolation, the suppression of her cavalier's letters and equally important, the suppression of any other letters from friends or relatives puts the focus on the unassisted subjectivity of the writer herself. It makes her letters essentially a diary. It is no accident that the strategy should have emerged, and to such popular enthusiasm, at the point that it did in literary history. Its appearance roughly coincides with what both Trilling and Lars Gustafsson have identified as the emergence of sincerity as a valued human trait.[7] The device allows one a privileged glimpse into the writer's inner world.

Guilleragues's genius, as I have tried to show, was to create a reflexive text as well and in so doing to achieve an intensity of interest that far exceeds the fully validated sincerity of his imitators' nuns. He went beyond the simple appeal of sincerity to the more complex appeal of authenticity, creating as it were a hermetic experiment

---

[7]Lionel Trilling, *Sincerity and Authenticity* (Cambridge: Harvard University Press, 1972), esp. 1–25; Lars Gustafsson, *Le poète masqué et démasqué: Etude sur la mise en valeur du poète sincère dans la poétique du classicisme et du préromantisme* (Uppsala: Almquist and Wiksells, 1968). See also Paul Delany, *British Autobiography in the Seventeenth Century* (London: Routledge, 1969).

designed for a culture increasingly concerned with the internal character of honesty. The work takes us into a sealed chamber to observe the actual chemistry of self-deception and insight. In the process it reveals how fully implicated in this chemical process is that principal vehicle of sincerity, the passionate letter. From one moment to the next the nun endows her words with an energy that comes back to her, to alter or maintain the shape of her self-awareness. As I have argued, the self-revelatory power of her letters is overbalanced, if only barely, by their power to sustain for the nun a fixed interpretation of her passion. As she admits, she is essentially writing letters to herself.

We have, then, a distinction, introduced right at the start of the prolific development of the diary or single letter-writer mode: a distinction between the rare instances of the special reflexive text and the densely stocked category of the sincere or purely expressive text. The latter is the text the nun *would* compose. Thanks to her intelligence and, more crucially, to the division of her needs, it is a text she cannot achieve. It may well be, of course, that the purely expressive text is a text no one, in reality, can achieve, but we are speaking here of a vogue in literary culture, a vogue that reflected a popular ideal. As would happen a hundred years later with *The Sorrows of Young Werther*, the *Portuguese Letters* was read as an expressive text and spawned a host of imitation nuns who, unlike the original, loved and wrote with a pellucid sincerity. As they were sincere, so their language was transparent, for in the expressive text there is no reciprocal exchange of energy between writer and text. Instead the energy all goes in one direction: from the writer to the reader. As we have noted, this belief in an achievable transparency of language goes hand in hand with the ideal of sincerity. It accompanies it right through the next century and is as much the equipment of those Peruvian princesses who wrote in imitation of Mme Graffigny's *Lettres d'une Péruvienne* (1747) as it was of the imitation nuns.

The expressive text thrives on a fatalism that does much to eliminate the significance of willed human activity. Consequently, the heroism of the writer is achieved not in acts but in self-expression. Much of the originality of the three works discussed in this chapter and the last rests in the way they hold such an art up to scrutiny. The art of spontaneous self-expression becomes at once more interesting and more treacherous, because in these works it has been reconnected to plot. Thus, from Werther's point of view, Werther is composing in his letters an expressive text in which the medium is transparent and the self shines through; but from Goethe's point of view, Werther's is also a self-concealing text in which the medium serves to prevent in its author a reperception of self that might bring on extensive changes. The transformation of a journal of self-expression into a journal of self-concealment is the transformation of a tale of fixed destiny into one that features the *possibility* of another plot. It is a metaphysical shift, a shift from fatalism to free choice, that maintains in the wings a secularized Augustinian tale of will and insight. The tensive brilliance of the *Portuguese Letters* lies in the way this latter possibility glides in and out of the text, unresolvedly, almost from sentence to sentence.

5

Textual Healing

The Werther approach to intercalated writing—the purely expressive ideal—not only antedates the nun, but carries past the jaded Byronic sincerity of Pechorin and on through the nineteenth century. With the publication of numerous journaux intimes in France during the last two decades of the century, it was given a new popularity with a new coloration. Nineteenth-century intimistes were moved increasingly by a vacancy (not a superabundance) of feeling to turn to their diaries. This sense of an interior blank was aggravated by the tendency (epitomized in the journals of Henri Amiel) to turn the diary itself into a battleground on which what emotion and will to action remain in the diarist are defeated by a constant barrage of intellectual analysis. These tendencies were in turn reflected in the fictional counterpart of the journal intime. Werther's fin de siècle cousin (in novels by Garborg, Rod, Söderberg) is generally drier, more abstract, disenchanted from the start, and cursed not by too much but by too little feeling.

An exception of note to this prevailing desiccation is the diarist hero of Gide's first novel, *The Notebooks of André Walter* (*Les cahiers d'André Walter*, 1891). Gide read *The Sorrows of Young Werther* at the same time he was composing *The Notebooks*, and it is hard to doubt that the twenty-one-year-old lover read that book more in the spirit of Werther than of Goethe. More precisely, he must have read it as a document of the legend that grew up around it, which stressed the similarity of the names Werther and Goethe, Lotte and Charlotte. So closely does Gide's first novel render his thoughts as lover and aspiring novelist that the alteration of "Gide" to "Walter" in

83

the title is (at least in the first notebook) almost gratuitous. Gide, in fact, lifted passages from his own journal to write his novel. At other times during its composition, he watched his face in a mirror. As noted in Chapter 1 the mirror scene is standard in the diary novel, but I doubt that it has ever achieved a more direct transcription. Unlike *The Sorrows of Young Werther*, no distance is invited in this text. Entirely unreflexive, it is dedicated to the service of "emotions too pure to be spoken,"[1] emotions holy enough to be venerated and relived as ends in themselves.

It is not far from this point to what is probably the apotheosis of the expressive text: the automatic writing and dream journals of the surrealists. The whole bias of the diary tradition against plan, order, form, in short against art, culminates in the uncompromising efforts of the surrealists against consciousness itself. André Walter's ideal of writing badly on purpose ("I wish to write badly on purpose. I will destroy all harmonies")[2] becomes André Breton's "pure psychic automatism":

> Tell yourself that literature is the saddest path that leads to everything. Write quickly, without a preconceived subject, fast enough not to remember and not to be tempted to read over what you have written....Continue as long as you like. Trust in the inexhaustible character of the murmur. If silence threatens to take over because you have made a mistake...following the word whose origin seems suspect to you, put down any letter, the letter l for instance, always the letter l, and restore the arbitrary by imposing this letter as the initial of the word that will come next.[3]

Yet there were, during this same long period in which expressive texts thrived, two manifestations of cloistered, inward, and intercalated writing that were intended to be neither "expressive" nor "self-concealing" but positive reflexive texts. The contrast between them is sharp, but they are both English, both rooted in a basically Christian paradigm of human development and both prepsychoanalytic forerunners of the popular modern therapeutic diary.

[1] André Gide, *Les cahiers et les poésies d'André Walter* (1891; reprint, Paris: Gallimard, 1952), 18, my translation.
[2] Gide, *Les cahiers*, 19.
[3] From "The Surrealist Manifesto," quoted in Maurice Nadeau, *The History of Surrealism*, trans. Richard Howard (New York: Macmillan, 1965), 89–90.

Richardson and the Puritan Diary

The Puritan diary, which caught on most vigorously in England and America, is in many ways the polar opposite of the journal intime, which did not catch on in either country. Where the latter is a much more immediate end in itself, the former is preeminently *useful*. Where the journal intime tends to relish particulars for their own sake, the Puritan diary seeks the universal or abstract structure of the diarist's life. Where the one (in the spirit of Rousseau) is individuating, the other is conforming. Where the one is generally shapeless, the other is dominated by the moment of conversion. In essence, where the Puritan diary is a tool or guide to be used for a life going on outside it, the journal intime is in many cases identified with life itself. When Julian Green, at the near end of the journal intime tradition, writes, "In what concerns me, writing is confounded with being,"[4] he echoes very closely the sentiment of Joseph Joubert at the far end: "[To keep a journal] is at once to lead and contemplate one's life. It is living itself."[5]

The Puritan Protestant found in the diary a tailored instrument for self-observation.[6] It became the superior Puritan counterpart of the Catholic confessional, more scrupulously attentive to all daily acts and more purely private—a record for the eyes of God and the communicant alone, without clerical mediation. The diary, moreover, enjoyed a distinct additional advantage over the confessional in that it established a record. It was both a written confession of sins before God *and* a mirror in which the confessor could review for himself those sins combined with all of his other deeds and thoughts. In his diary, the Puritan's life became inescapable. Thus, it allowed the communicant to determine the true character of his spiritual—in other words, his essential—existence.

Early in the history of the form, then, the Puritan appropriated

[4]Julian Green, *Journal*, vol. 6, *1950–1954* (Paris: Plon, 1955), 32, my translation.
[5]Quoted in Béatrice Didier, *Le journal intime* (Paris: Presses universitaires de France, 1976), 39, my translation.
[6]Good sources of information about Puritan diaries are William Haller, *The Rise of Puritanism* (New York: Harper, 1957), 96–100; J. Paul Hunter, *The Reluctant Pilgrim: Defoe's Emblematic Method and the Quest for Form in Robinson Crusoe* (Baltimore: Johns Hopkins, 1966), 76–92; K. Murdoch, "The Personal Literature of the Puritans," in his *Literature and Theology in Colonial New England* (Cambridge: Harvard University Press, 1949), 99–135; and G. A. Starr, *Defoe and Spiritual Autobiography* (Princeton: Princeton University Press, 1965), 29–33.

the diary and converted it to a powerful instrument for the determination of personal identity. Identity, of course, is defined here in strictly spiritual terms and with salvation in mind. That it was a laborious and challenging enterprise was predicated on the idea that one's spiritual identity, in contrast to one's public or familial identity, was difficult to determine, easily obscured, buried in the world of appearances. Yet it was only *through* appearances that this essential reality could be found. The Puritan diarist in consequence developed the habit of minute scrutiny, recording details many of which could not at the moment be interpreted. Preserved in the text, they allowed him at a later date to read himself, as it were, with an enlightened eye.[7]

It is most likely this concern to achieve a correct, retrospective interpretation of events that accounts for the, to modern readers, curiously awkward management of the diary in its first known insertion into fiction in *Robinson Crusoe* (1719). In Defoe's novel, the journal commences, strongly enough, shortly after Crusoe lands on the island. But no sooner is it well established than it becomes laced at gradually increasing length and frequency with retrospective intrusions until at last, roughly twenty pages from where it began, the journal dissolves into the narrative for good. There is no doubt impatience and failure of craft involved here. In some passages, the modulation to a retrospective narrative is so casually accomplished that the reader awakens with a kind of jolt to the fact that what he or she is reading is no longer, at this point, the imitation of a journal. But, as both J. Paul Hunter and Everett Zimmerman have persuasively argued,[8] it is because the Puritan diarist is incapable of reading the spiritual significance of what he does and

---

[7]The gift of insight, of course, could never be presumed. It is this presumption that James Hogg unveiled in his attack on the Antinomian Heresy, *The Private Memoirs and Confessions of a Justified Sinner* (1824). From the moment his father tells him that the Lord has answered his prayers and assured his son of sainthood, Robert Calvin gets *everything* wrong, including the true identity of his friend (the devil). One could read, in short, as incorrectly as correctly. A genuine conversion might begin one's career as an interpreter, but true interpretation required time and reflection. This may also be what Duhamel was parodying in *Salavin's Journal* (1927). At the moment Salavin decides to become a saint, he begins his diary and at the same time begins looking for the signs of his sainthood.

[8]Hunter, 144–147; Everett Zimmerman, *Defoe and the Novel* (Berkeley: University of California Press, 1975), 40–41.

what happens to him that the Puritan autobiographer feels compelled to intrude with his present understanding:

> The growing up of the Corn, as is hinted in my Journal, had at first some little Influence upon me, and began to affect me with Seriousness, as long as I thought it had something miraculous in it; but as soon as ever that Part of the Thought was remov'd, all the Impression which was rais'd from it, wore off also, as I have noted already.
>
> Even the Earthquake, tho' nothing could be more terrible in its Nature, or more immediately directing to the Invisible Power which alone directs such Things, yet no sooner was the first Fright over, but the Impression it had made went off also. I had no more Sense of God or his Judgements, much less of the present Affliction of my Circumstances being from his Hand, than if I had been in the most prosperous Condition of Life.[9]

Defoe slips back into the retrospective mode here because he feels an urgency, in spite of the advantages of realism and immediacy that the diary gave him, to show the true spiritual character of what was happening to his hero. As Crusoe the diarist was not equipped to do this, Crusoe the mature autobiographer had to do it for him.

Technically, Crusoe's is not even a proper Puritan diary. It is not undertaken as a religious duty. It is begun as a record of his stay on the island and *just happens* to include that period, early in his stay, when he is awakened to "Seriousness" by a dream, a fever, some hard thinking, and his first spontaneous prayer. For the novelist, it serves in part the functions of realistic "validation" and documentary immediacy. It may also have been introduced as a signal, recognizable in the Puritan "code of meaningful actions," to indicate that "a process of spiritual betterment is underway."[10] But for Crusoe himself, the diary is an instrument to define and maintain his spiritual identity. Though the converted Puritan did not write it, the converted Puritan now puts it to Puritan use. In providing the documentary testimony of that "certain Stupidity of Soul" that characterized him of old, Crusoe defines the distance between what he was and what he is now. Intruding the diary at

[9]*Robinson Crusoe*, ed. Michael Shinagel (New York: Norton, 1975), 72.
[10]Lorna Martens, "The Diary Novel and Contemporary Fiction: Studies in Max Frisch, Michel Butor, and Doris Lessing" (Ph.D. diss., Yale University, 1976), 38.

this point helps maintain that distance. It also helps him maintain vigilance against the very blindness it gives evidence to. And finally, since the diary contains the awakening of his conscience, it serves as documentary evidence of God's Grace, evidence made even more vivid and dramatic because it is extended to the "hardned, unthinking, wicked Creature" (71) who keeps the document that records it. The diary, then, is an *object* in this tale, submitted in evidence to characterize an earlier state of being, and thus functions like the other recalled acts and events of the narrative. It does not, in other words, take part in the kind of immediate, dynamic reciprocity of writing and living we have been examining so far. And though it plays a vital, kinetic role in maintaining the identity of the *present* Crusoe—the mature Puritan writing his life story—it does not function actively *in* that story.

The letters of Richardson's Pamela, which appeared twenty-one years after *Robinson Crusoe*, are, if anything, the work of a more orthodox Puritan self-transcriber. Once Pamela is married to Mr. B, for example, she characteristically acquires a blank journal and, echoing the mercantile terminology of Puritans, vows to keep it "quarter to quarter; and I will, if any be left, carry it on, like an accomptant, to the next quarter, and strike a balance four times a year, and a general balance at every year's end.—And I have written in it, *Humble* RETURNS *for* DIVINE MERCIES."[11] But this journal will be, essentially, a continuation of the same daily exercise she has been carrying out all along in her letters to her parents. As Hunter points out, Richardson capitalized on the immediacy of letters to allow his heroine to compile, in the Puritan manner, an inventory of all the potentially emblematic detail in her life.[12] In her study *Samuel Richardson and the Eighteenth-Century Puritan Character*, Cynthia Griffin Wolff expands on this insight by showing how both Pamela and Clarissa appear to be writing their letters as much for

---

[11]Samuel Richardson, *Pamela, or Virtue Rewarded*, ed. William M. Sale, Jr. (New York: Norton, 1958), 501.

[12]"A close reading of Richardson in historical context reveals the same rhythms, the same providential control of events, the same detail-become-emblem [as Defoe]. Richardson's 'writing to the moment' technique becomes, in fact, the ultimate (but inadvertent) *reductio* of the emblematic method, a point which did not escape Fielding when he had Shamela record her seduction moment by moment as a good diarist searching for 'meaning' should" (Hunter, 208–209).

themselves as for the recipients, if not more. Often they write regardless of whether or not a letter can be sent, treasuring their letters as if they had a significance or use far beyond that of communication. And they obsessively record everything: "The letters serve their writers in much the same way that the spiritual diary served their Puritan ancestors. They are the record of a trial— overfull of detail so that no morally incorrect interpretation might be imposed upon them."[13]

It is clear, then, that in contrast to *Robinson Crusoe*, which is the imitation of a Puritan spiritual autobiography that makes use briefly of a journal, much of Richardson's first novel is the imitation of a Puritan diary. Moreover, where Crusoe's journal had no effective role to play in the development of his story, Pamela's letters play a pivotal role in hers. One could quite reasonably argue, for that matter, that they are the single most important element in diverting the tale from its tragic course to its "comic" outcome, because Mr. B, who has been bent upon stealing Pamela's virginity, along the way steals her letters, reads them, and changes his object. When he takes her letters, Mr. B. jestingly animadverts on precisely the position they occupy in the story, little realizing how true his words will be: "Besides, said he, there is such a pretty air of romance, as you relate them, in *your* plots, and *my* plots, that I shall be better directed in what manner to wind up the catastrophe of the pretty novel."[14] So great is the combination of truth and affective power in Pamela's letters that Mr. B is, quite literally, converted. Like any spiritual rebirth, his is a conversion in the heart, where it counts. As Lady Davers, his sister, says, he is "turned *Puritan*."[15] This, too, has its dramatic irony, since, much as she is undisposed to the unfavorable marriage of her brother, she herself is eventually converted—and by the same textual agency.

What Richardson has come up with, among other things, is a book in which the book itself is vitally engaged in determining its own outcome. In reading the story as we have read it, that is, through Pamela's letters, Mr. B experiences a rewriting of the history in which he had a part. The plot he had been spinning in his

[13]Cynthia Griffin Wolff, *Samuel Richardson and the Eighteenth-Century Puritan Character* (Hamden, Conn.: Archon, 1972), 38.
[14]Richardson, *Pamela*, 242.
[15]Richardson, *Pamela*, 449.

imagination depended on a certain cliché of the servant girl—and of the master. By reading her letters he discovers a character of quite a different depth and a plot, too, of an altogether different shape. He discovers that what had been for him an amusing tale had really been a harrowing one—on the brink of tragedy. Character and plot thus lock together. They do so with an added twist: as Mr. B. reads the letters, his own character undergoes a transformation in depth, which in turn allows him to step in and effect yet another transformation in the plot.

Essentially Richardson has drawn upon the tradition of public utility that belongs to the Puritan spiritual autobiography (the improving book). He has combined this tradition with sentimental confidence in the power of spontaneous utterance. The work is a *feeling record*, doubly powerful because the emblematic spiritual record is communicated by a pen charged with the feelings of the moment. But, to repeat, it is in its communicative, that is, its extra-subjective, outwardly directed, and (by the end of the story) thoroughly public, role that Pamela's collection of letters functions. The letters are not, in other words, a text vitally engaged in the personal evolution of the one who keeps it. As in the case of *Robinson Crusoe*, so too in *Pamela* we do not have the kind of close interplay between writing and the behavior of the one who writes that we find in paradigmatic reflexive diaries. When Pamela is taken prisoner on Mr. B's Lincolnshire estate, she does keep her letters "journal-wise," as her editor remarks, so that she might at some later date "examine, and either approve or repent of her own conduct in them."[16] But as her letters are, after all, a record of her own virtue under distress, there is little she can learn from them—little of significance for her story—that she does not already know.

Seven years later, in Clarissa's letters (for their composer, essentially a letter journal—as are Pamela's), Richardson developed a demonstrable reflexivity of the kind on which we have been focusing in this study.[17] Studies of the epistolary character of Richardson's

---

[16]Richardson, *Pamela*, 98.

[17]Wolff has argued that for Pamela, as much as for Clarissa, letters serve as expressions or objectifications of her identity, providing her with a sense of the continuity of her self (Wolff, 31–40). In *Pamela*, I find this function is more implicit; in *Clarissa*, more explicit. For Wolff's provocative treatment of the role of letters in *Clarissa*, see Wolff, 39–40, 127–135, 156–167.

work have generally made much, and quite rightly, of the *outward* power of writing as a theme. In Richardson's novels, as in Choderlos de Laclos's *Les liaisons dangereuses*, letters are instruments of influence. Clarissa's odious sister puts her finger on it: "You had always a knack at writing; and depended upon making every one do what you would when you wrote."[18] But from our perspective, the important power of these letters is their reflexive power; the important addressee, Clarissa herself. They are vitally important to her in that they constitute, to use her own phrase, her "written mind" (125). In this regard, the sequel to *Pamela* (1742) is an important work in the transition to *Clarissa*. It allowed Richardson to provide the intellectual record of a mature woman, of tested and proven virtue, who extends her thoughts like rays outward from the core of that virtue. Much has been made, and rightly, of the emotive or sentimental expressiveness of Richardson's "writing to the moment" technique, including a good deal by Richardson himself. But the daily record in letters is equally useful as an ongoing, continually expanding elaboration of *views*. Given the manifold trials of marriage—the threat of her husband's infidelity, childbirth, the raising of children—the letter writer methodically accommodates them to her confident assumption of an ultimate moral order, an order in which she in turn has her own high place. As continual assertions of order, the letters reinforce her own substantiality. Developed in the mature Pamela, this bent is continued in the letters of Clarissa.

In her letters, Clarissa must continually and dutifully set down what she thinks on whatever topic is at hand. The letters are an almost limitless instrument for extending her moral self-conception out into the universe. She defines precisely the proper conditions of marriage, the duties of a daughter to her father, the necessary qualifications of a suitor. In this way she pursues, with an urgency shared by her author, the effort of establishing the sufficiency of her moral—that is, ultimately, her spiritual—views. It is a project that requires the preparedness and courage to argue, and in this Clarissa never fails. She must show how all areas of life can be

[18]Richardson, *Clarissa* (1747–1748; reprint, London: Dent, 1932), 4:82. Two studies that include extensive exploration of this outwardly directed force of the letter in the correspondence novel are Tzvetan Todorov's *Littérature et signification* (Paris: Librairie Larousse, 1967) and Janet Gurkin Altman's *Epistolarity: Approaches to a Form* (Columbus: Ohio State University Press, 1982).

rationally accommodated by her beliefs, because both her virtue and her salvation are located within those beliefs. And they must be shown on paper, for set down in ink they at once commit and authenticate the believer.

Clarissa's concern to extend in thought an order, on her own, in which her moral identity can be found—and her use of daily letters to this end—is an aspect of her character very closely related to her pride. Clarissa's pride is still an interpretive crux, but it would appear at bottom to be a pride of autonomy or self-completeness. Her pride enables her to construct a comprehensive moral and intellectual order. Thus, the plot is built on a continual series of threats to the integrity of that order—an order that at once includes and is governed by herself. Like others before and after her who have had little effective power—social, political, economic, physical—she continually and vigilantly buttresses this integrity with her pen. She wields her pen against the threat of her family, and later against the far more serious threat of Lovelace, who, compared with her family, is better equipped for combat in every way, though perhaps in none so much as his appeal to her sexuality—the potential traitor within.

When Lovelace rapes Clarissa, he pushes his assault on her integrity to its furthest limits. It is after this point that the reflexive importance of pen and paper is vividly dramatized. When we next see her, she is observed writing on scraps of paper that she then tears and throws on the floor. As critics have frequently noted, it is in one of these brief and chaotic ramblings that she manages to assert her still inviolate will: "Yet, God knows my heart, I had no culpable inclinations! I honoured virtue! I hated vice! But I knew not that you were vice itself!"[19] But it is the scraps of paper themselves (a dramatic and imaginative response to the exigencies of the epistolary mode) that express the character of this will; for it is in the authority of writing that she seeks the authority of her self. At this point in the novel, Clarissa is as close to complete internal disintegration as she will ever come. By turning in her confusion to the written word, she is clearly trying to reinstate order. In a sense, to go on writing is to go on living. Fragmentary and confused as they are, these scraps of writing hold out the

[19]Richardson, *Clarissa*, 3:208.

promise of that universal coherence that she had spent her life composing in the same medium. Thus, significantly, in the final scrap of paper, she turns to verse. The poem she writes expresses the gradual coming to order of her mind. Beginning with un-rhymed lines of uncertain meter, she builds by the end coherent stanzas.

The importance of her letters, and particularly the whole body of her letters, as the completed edifice of her self is underscored when, in the last weeks of her life, knowing the end is not far off, she devotes no little of her remaining energy to ensuring their preservation. Belmont, her antagonist's close friend, now "con-verted," is asked to be her literary executor—to be, that is, "the protector of my memory." Belmont accepts with the devotion of a hagiographer; and hagiography is, after all, quite literally what he will pursue, since the memory preserved will be that of a martyred Protestant saint. But for Clarissa, it is apparent that the desire to preserve the story of her life for its instructional value is equaled (if not surpassed) by the desire "for my honour's sake" to have the record preserved, period. Belmont is chosen because he has not only her letters but also the contrasting ones of Lovelace. As she says, he will be "the *only* person possessed of materials that will enable him to do my character justice."[20]

There is, then, a clear emphasis on the identity-sustaining func-tion of the letters in *Clarissa*. Whether or not her letters also par-ticipate in Clarissa's *growth* is much more open to debate. There is no doubt that Clarissa does grow, and profoundly, during the course of the novel—particularly as she moves from a self-obscuring and obscured pride to what Richardson wished to be seen as true hu-mility. Her winning her way to a perception of her pridefulness is one of the dramatic aspects of the tale, but I am not convinced that she is greatly assisted in this by an active reflection on what and how she writes. Though, as I have argued, her writing is a means of confirming and sustaining, even of casting a critical eye in true Puritan fashion, on her character, she does not examine herself *in* her writing. She is, moreover, blessed with the lively Anna Howe for a correspondent. In Miss Howe she finds a good mirror. Anna reads Clarissa's letters with a sufficiently critical eye that Clarissa

[20]Richardson, *Clarissa*, 4:78.

is brought to a recognition of her failings. In short, as *Clarissa* is a correspondence novel it is predictably lacking in the test of literary self-analysis that can be dramatically developed in a true diary novel.

In its first appearances in fiction, then, the Puritan diary or letter journal functions primarily to maintain identity. It is an agent of character preservation—in Defoe, by contrast with the old self; in Richardson, by continuity of thought and feeling. Though these texts do not show the complex reciprocal role in the action that we analyzed in Lurie's novel, in *Clarissa*, at least, it is clear that the text is a stay against inner collapse (especially after Clarissa is raped). Clarissa's letters keep her story from having a different, less heroic, outcome. In *Clarissa*, the written record is a positive version of the kind of textual self-support seen in *The Sorrows of Young Werther* and *A Hero of Our Time* and that one can find again in the letters of Clarissa's antagonist, Lovelace. All four fictional writers employ the written images of themselves embedded in their versions of the narrative to withstand shocks to the character structure they strive to preserve. All four succeed in preventing internal collapse. But where Werther, Pechorin, and Lovelace exploit their texts unconsciously to this end, where they are to a degree controlled by a literary manner, where they engage in self-deception, and where it is strongly suggested that internal collapse would be in their cases a step toward rebirth, in Clarissa's letters the text is "pure," the writer is conscious and undeceived, her eye for moral failure is sharp, and (from her point of view and from Richardson's) the collapse she averts would not have been a birth but a death.

The Organic Elegy: Tennyson's Verse Diary

With the possible exception of *Childe Harold*, Tennyson's long elegy, *In Memoriam*, is the first significant verse diary in English. It is also, I believe, the first full-blown example of a reflexive diary of self-discovery, in either poetry or prose. In adapting the diary to verse, Tennyson added his own stamp to the tradition of emotive spontaneity that extends back to the seventeenth century. In the process, he refashioned the conventional reversal of mood (from grief to rejoicing) that one finds in the pastoral elegy, adapting to it what is basically a Coleridgean model of organic process.

Especially important in this model is Coleridge's elaboration of what Edward Young called the "vegetable" nature of artistic genius[21]: harvesting works that are "grown" rather than forcing works into being. The final formulation of the difference between "mechanic" and "organic" form that Coleridge arrived at, relying heavily on the thought of A. W. Schlegel, employed a "vegetable" terminology of *coming into being*: "The form is mechanic, when on any given material we impress a predetermined form, not necessarily arising out of the properties of the material. . . . The organic form, on the other hand, is innate; it shapes, as it developes, itself from within, and the fulness of its development is one and the same with the perfection of its outward form. Such as the life is, such is the form."[22] As a critic, one can identify whether or not a work is organic or mechanic only by signs in the finished product. In an organic poem, for example, the various parts will be seen to "mutually support and explain each other."[23] One will appreciate it as one does a flower, seeing not only "the connexion of parts in and for a whole" but also how "each part is at once end and means."[24] But, Coleridge argues, we are also aware of such form *as the product of growth*. Thus, our attention is directed as much toward the poet as it is toward the poem. We see the poem as an expression of its growth in the poet. For this reason many of Coleridge's key critical concepts describe the poet as much as they do his poetry: "What is poetry? is so nearly the same question with, what is a poet? that the answer to the one is involved in the solution of the other."[25]

The theoretical bias toward the inner state of the author is, of course, one of the many manifestations of that turning inward to the individual in his own right that moves like a tide through the

---

[21]"An *Original* may be said to be of a *vegetable* nature; it arises spontaneously from the vital root of genius; it *grows*, it is not *made*; *Imitations* are of a sort of *Manufacture* wrought by those *Mechanics*, *Art* and *Labour*, out of pre-existent materials not their own" (Edward Young, *Conjectures on Original Composition* [1759; reprint, Leeds: Scolar Press, 1966], 12).

[22]*Coleridge's Literary Criticism*, ed. J. W. MacKail (London: Humphrey Milford, 1921), 186.

[23]*Biographia literaria*, ed. J. Shawcross (London: Oxford University Press, 1907), 2:10.

[24]*Coleridge's Literary Criticism*, 185.

[25]*Biographia literaria*, 2:12.

eighteenth and nineteenth centuries. It is, among other things, that new concept of the self ("sentiment nouveau de la personne") that, as Alain Girard has argued, accompanied the widespread keeping of the journal intime in France.[26] Among the English romantics, the primary literary instrument of this inward turn toward the autonomous legitimacy of the subject's inner life was the lyric poem. And in certain of what have come to be called Coleridge's "conversation poems"—those distinctively Coleridgean adaptations of the verse epistle and the late Augustan reflective mode—one can find a close approximation in poetry of the novelistic method of "writing to the moment." If they do not, collectively, constitute a diary, they are in themselves what could be called diaristic moments. As they are monologues, they express the kinetic engagement not of writing but of words in the outcome of the poem. Nonetheless, the words themselves are representations of thoughts *in the moment*. The poet is *there*, usually (if vaguely) troubled, more or less at the mercy of his associating mind, and seated somewhere in the scene of which he makes detailed inventory. The lines of the poem thus enjoy the romantic promise of the apparently disorganized. Fragmentary, spontaneous, they are, like the fictional diary, approximations of a mind freed of the arbitrary conventions of literary form—mind in the present, as yet unaccommodated by art.[27]

They represent a mind, for example, overcome by mawkish self-pity:

> Well, they are gone, and here must I remain,
> This lime-tree bower my prison! I have lost
> Beauties and feelings, such as would have been
> Most sweet to my remembrance even when age
> Had dimm'd mine eyes to blindness! They, meanwhile,
> Friends, whom I never more may meet again,

[26]Alain Girard, *Le journal intime* (Paris: Presses universitaires de France, 1963).
[27]It may be objected that I have narrowed my focus here too exclusively to Coleridge, slighting such kindred efforts as Wordsworth's "Tintern Abbey," Keats's "Ode to a Nightingale," and Shelley's "Mont Blanc." But compared at least to Coleridge's, these poems are less the imitations of a mind growing in a particular passage of time than they are contemplative or rhapsodic oratory. Wordsworth's *The Prelude* suggests in its opening lines what Coleridge does in the conversation poem: "Oh there is a blessing in this gentle breeze, / A visitant that while it fans my check / Doth seem half-conscious of the joy it brings."

> On springy heath, along the hill-top edge,
> Wander in gladness, . . .

These are the opening lines of Coleridge's 1797 conversation poem, "This Lime-tree Bower my Prison." They express what could be called the child state of the poem. But part of what the poem goes on to demonstrate is that even in this restricted, self-absorbed, highly passive condition, the poet has in his wandering mind and latent affections the capacity for later wholeness—at once a wholeness of the poem and a reintegration of the poet with the world.

Allowing his mind to wander as his friends wander, Coleridge idly imagines the natural beauties they are at that moment enjoying. Focusing more particularly on the friend to whom the poem is addressed, Charles Lamb, Coleridge is inspired with such empathy that he not only sees through Lamb's eyes but engages (as it were in coordination with Lamb's own imagination) in an act of scene transformation whereby the universal is perceived in the particular:

> till all doth seem
> Less gross than bodily; and of such hues
> As veil the Almighty Spirit, when yet he makes
> Spirits perceive his presence.

These lines in turn lead reflexively to Coleridge's sudden awareness of a transformation that has been working in him during his flight of mind:

> A delight
> Comes sudden on my heart, and I am glad
> As I myself were there!

And in this new delight he inventories the immediate scene—the vicinity of his "prison"—noting sensory pleasures that have been affecting him during his "idleness" and that may have had no little role in his mental construction of the scene in which his friends wander. Finally, from this catalogue of pleasures comes a generalization to account for the whole experience (that is, for the poem itself): "Henceforth I shall know / That Nature ne'er deserts the wise and pure." One may, perhaps, blush for the poet at this point, but in his way he is doing what the Puritan did before him, drawing a moral from his experience, which praises God as it praises himself.

Unlike Puritan texts, however, the poem is an expression not only of the moral but of its emergence. To put this in other words, the generalizing power that is evident in the moral is shown to be united with and dependent on the sensory, imaginative, and emotional business that precedes its coming into action. Reflecting back on himself, he is reflecting back on what we have read, all the way back to the present-tense sensation of misery with which the poem began, now made emblematic in retrospect:

> sometimes
> 'Tis well to be bereft of promis'd good,
> That we may lift the soul, and contemplate
> With lively joy the joys we cannot share.

What distinguishes such a poem as this from almost all the others in the romantic canon is that it presents itself both as an organic object and as an organic coming into being. It is itself the expression of a mind in the present, moving by stages from the apparent disorder of its child state to the broad poetic integration of its maturity. Recalling how Coleridge distinguished organic from mechanic form in terms of how it *became* what it is, we can see how the conversation poem indulges the theorist. In it we have both the achieved object in which part relates to part in a "spatial" unity and the "temporal" unity of poem *production* imitated in the gradual emergence of the transformed poet. The latter creates the former. The organicism of growth creates the finished unchanging organicism of the poem. We have at once both flower and history of the seed.

If Coleridge's conversation poems are meant to be imitations of speech, not writing, they are nonetheless monologues the earlier parts of which play an active part *by their expression* in the making of the conclusion. This can be seen equally clearly in "The Eolian Harp" and "Frost at Midnight."[28] The specific acts of self-expression at once generate and submit to what follows. Like the reflexive

---

[28]This kinetic involvement of the monologue in its own completion is perhaps most evident in "Frost at Midnight," with that poem's even more restricted focus on the mind's innate capacities for self-healing and creation.

texts of the novels I have been discussing, Coleridge's conversation poems take us through a drama in which the key dramatic element is the possibility of change or growth in the central figure. Moreover, as they are imitations of a mind thinking, the natural mind of a human being in an empirically validated scene, the conversation poems are a late development in verse of the "formal realism" Ian Watt ascribed to the eighteenth-century novel (to, among others, the novels of Samuel Richardson). This concern to render the organic operation of an actual mind distinguishes the dramatic change in these poems from the conventional alteration of mood in certain traditional lyrics, notably the pastoral elegy. Change is spread out over the poem as an evolution, rather than a "mechanic" application of a convention of reversal. Such poems are odes to the reflexive power of utterance.

A line is traceable from Coleridge to *In Memoriam*. It runs through the Cambridge Apostles, a society strongly influenced by Coleridge to which Tennyson belonged in 1829–1830. It runs more distinctly through Tennyson's friend Arthur Hallam, the Apostle whose death was the occasion of Tennyson's elegy. Particularly in their thinking on education, both the Apostles and Hallam elaborated Coleridge's allied emphases on organic development and the centrality of emotion in knowing. This combination of emphases drew Hallam toward a method of learning, like Plato's dialogues, that stressed growth rather than indoctrination. It was wrong, he argued, to suppose that Plato sought by his method "any inculcation of complete notions by the way of argument. . . . Not that he was indifferent to truth; but he chose to convey it dramatically, and trusted more to the suggestion of his reader's heart than to the conviction of his critical understanding."[29]

This dialectical view of learning is in perfect accord with the motive behind the society of Apostles itself. The society arose primarily in reaction to the appalling state of education at Cambridge, and particularly in reaction to an almost exclusive reliance on rote memorization. The Apostles' alternative was the principle of de-

[29]Arthur Henry Hallam, *Remains in Verse and Prose* (Boston: Ticknor and Fields, 1863), 304–305.

bate, predicated on the belief that conflict—encountering views dia-
metrically opposed to one's own—was essential to learning. Learning, in other words, was not a matter of mechanically storing the
tabula rasa with information, but of challenging the free imagination through opposition. The principle of necessary opposition
carried to its extreme became the principle of necessary suffering,
and this was applied not only to the individual but to society as
well. In the words of one Apostle (John Sterling), England would
not experience a "reform of thought and feeling . . . until she has
been taught by much sorrow, been disciplined into wisdom by suffering, and learnt to listen to the voices of the teachers, of such
men as Wordsworth and Coleridge."[30]

As Tennyson himself matured, the necessity of painful resistance
in the organic process of learning became a central conviction. In
addition to what he may have picked up from the views of the
Apostles, he had a personification of this necessity in Hallam himself, who during his first year at Cambridge had fought and eventually overcome a severe depression heavy with metaphysical doubt.
In the elegy, Tennyson, responding to the argument that doubt is
of the devil and should be avoided at all costs, refers directly to
the example of Hallam.

> Who touched a jarring lyre at first,
> But ever strove to make it true:
>
> Perplext in faith, but pure in deeds,
> At last he beat his music out.
> There lives more faith in honest doubt,
> Believe me, than in half the creeds.
>
> He fought his doubts and gathered strength,
> He would not make his judgment blind,
> He faced the spectres of the mind
> And laid them: thus he came at length
>
> To find a stronger faith his own;
> [Sec. 96, ll. 7–17][31]

[30]Quoted in Peter Allen, *The Cambridge Apostles: The Early Years* (Cambridge: Cambridge University Press, 1978), 80.
[31]All quotations from *In Memoriam* are taken from Christopher Ricks, ed., *The
Poems of Tennyson* (London: Longmans, 1969).

Hallam, then, provided not simply the subject of the elegy but an example of human development that Tennyson could apply to himself—could apply to himself quite specifically as the author of an elegy in progress.

At what point Tennyson became aware that he was composing a diary in verse is difficult to determine. In later years he came deeply to resent questions about the genesis and true chronological order of the entries, 131 of them, which he composed between 1833 and the poem's publication in 1850.[32] But it is clear that whether the actual evolution of the poem roughly corresponds to the progression we have or whether the appearance of evolution was "assisted" in retrospect, the poem reflects quite self-consciously on its status as something that is "natural" in the sense of being unplanned and therefore obedient to the laws that govern spontaneous utterance. Correlatively, it overtly endorses the diary mode—its immediacy, its lack of imposed or "mechanic" form, its unconstraint—as an agent of soul expression (and later as an agent of the soul's discovery of the truth). In reflecting on the mode he has chosen, Tennyson creates his own version of what we called in our discussion of Coleridge, the "child state" of the poem.

> If these brief lays, of Sorrow born,
>   Were taken to be such as closed
>   Grave doubts and answers here proposed,
> Then these were such as men might scorn:
>
> Her care is not to part and prove;
>   She takes, when harsher moods remit,
>   What slender shade of doubt may flit,
> And makes it vassal unto love:
>
> And, hence, indeed, she sports with words,
>   But better serves a wholesome law,
>   And holds it sin and shame to draw
> The deepest measure from the chords:

---

[32]For more on the vexed issue of chronology see Eleanor B. Mattes, "Chronology of *In Memoriam*," in Alfred, Lord Tennyson, *In Memoriam: An Authoritative Text, Backgrounds and Sources, Criticism*, ed. Robert H. Ross (New York: Norton, 1973), 137–149. See also Stuart F. C. Niermeier, "The Problem of the *In Memoriam* Manuscripts," *Harvard Library Bulletin* 19 (1971), 149–159, and Joseph Sendry, "The *In Memoriam* Manuscripts: Some Solutions to the Problems," *Harvard Library Bulletin* 21 (1973), 202–220.

> Nor dare she trust a larger lay,
> But rather loosens from the lip
> Short swallow-flights of song, that dip
> Their wings in tears, and skim away.
>
> [Sec. 48]

The difference between the Tennysonian and the Coleridgean child state is that the former includes (as in the passage above) endorsements of what the poet is, *at the moment*, doing in verse. Tennyson repeatedly defends the special superiority of the diary's departure from the pretensions of public genres: an apology, as it were, for this kind of poetry, composed under this kind of stress. No use to chide him, to demand greater thought or self-control. His privilege is that of any natural and unconstrained being. "I do but sing," he says, "because I must, / And pipe but as the linnets sing" (sec. 21, ll. 23–24). What we read is (or is intended to appear to be) the uncontaminated response of a man who has, in a sense, decivilized himself. He has shed sophisticated structures of philosophical thought and with them his self-consciousness. He has become his feelings of the moment, "An infant crying for the light: / And with no language but a cry" (sec. 54, ll. 19–20).

But if these "wild and wandering cries" are the outpouring of one who has given over his whole self to the immediacy of grief ("I cannot understand: I love"), what gives the poem much of its complexity, and what accounts for its mid-century urgency, is that Tennyson's grief is colored throughout by shocks to his *understanding*. He is more than a linnet, or an infant, and this is, basically, his problem. He is a consciousness and as such cannot simply take the death of his friend as a loss but must also take it as a statement— one that bears on the whole meaning of human life. In other words, he is not merely crying because of the death of a beloved friend but also because of the nihilistic implications of that death, especially as they impinge on a Victorian consciousness saturated with the geological and astronomical revelations of Sir Charles Lyell and the Herschels. He has lost not simply Hallam but also a harmonious universe. The age has outgrown Wordsworth's confidence in nature. Hallam's death is but an outstanding example of her carelessness in all particulars, a carelessness that extends to the human race itself.

From scarpèd cliff and quarried stone
She cries, "A thousand types are gone:
I care for nothing, all shall go.

"Thou makest thine appeal to me:
I bring to life, I bring to death:
The spirit does but mean the breath:
I know no more."

[Sec. 56, ll. 2–8]

This cosmic carelessness puts the pressure of critical scrutiny back upon the lyrical enterprise itself. Because the poet thinks, he cannot avoid awareness of the possible absurdity of his poem. The dilemma of loss is a dilemma of poiesis, and continually as he asserts his privilege of voiced unhappiness he cannot avoid the counterassertion that this is merely "private sorrow's barren song" (sec. 21, l. 14), and as such an enlargement of futility.

What hope is here for modern rhyme
To him, who turns a musing eye
On songs, and deeds, and lives, that lie
Foreshortened in the tract of time?

[Sec. 77, ll. 1–4]

Not simply "modern rhyme"; the very tradition of spontaneous verse out of which the poem comes—the unpretentious, "natural" voice that the poet seeks to endorse—now provides a model for the worst kind of divinity:

This round of green, this orb of flame, [were]
Fantastic beauty; such as lurks
In some wild Poet, when he works
Without a conscience or an aim.

[Sec. 34, ll. 5–8]

To operate in the same spontaneous mode would be to compound by collaboration the universal crime. In such a world, it would be better to keep silence—absolute silence:

'Twere best at once to sink to peace,
Like birds the charming serpent draws,
To drop head-foremost in the jaws
Of vacant darkness and to cease.
[Sec. 34, ll. 13–16]

The antidote to such thoughts is the great length of the poem—
its length, coupled with its diarylike character as a record of actual
moments that make up that length. Such thoughts as those above
are allowed to occur, but not to deter, so that simply by going on,
the poem manifests the best defense of the spontaneous mode. The
poem, in effect, is what happens, but it is also what makes what
happens happen. It is a natural drama of expression. However
inept language may be to convey psychic truth ("For words, like
Nature, half reveal / And half conceal the Soul within" [sec. 5, ll.
3–4]), giving voice to grief is what eventually generates the change
from grief to joy. Even the curse of rational awareness is no match
for the redemptive powers of suffering when suffering is given full
voice. By sheer persistence, Tennyson faces down his rational mind—
even those powers of logic that have so often lent their assistance
in the history of human affirmation. As his new conviction emerges
in the last thirty sections, Tennyson underscores his thoroughgoing
emotive bias: he did *not* find God by rational deduction. He is no
Newtonian deist. "Nor through the questions men may try, / The
pretty cobwebs we have spun" (sec. 124, ll. 7–8). Instead,

If e'er when faith had fallen asleep,
I heard a voice, "believe no more"
And heard an ever-breaking shore
That tumbled in the Godless deep;

A warmth within the breast would melt
The freezing reason's colder part,
And like a man in wrath the heart
Stood up and answered "I have felt."

No, like a child in doubt and fear:
But that blind clamour made me wise;
[Sec. 124, ll. 9–18]

It was the blind clamor of an up-to-date mind, but blind clamor nonetheless, and it is the argument of the poem—or rather, the argument the poem comes upon—that in the spontaneity of that clamor lay the seeds that eventually flower in the late entries. The brute survival of the fittest is transformed into evolutionary meliorism, Hallam is reconceived as a Christlike foreshadowing of future man, and God is rediscovered—all precisely because Tennyson has repeatedly allowed himself a free, passionate response to absurdity.

If Tennyson's poem lacks the concentration of a poem like Coleridge's "Frost at Midnight," and if, too, it represents an adherence to a much more elementary view of the virtues of natural spontaneity,[33] it is the last major step in shaping the myth of reflexive textual therapy. It does this by raising the spontaneous tradition to the level of theodicy. The justification of suffering and evil is not represented but manifested in the growing of the text itself. The unpremeditated structure of the poem is its philosophical argument. The "fuller minstrel" who sings the later lyrics can evolve—the term is especially appropriate—only because the child poet was given free license to cry. However fictional the poem—whether it actually evolved this way or whether the original effect was "assisted" in retrospect[34]—the intention of the poet was to show in his verse diary a case history of evolutionary meliorism: the beneficent operation in verse of the poet's innate powers of recovery and growth. And from this he generalizes in the embracing organic vision that concludes the poem. Blind nature is accommodated to a higher organicism, working on the same principles as the poet. Society, the human race, the earth itself are not like "idle ore,"

> But iron dug from central gloom,
> And heated hot with burning fears,

[33]The extent of Tennyson's difference from Coleridge in this—especially in his near contempt for the reasoning faculties—ought not to be underestimated. Tennyson confided to James Knowles that he was thinking of adding yet another speculative poem to show "that all the arguments are about as good on one side as the other, and thus throw man back more on the primitive impulses and feelings" (*Poems*, 860).

[34]That there was "mechanic" alteration of the original is suggested in Tennyson's comment, quoted by his son, that the elegy "was meant to be a kind of *Divina commedia*, ending with happiness"—a comment that one may read in tandem with Tennyson's confidence to James Knowles: "It's too hopeful, this poem, more than I am myself" (*Poems*, 859).

> And dipt in baths of hissing tears,
> And battered with the shocks of doom
>
> To shape and use.
>
> [Sec. 118, ll. 21–25]

In his own way Tennyson seeks what we have had occasion to observe generally among the authors of reflexive diaries: he tries to erase any fundamental distinction between art and life. The difference between him and the others, a difference he shares with Coleridge, is the metaphysical extent of his erasure:

> I see in part
> That all, as in some piece of art,
> Is toil cöoperant to an end.
>
> [Sec. 128, ll. 22–24]

6

Textual Madness:
The Golden Notebook

But there will come a day when my hand will be distant from me,
and when I bid it write, it will write words I do not mean. The
day of that other interpretation will dawn, when no word will
properly follow another, and all meanings will dissolve like clouds,
and fall down like rain.
— Rilke, *The Notebooks of Malte Laurids Brigge*

With the advent of psychoanalysis, its stress on an unconscious
self and its promulgation of discovery techniques like free association, the keeping of a diary has become a common therapeutic
practice. If the Christian assurance of Tennyson is lacking, the
textual paradigm remains basically that of *In Memoriam*: the discovery of one's inner nature and the recovery of psychic wholeness
by a persistent effort of spontaneous, periodic writing. Largely
through the advocacy of a trio of closely allied diarists—Anaïs Nin,
Marion Milner, and Tristine Rainer—diary-keeping has become
both a teachable pursuit and a cause.[1] Nin, as a novelist, saw in the
diary a key recuperative weapon against what she called the "dis-
memberment of man" evidenced in the work of modernists like
Joyce:

The Diary dealing always with the immediate present, the warm, the
near, being written at white heat, developed a love of the living moment, of the immediate emotional reaction to experience, which re-

[1]Perhaps the single most influential event has been the publication in recent years
of seven volumes of Anaïs Nin's diary. During the last years of her life, Nin and
Tristine Rainer taught a course in journal writing at the International College in
Los Angeles out of which came the latter's guide to diary keeping, *The New Diary*
(1978). Marion Milner's work in the field can be found in *A Life of One's Own* (1934),
An Experiment in Leisure (1939), and *on not being able to paint* (1957).

vealed the power of recreation to lie in the sensibilities rather than in memory or critical perception.... this tale without beginning or end which encloses all things [is] a strong antidote to the unrelatedness, incoherence and disintegration of the modern man. I could follow the inevitable pattern and obtain a large, panoramic view of character.[2]

Character, plot, and author—all three—come together again and are made whole in much the same way as they were for Tennyson: not through the rational, critical faculties but through the hot, recreative work of the sensibilities as they make free use of the page.

Perhaps the single most important influence behind this development is Carl Jung's psychotherapeutic concept of "Active Imagination": the quasi-artistic objectifying of contents of the unconscious. As a form of concentrated repetition, active imagination was developed as an adjunct to dream interpretation, and considered by Jung to be superior to Freudian free-association because it was at once more focused and less overwhelming. Active Imagination was meant to assist what Jung called "the transcendent function"—a "collaboration of conscious and unconscious data" to the end of integrating and renewing personality.[3] By actively and repeatedly working at this objectification, the patient develops a reciprocal kinetic relationship with his medium, which, if successful, becomes "a living birth that leads to a new level of being, a new situation":[4] "By objectifying his impersonal images, and understanding their inherent ideas, the patient is able to work out all the values of his archetypal material. Then he can really see it, and the unconscious becomes understandable to him. Moreover, this work has a definite effect upon him. Whatever he has put into it works back on him and produces a change of attitude."[5] Active Imagination was meant to work with any of a variety of media, and in therapeutic practice today it can be found in painting, sculpture, and poetry. But in the medium of the diary, it has achieved almost an institutional status, particularly in such programs as Ira Progoff's patented "Intensive

[2]Anaïs Nin, On Writing (Yonkers: Oscar Baradinsky, 1947), 21–22.
[3]"The Transcendent Function," in The Collected Works of Carl G. Jung, trans. R. F. C. Hull (Princeton: Princeton University Press, 1969), 8:82.
[4]Jung, "The Transcendent Function," 90.
[5]Jung, "The Tavistock Lectures," in The Collected Works, trans. R. F. C. Hull (Princeton: Princeton University Press, 1976), 18:173.

Journal." The Intensive Journal, Progoff writes, allows "all the events and relationships of our life to show us what they were for, what their purpose was in our lives, and what they wish to tell us for our future. . . . We see the inner myth that has been guiding our lives unknown to ourselves." And at special moments we find ourselves writing "in the language of the Spirit," moments of great depth when our entries take on "the style of natural poetry or personal prophecy, the language of the self discovering itself."[6] In yet another twist in the history of spontaneity, Progoff's approach is conducted in "Journal Workshops" and makes use of a systematic journal organized into seventeen different color-coded sections. In the history of journal-keeping it is a twist that is also a return, especially among those Americans whose Puritan forebears systematically kept a journal as a regular discipline of self-scrutiny.

Endemic in the popular therapeutic diary is the tendency to objectify or hypostatize an inner self (witness the title of Lucia Capacchione's 1979 manual, *The Creative Journal: The Art of Finding Yourself*). This tendency and the attendant myth of being able to find and bring forth a nameable inner reality has provoked some of the sharpest reactions among modern novelists who have written, as it were, against the therapeutic model (Sartre, Bellow, Beckett, Beauvoir, Lessing). Simone de Beauvoir's *The Woman Destroyed* is the fictional transcript of a diary, undertaken at the suggestion of a psychiatrist, which leads its keeper not to an inner self but to an inner vacancy. At its terminal point, the diarist sits alone, terrified, watching the door to her room:

> Closed. A closed door: something that is watching behind it. It will not open if I do not stir. Do not stir: ever. Stop the flow of time and of life.
> But I know that I shall move. The door will open slowly, and I shall see what there is behind the door. It is the future. The door to the future will open. Slowly. Unrelentingly. I am on the threshold. There is only this door and what is watching behind it. I am afraid. And I cannot call to anyone for help.
> I am afraid.[7]

[6]Ira Progoff, *At a Journal Workshop* (New York: Dialogue House, 1975), 11, 12.
[7]Simone de Beauvoir, *The Woman Destroyed*, trans. Patrick O'Brian (New York: Putnam's, 1979), 253–254.

In Doris Lessing's ambitious diary novel, *The Golden Notebook* (1962), there is no vision of inner vacancy—quite the reverse—but the same problem of the therapeutic journal that disturbed Beauvoir, its naming of "the within," is what gives Lessing's book much of its strange shape. It is even possible that when she chose to cast *The Golden Notebook* in the form of a novella and a variety of color-coded notebooks, Lessing had Jung in mind. When Jung finally published his autobiography, he revealed that he had kept two notebooks of his dreams: the Red Book and the Black Book.[8] Lessing's Anna Wulf keeps five: a Red, a Black, a Yellow, a Blue, and a Golden Notebook. If one could find a veiled belligerency in this, however, it would not be directed at Jung, whom Lessing greatly admired, but at the popularization of Jung—that clinical use of the diary of self-discovery in which the patient is led by her analyst to certain preconceived categories of selfhood. In *The Golden Notebook*, the representative of this procedure is Anna's Jungian psychoanalyst, Mrs. Marks. If Lessing intends no comment in the coloration of the notebooks, she does pointedly use the analyst to play her character's quest off against the common therapeutic quest. As Mrs. Marks, in their sessions together, seeks to bring her patient to a discovery of her own preexistent form, Anna seeks in her private notebooks a self that stands beyond form.

Mrs. Marks peddles form in its commonest mode: as the repeatable, or recognizable. She finds in Anna not simply a predetermined idea of Woman, but pries from the creative activity of Anna's imagination the inherent, repeatable shadows of all those who have imagined before her. " 'Look,' " Anna challenges her,

> "If I were sitting here, describing a dream I'd had last night, ... there'd be a certain look on your face. And I know what the look means because I feel it myself—recognition. The pleasure of recognition, of a bit of rescue-work, so to speak, rescuing the formless into form. Another bit of chaos rescued and 'named.' Do you know how you smile when I 'name' something? It's as if you'd just saved someone from drowning."[9]

[8]See Carl G. Jung, *Memories, Dreams, Reflections* (New York: Pantheon, 1963), 188. In Lessing's adaptation there is perhaps the faint glow of a literary subtype. Lars Gustafsson's *The Death of a Beekeeper* (1978) is made up of three notebooks: "The Yellow," "The Blue," and "The Damaged."
[9]Doris Lessing, *The Golden Notebook* (New York: Bantam, 1973), 470.

What is drowning for Mrs. Marks is the only way of coming to life for Anna. She wants to "leave the safety of myth." Yet Mrs. Marks is a very powerful antagonist. She has power not only because of the intelligence and direct personal concern she trains on her patient but also because in her advocacy of form she fights for something that part of Anna wants very badly: belonging in a world of forms, a label, a place in history. Anna's anger at her therapist is in direct proportion to the lure she feels. Moreover, the form-finding she repudiates is what she also, as a writer, is in the business of doing. She is a professional "namer."

Her conflict with Mrs. Marks brings into the sharpest focus her conflict with herself: her need to name what she needs to leave unnamed. Mrs. Marks has her own name for Anna. The name is "artist." Throughout the later stages of her analysis, Anna staunchly repudiates the name whenever Mrs. Marks attempts to apply it to her and busily seeks to unravel its illusion of coherence in the notebooks she keeps privately at home. When by chance she reveals to Mrs. Marks that she is keeping these notebooks, she sees the old familiar light come on in Mrs. Marks's eyes. Behind the light she sees another form taking shape in the analyst's mind, another name: the blocked-artist-keeping-a-diary-to-end-the-block. Like a child, Anna then determines to stop writing altogether, even in her notebooks. But incorrigibly the notebooks keep going on, seeking in their discontinuous way some route in the opposite direction from Mrs. Marks: beyond both art and the artist, beyond language itself, to the paradox of textually generated wordlessness.

The problem that divides Anna divides the book as a whole. It is Lessing's problem. We are asked to accept neither the existential dissolution of the self nor its Christian or psychiatric elaboration but the sheer force of its presence. It absorbs attention by the combination of its undeniability and its gratuitousness. Yet the literary art that serves this version of the self must somehow express not only what cannot but what must not be expressed. Cannot, because the observer (diarist and reader) is like the student of subatomic particles who cannot ever see the object of his study but must be content with the evidence of its passing. Must not, because even the textual tracing of its passage runs the risk of placing limits on its freedom. Freedom here lies not simply in unpredictability of movement but in an absence of any formal properties. It is a raw freedom, at once exotic and distressing. In this literary universe we are granted one metaphysical fact; yet having been granted it and directed to pay homage to it, we are denied all categories of significance save that of its categorical freedom.

We can gain some idea of how this opposition between form and content divides *The Golden Notebook* by looking at its shape. Sighted from a distance, it is an exploded novel: a novella entitled *Free Women*, covering a critical period in the life of a novelist, roughly 150 pages in length but cloven into five parts. In the four spaces between the five parts, the author has wedged great masses of material from the novelist's notebooks, five notebooks in all, so that the length of *The Golden Notebook* exceeds that of the novella by more than 400 pages. Though the novella is rendered from an omniscient perspective and speaks of the life of its novelist, Anna Wulf, in the third person, the diaries are composed in the first person and comprise, imperfectly, the material out of which the novella, *Free Women*, comes.

Though *Free Women* is a part, then, of the much longer novel, *The Golden Notebook*, the notebooks are not a part of the novella, *Free Women*. More exactly, they are a pointedly suppressed part of the novella. We learn of their existence in the novella, but throughout that short work they are kept in a drawer, out of sight, and are glimpsed by only one character aside from Anna. Thus, in *Free Women*, any reflexive exchange between the protagonist and her text is suppressed. The relationship between Anna and her notebooks is a veiled theme, and the inchoate, often suicidal material that her notebooks contain is only implicitly connected with the mental breakdown that Anna goes through at the climax of the novella. When challenged as to why she does not publish this private, fragmented material, Anna argues that she does not precisely because it *is* private material and not meant for public consumption. As the plot of *Free Women* develops, it develops at the same time a cautionary tale on the danger of the inchoate notebook, in a way supporting the argument that Anna makes. The principal subject of the cautionary tale is her friend's son, Tommy, who finds and reads the notebooks and, it would appear, seeing in them a despair and incoherence that matches his own internal disintegration, goes home and puts a bullet in his head. The whole incident bears an eerie resemblance to the similarly painful experience of Goethe, who, as we have noted, found that a good number of his readers responded to *Werther* not on the level of Goethe but on the level of the deeply disturbed other self that Goethe had transposed to the novel.

The author of *Free Women*, however, adds an ironic twist to this cautionary incident by having Tommy succeed not in committing suicide but in permanently blinding himself. Tommy's blindness would appear to correlate to a subsequent, willfully self-imposed psychic blindness. He proceeds to become the male guru for his father's second wife, the alcoholic Marion, in whom he encourages a childlike and ineffective enthusiasm for the oppressed masses of Africa. He practices on her the kind of therapy that puts truth below psychological wholeness. Marion in her enthusiasm for the "poor dears" in Africa has now a myth, which keeps her from disintegration. The final twist in Tommy's story comes at the end of the novel when we learn that he is stepping into the shoes of his father, taking over as a captain of industry, so that his father may retire in the company of his secretary, with whom he in turn hopes to sustain into the late afternoon of his life the illusion of his male potency. The caution in this tale of Tommy is like that of Plato's Myth of the Cave: that a glimpse of the truth is blinding— though unlike Plato's truth, in this tale the truth is that of an underlying formlessness. Even the lives of the principal characters in this novel, Anna and her friend Molly, would appear to bear out this caution. After undergoing in the last chapter of *Free Women* a complete mental breakdown, Anna recovers, abandons writing and politics, and becomes a welfare worker; at the same time her friend Molly leaves the Communist party to marry a millionaire.

This is the shape and the argument of the novella. But as we noted, the overwhelming bulk of the novel *The Golden Notebook* is made up not of the novella but of the notebooks that are the buried material out of which the novella came. As they develop, moreover, the notebooks gain ascendancy over the novella, not only in quantity but in quality as well. Furthermore, as we read through the notebooks, certain clues gradually apprise us that the novella and the notebooks inhabit different factual universes. Tommy, for example, is younger than he should be in *Free Women*. We learn late in the notebooks that Tommy is married, though he never has a wife in *Free Women*. In the notebooks Tommy is actually engaged in radical social activity, whereas at the end of *Free Women* Tommy is beginning a career as a captain of industry. Tommy, who is blind in *Free Women*, is never referred to as blind in the notebooks. If we are not sufficiently aware of the discrepancy between the two universes by the end of the fourth immersion in the notebooks, the truth of the matter is made baldly apparent in the brief, climactic Golden Notebook, in the course of which Anna's schizophrenic lover, Saul Green, provides her with the first sentence of her next novel: "The two women were alone in the London flat." This, as it turns out, is the first sentence of the novella, *Free Women*— a novella which, on our first reading, we had confidently assumed was a story by Doris Lessing. Thus the omnisciently narrated, comfortably true, novelistic work *Free Women*, which had, by its placement, enjoyed the requisite suspension of disbelief—the status of a fixed frame of reference by which we could evaluate the notebooks—becomes by the end of our reading a subsidiary accessory to the notebooks. Lessing has, in effect, turned the novel inside out. Or, to put it another way, she has demoted the novella *Free Women* to an inferior status in whatever it is one wants to call *The Golden Notebook*. Indeed, in terms of fictional credibility, compared with any of the five notebooks, *Free Women* becomes the most inauthentic, the least credible prose in the book, itself a kind of commentary by contrast on the more honest and more interesting notebooks. In the book as a whole we are made to call upon this fact, to experience (at least in our first reading of it) our own betrayal, and to recognize the honored status which we had conferred upon what is essentially an inferior form and an inferior content.

Lessing has, since the composition of her novel, in several interviews and other public statements, made what is implicit in *The Golden Notebook* explicit.

You know, the Free Women section in *The Golden Notebook*—the envelope—I was really trying to express my sense of despair about writing a conventional novel in that. Actually that is an absolutely whole conventional novel, and the rest of the book is the material that went into making it. One of the things I was saying was: Well, look, this is a conventional novel. God knows, I write them myself and doubtless will again. One has this feeling after writing a novel. There it is: 120,000 words; it's got a nice shape and the reviewers will say this and that. And the bloody complexity that went into it. And it's always a lie. And the terrible despair. So you've written a good novel or a moderate novel, but what does it actually say about what you've actually experienced? The truth is—absolutely nothing. Because you can't. I don't know what one does about novels.[10]

Thus, her intention was "to write a short formal novel which would enclose the rest in order to suggest what I think a great many writers feel about the formal novel; namely, that it's not doing its job any more. So I thought that the only way to do this would be to write the short formal novel and put in the experience it came out of, showing how ridiculous the formal novel is when it can't say a damn thing."[11]

That the formal novel is "ridiculous" is borne out by the warfare between the two principal divisions of *The Golden Notebook*: novel and notebooks. But as the book progresses it becomes quite clear that the ridiculousness of the "formal" novel is only one expression of a far more serious and extensive problem. This is the problem of form itself, a problem that extends deep into the territory of the notebooks. In this way, Anna's situation is strikingly similar to that of Sartre's Roquentin, the diarist of *Nausea*. Like him, she has discovered that the world she grew up in, the one that starts with words and includes all the larger forms they assist—myths, stories, history, ideologies—is a kind of gnostic world of illusion, a comfortable prison in which she is kept from the truth. Like Roquentin, she reverts from "literature" to the keeping of a diary, hoping to find in the latter's apparent freedom from form a more authentic mirror of her experience. Like Roquentin, she at the same time fears this pushing on through the barrier of form—fears it as she would fear suicide, for abandonment of form would appear to be the abandonment of self. And so—and again like Roquentin—she finds in these notebooks, for all their wonted authenticity, a traitor

[10]Doris Lessing, *A Small Personal Voice* (New York: Random House, 1975), 81–82.
[11]Doris Lessing, quoted in Paul Schlueter, *The Novels of Doris Lessing* (Carbondale: Southern Illinois University Press, 1973), 82.

to the cause of truth—a negative reflexive agency collaborating with her own fears. Even the most disorganized of her notebooks (the Blue Notebook), with its apparent disjunctive formlessness, its incursions of insanity, its subversive, antinovelistic qualities, can be a stay against disintegration: an attempt to preserve form and to preserve Anna's existence in the world of words.

> Every evening I sat on the music-stool and wrote down my day, and it was as if I, Anna, were nailing Anna to the page. Every day I shaped Anna, said: Today I got up at seven, cooked breakfast for Janet, sent her to school, etc., etc., and felt as if I had saved that day from chaos. Yet now I read those entries and feel nothing. I am increasingly afflicted by vertigo where words mean nothing. Words mean nothing. They have become, *when I think*, not the form into which experience is shaped, but a series of meaningless sounds, like nursery talk, and away to one side of experience. Or like the sound track of a film that has slipped its connection with the film. [476]

In spite of this reflexive treachery in the notebooks themselves, the book as a whole, finally, endorses the notebooks. It does not endorse them as a mimetic expression of the sought-for truth, but it does endorse them as a positive agent in the quest for it. In helping Anna pursue what is in effect an ideal of mental breakdown, the notebooks help her move beyond their words toward an ideal of textual vacancy or silence. In part this is effected by the same treachery referred to above. In the passage just quoted, for example, Anna the writer is disabused by Anna the reader. The weapons of form become the weapons of formlessness, because Anna is forever rereading what she writes and, in consequence, sharpening her awareness of verbal discrepancy. In writing and rereading the Black Notebook, her record of the background material for her first novel (*Frontiers of War*), she finds not only how far the novel was a romantic departure from the facts, but also how much those recollected "facts" are themselves warped by nostalgia. Correlatively, in the Yellow Notebook, each successive attempt to compose a new novel arises out of a rereading and cancellation of the last. Each notebook is the track of a finite regression, a course of increasingly exacerbated discontinuity, that culminates in the successive abandonment of each one of them. What takes their place is the Golden Notebook, the text of Anna's schizophrenia, in which discontinuity has moved into the language itself. All temporal and referential fixity is undermined. That minimal separation of points in time characteristic of diaries is abandoned as the jottings from one hour or day blend into those of another. Through a grammatical confusion of personal pronouns, the text of this notebook would appear also to lose any consistent implication of a perceiving subject. By these means, Lessing constructs not a "dehumanized" text, but a text governed from outside itself and indicating by its mutation a presence beyond form.

There is another way in which Anna's notebooks operate in a positive reflexive fashion. One can find it in the Yellow Notebook, the notebook in which Anna pursues her fictional work in progress. At the conclusion of the third and final attempt to write a novel (tentatively entitled *The Shadow of the Third*), Anna describes her fictional counterpart, Ella (also a writer; also struggling to compose a novel), coming upon an insight that may yet lead to a solution of her creative problems—a story with a new twist:

> I've got to accept the patterns of self-knowledge which mean unhappiness or at least a dryness. But I can twist it into victory. A man and a woman—yes. Both at the end of their tether. Both cracking up because of a deliberate attempt to transcend their own limits. And out of the chaos, a new kind of strength.
>
> Ella looks inwards, as into a pool, to find this story imaged; but it remains a series of dry sentences in her mind. She waits, she waits patiently, for the images to form, to take on life. [467]

The whole idea is so much like what it happens later in the "real" life of Anna and Saul Green that it is hard to avoid the implication that there is some kind of predictive or even determinative power residing in the notebook itself. In Part Four, when Anna picks up the Yellow Notebook again and begins jotting down a series of ideas for short stories and novels, there again emerge a number of suggestions that come eerily close to what will happen between her and Saul, including a situation in which two lovers secretly read each others' private diaries—a detail that becomes literally the case shortly thereafter. The presence of these elements has, for several critics, been the final, devastating blow to any secure point of reference in this book. They have been taken to disqualify even the

Blue Notebook as the foundation stone of the "real" reality of the fictional universe of *The Golden Notebook*. Perceived in this way, the book would appear to be, finally, an endlessly elusive four-dimensional puzzle, a nest of ivory boxes in which the innermost box is seen to contain within it the shadowy contours of the outermost box.

We do not need to view the work quite this radically. Part of Lessing's complex effort is to erode the boundaries between writing and living one's life. Indeed, the anticipatory suggestive elements in the Yellow Notebook, by their placement before the incident they anticipate, vividly express the kinetic interrelationship of Anna's inner life and writing. Seen as such, they are instances in which Anna, collaborating with her text, creates within her a preparedness, a set, as it were, for just the opportunity that Saul Green provides when he arrives at the door of her apartment. She improvises her future in her fiction. It is important to note that Anna has been unwilling to rent her apartment. After asking her last boarder to leave, she has refused to take on a new one. It could be, then, that what induces Anna to rent her apartment to Saul Green are the obvious manifestations of his own mental fragmentation, evidenced in the very first contacts he has with her, coupled with ideas she has already allowed herself to express fictively. "A man and a woman—yes. Both at the end of their tether." With Saul's arrival, Anna understands that she is now at a point she has already selected—a point where she must face her inner formlessness by immersing her whole conscious self in it. She has also, in yet another idea for a short story, thought of the situation in which one mentally ill person infects those around him with his disease. So she recognizes in Saul Green the catalyst she has been waiting for. Taking him on as a boarder, she commits herself, with what could be considered heroism, to those final stages of disintegration of herself and her art that Lessing makes the doomed attempt to follow through Anna's words.

There are many difficulties with this long and frustrating work, not the least of which is the quality of the writing itself in *Free Women*. It is as if Lessing had followed the theory of imitative form with such austerity that she could stay the hand capable of such vigor and invention as are found in *The Grass Is Singing* and *The*

Summer before the Dark. Were this her intention, one could find at least a certain intellectual (if not aesthetic) justice in the quality of *Free Women.* For if leaden prose and stereotypical characterization can be said to express anything, it would have to be the deadly triumph of form over truth ("how ridiculous the formal novel is, when it can't say a damn thing").

If *Free Women* represents an aesthetic difficulty, it also represents—thanks to the ingenuity of Lessing's design—an interpretive difficulty. It brings us back to the doubleness of this book. So far we have placed our entire interpretive emphasis on Anna's quest for self beyond form, on how that quest is assisted by the reflexive agency of her notebooks and at the same time thrown into relief by the novella that frames it. The difficulty I want to turn to now arises from the fact that it is Anna who composes the framing novella. She not only composes it, but she composes it *after* the breakdown recorded in the Golden Notebook. Moreover, the structure of the book as a whole, particularly the series of efforts recorded in the Yellow Notebook, strongly suggests that *Free Women* represents a revitalization of Anna's art, a creative breakthrough for which all the business of the notebooks and mental breakdown was a necessary gestation. Throughout the later stages of the book, and particularly in the Golden Notebook, there are strong Nietzschean suggestions that the destruction she undergoes is a necessary stage in any truly creative process. During the period of her insanity, her dreams are presided over by a figure, at once attractive and frightening, which she calls "the principle of joy-in-destruction." Out of its ruinous work is to come new life and new integration: "war [is] working in us all towards fruition" (594).

What arises from the ruins is *Free Women*, a novel manifestly inferior, both in form and content, to the record of the destructive process that precedes it. Moreover, it features a novelist who denies both her trade and her notebooks to pursue the security of form. At the end, the Anna of *Free Women* abandons both writing and political commitment for welfare work. There is always the temptation, mentioned above, to take this outcome as a final cutting back in the endless and exitless labyrinth that is the book as a whole. This would make *The Golden Notebook* a kind of *nouveau roman* by default, ending where it began. But I do not think this is the case. For one thing, Lessing has given clear indications, in comments that she has made since writing *The Golden Notebook*, that for all her intention to expose the inadequacies of "the formal novel," she also took *Free Women* seriously as a mimetic act.[12] More important is the fact that Anna herself comes in the Golden Notebook to accept the distance between telling and true knowing. Though the latter can be approached only through insanity, sanity still matters. Though genuine illumination is attained by passing beyond words, in this world all we have is words.

> The people who have been there, in the place in themselves where words, patterns, order, dissolve, will know what I mean and the others won't. But once having been there, there's a terrible irony, a terrible shrug of the shoulders, and it's not a question of fighting it, or disowning it, or of right or wrong, but simply knowing it is there, always. It's a question of bowing to it, so to speak, with a kind of courtesy, as to an ancient enemy: All right, I know you are there, but we have to preserve the forms, don't we? And perhaps the condition of your existing at all is precisely that we preserve the forms, create the patterns—have you thought of that? [633–634]

There is more on this side of the argument than simply preserving the forms. One of Lessing's favorite figures for her kind of artist—a figure that Anna also employs—is that of the "boulder-pusher." Out in the world, this is their job of work: pushing the boulder slowly upward. Unlike those who spend their time on the top of a mountain looking at the truth, the artist in the world seeks to be out among the people of society working on what goes by the name of Progress. Her condition is like that of Sisyphus, only with this qualification: she pushes the boulder up the slope, but every time it rolls down again it stops at a point a little higher than before. Considered in the light of this figure, *Free Women* can be seen as just such a consequence of Anna's insight. The boulder has fallen far below the height of the insight that Anna gained in her notebooks, but it does not roll all the way back. It is not, in short,

---

[12]In one interview, for example, she made this comment about the conclusion of *Free Women*: "The scene at the end when Molly goes off and gets married and Anna goes off to do welfare work and joins the Labor party was intended as a sign of the times. I was being a bit grim about what I observed about me. Women who had been active for years in socialist movements gritted their teeth and said, 'Right, the hell with all this politics, we'll go off and be welfare workers' " (Lessing, *A Small Personal Voice*, 75).

as false as Anna's first novel, *Frontiers of War*. It clearly rests above that romantic work and is truer to the life out of which it comes. And though the Anna of *Free Women* rejects her craft and goes off into welfare work, it is more than probable that the Anna who wrote *Free Women* will start pushing the boulder back up again.

The Golden Notebook, nevertheless, remains a restless work. It comes at the midpoint between two principal phases of Lessing's development. It expands the metaphysical intuitions of the essentially realistic novelist of the fifties and it precedes the metaphysical vision of the gnostic fantasist who begins to emerge in *The Four-Gated City*. As such, it is an unstable book, exploratory and unresolved. Nowhere is this clearer than in the persisting dilemma of the relations between the novella and the notebooks. If, as we have just argued, *Free Women* can be granted some degree of mimetic validity as a novel, then can we ever successfully override the sense of flat contradiction between it and the notebooks? The problem can be brought into sharper focus by observing that the thematic melange of breakdown/disharmony/disintegration so central to the notebooks is also central to *Free Women*. In the notebooks, as mentioned, breakdown becomes an ally in the search for interior truth. Conversely, the enemy is form, per se. In the novella (and even in parts of the notebooks), the terms appear to be reversed: the enemy is fragmentation. Moreover, this enemy is a particular historical evil. Whatever the causes of fragmentation, socioeconomic or otherwise, it would appear to be a uniquely modern condition, extending inward, into the psyche; outward, into relations between people; socially, between economic classes; sexually, between men and women; internationally, between the nations of the world; and epistemologically, between the world and words. With this last manifestation of it especially in mind, Lessing has called the theme of the artist "the theme of our time." The experience of fragmentation undergone in the modern self is experienced most acutely by the artist whose métier is the creation of representative form. Among artists, it is the writer who experiences this modern crisis most deeply, her identity itself being so closely bound to the words that have been torn from the world.

If one puts the two sides of this book together, the question arises, Have words been torn from the world and is our cultural evolution the cause of it, or have modern conditions merely exposed the age-old illusion of words' unity with the world? To put this in other terms, Is neurosis a disease (the modern consequence of sick etiology and sick, unequal relations) or is it the consequence of insight? Ernest Becker, in his bleak and eloquent book *The Denial of Death*, argued that the breakdown of character evinced in a neurotic was not the sign of sickness but rather the result of a keen perception of the truth. The neurotic's awareness of the truth does not allow him to accept the arbitrary form of character.[13] His argument echoes that of Dostoevsky's Underground Man, who contended that his distinction from "the man of action" (that is, the man of character) was that he suffered from the "disease of lucidity." It is a condition that Anna too, in much fear and trepidation, attempts to turn into a badge. This is the central idea in the battle she wages with her psychoanalyst.

> "I'm going to make the obvious point that perhaps the word neurotic means the condition of being highly conscious and developed. The essence of neurosis is conflict. But the essence of living now, fully, not blocking off to what goes on, is conflict. In fact I've reached the stage where I look at people and say—he or she, they are whole at all because they've chosen to block off at this stage or that. People stay sane by blocking off, by limiting themselves." [469]

In short, "the condition of being highly conscious and developed" is simply not viable in the historical world of *Free Women*. By the logic of Anna's argument, a policy of "not blocking off" can lead only to insanity—from *Free Women* back to the Golden Notebook.

The source of the difficulty is, finally, that there are two contexts in which the fragmentation treated in the novel exists. Likewise, there are two Annas. There are on the one hand the historical context and the historical Anna and on the other hand the metaphysical context and the metaphysical Anna. The historical Anna is an alienated Anna, a neurotic, a fragmented Anna, but she suffers the pangs of alienation and fragmentation because there is no home for her in this world. This Anna seeks in the world recognition of the unique *form* that is hers and not the property of men at war

[13]Ernest Becker, *The Denial of Death* (New York: Free Press, 1975), 176–207.

with Mother, not a stale fiction, not a political caricature or a primordial dream. This is the Anna who repudiates Mrs. Marks's categorization of her because it does not do justice to her unique *historical* identity. Thus, she repudiates the categories "because I'm convinced that there are whole areas of me made by the kind of experience women haven't had before" (471). This Anna wants to isolate the new element that is hers by virtue of her position in history. " 'I want to be able to separate in myself what is old and cyclic, the recurring history, the myth, from what is new, what I feel or think that might be new' " (472–473). In the historical context (that is, in the world), such an identity, though it has been created by a world in fragmentation—a world under the threat of total annihilation—ends fragmentation by achieving a place in a field of mutually accepting forms. This, in short, is the goal of progress, a world in which men, women, nations, respect the formal autonomy of each individual identity. It is the Four-Gated City.

The metaphysical Anna, however, seeks a pure and terrible freedom of being that exists nowhere in history because it exists nowhere in form. Confined to the medium of words, she can only point to it in her diary by a kind of verbal triangulation. If this inner being is conceivable as a formlessness that is at the same time an end of fragmentation, to borrow Lessing's own formulation,[14] it is so in the traditional mystical sense of an oceanic oneness. As that rugged scientist Mrs. Marks fears and knows all too well, it is a genuine "drowning." To Anna's Marxist comrades, it would appear so equally. In the eyes of both, by choosing to drown, Anna chooses to leave history. The route she takes is the traditional one: the route of insanity—insanity, that is, by the standards of society. This is the route of the saints and martyrs and it is a route that leads right out of this world.

The conflict between these two contexts of fragmentation, and between the historical novelist and the metaphysical one, creates the tensions that in effect pull this novel apart. Lessing seeks at one and the same time to advance the boulder a notch and to put us on top of the mountain. She seeks to do so, but with an added

---

[14]In her 1971 Introduction, Lessing wrote: "In the inner Golden Notebook, things have come together, the divisions have broken down, there is formlessness with the end of fragmentation" (*Golden Notebook*, vii).

qualification: there may be not one mountain but in fact two mountains. And the mountain up whose steep side she pushes the boulder may not be the same mountain on top of which she already stands. For the one is a mountain of form, and the other is a mountain of formlessness. The one is a mountain of progress, and the other is a mountain of metaphysics. On top of the one mountain is the future, and on top of the other is the timelessness of inner being.

7

Textual Salvation

Bernanos's *Diary of a Country Priest*

In the 1930s, two Catholic novels appeared, both cast as diaries
and sharing such striking thematic similarities that together they
suggest a paradigm for the reflexive diary in the Catholic novel.[1]
Compared with Lessing's novel, Bernanos's *Diary of a Country Priest*
(*Journal d'un curé de campagne*, 1936) and Mauriac's *Vipers' Tangle*
(*Le noeud de vipères*, 1932) are stabler works, unambiguously devoted
to an established metaphysical point of view; but as in the notebooks
of Lessing's heroine, madness in these diaries has its metaphysical
privilege. The governing model here is that of the saint and his
martyrdom. In both works, the final moment of fullest self-awareness comes at the point of death; therapy is replaced by salvation.
The diary in both novels serves a range of customary functions,
but in its reflexive operation it contributes an additional distinction
that I wish to pursue further in this chapter. The reflexivity of these
diaries is used continually to open out the paradox that self-perception is self-transformation. For both diarists, moments of becoming are moments of a return to what they have always been.
We have seen this duality before, but these novels are distinguished

---

[1] If diary keeping did not have the importance among Catholics that it did among
Puritan Protestants, it did, in certain quarters of the faith, enjoy a quasi-institu-
tionalized status: "The habit of jotting down each evening my thoughts of the day
is the best discipline that remains to me from my Catholic education. The good
Fathers used it only for moral improvement . . . " (Hugues Le Roux, *Gladys* [Paris:
Calmann-Lévy, 1884], 1, my translation).

by the degree to which it is made a controlling concern. They are preeminently novels about depth: the self discovered is the self uncovered.

Bernanos's novel is the intimate journal of a young, a very young, priest whose internal struggle with doubt, pride, fear, the "hardness" of his heart, and his incapacity to pray, keeps pace with the growth of a stomach cancer that eventually kills him. The diary in this novel is taken up as a comforter, a companion, and a confessor, but in its emerging reflexive function as a mirror, it makes increasing demands on the priest's capacity for sincerity. As is so often the case in the spontaneous, self-expressive tradition, language and learning are a curse. Fulfilling his functions as a priest, the curé suffers this curse almost daily:

> Those people who think the Sacrament gives us instant power to read the hidden places of a soul are indeed credulous! If only we could ask them to try for themselves! Used as I am to confessions of simple seminary students, I still cannot manage to understand what horrible metamorphosis has enabled so many people to show me their inner life as a mere convention, a formal scheme without one clue to its reality.[2]

The diarist in his turn must fight the same disease. As he begins his journal, the curé finds that it is his very gifts that he must struggle against. His pen is still the pen of the accomplished student (he was first in his class), the well-trained writer, the rational thinker, in short, the antidiarist. All the watchwords of the popular conception of spontaneous utterance are implicit here:

> I have been looking over these first few pages of my diary without any satisfaction, and yet I considered very carefully before making up my mind to write it. But that is not much comfort to me now. For those who have the habit of prayer, thought is too often a mere alibi, a sly way of deciding to do what one wants to do. Reason will always obscure what we wish to keep in the shadows. [11]

[2]Georges Bernanos, *The Diary of a Country Priest*, trans. Pamela Morris (New York: Macmillan, 1962), 79.

His antidote is a familiar one: "I will . . . force myself to write exactly what comes into my mind, without picking and choosing (sometimes I still search for words, correct myself)" (26).

One of the ironies that governs this text is that this priest who must struggle so to find the language of sincerity, who has such difficulty seeing into himself, is nearly infallible in reading the inner truth of others. What he sees is almost always beneath the surface. He sees the "inner joy" beneath the Curé de Torcy's anguish (103). He sees Sulpice Mittonet's "real look . . . [in] his eyes, under the scum" (108). With X-ray vision he sees a letter to her father in Chantal's purse, and he not only reads the countess's heart but has a vision of her death the evening before she dies. A crack interpreter of others, he must still labor to get to the bottom of himself, against all his natural human fear to do so. So at the very least, the diary is a spur: "More than ever I need this diary. It is only during these snatched moments that I am aware of some effort to see clearly into myself" (159–160).

But how can he make this infallible insight work upon himself? A literal mirror is no help. With some amusement, I am sure, Bernanos returns more than once to this standard accessory of the diary novel. What the curé sees in his mirror is fearsome, a combination ogre and down-and-out: "my face drawn and more yellow each day, with its long nose and double furrows descending on either side of the mouth, its bristly chin which a bad razor cannot deal with" (71). It is, as he says, a face "made to be slapped" (161). Yet (complementing the irony discussed above) this appalling face has strange power over others. It draws them out. Dr. Delbende, Dr. Laville, Chantal, and the countess cannot resist it. In its presence they unburden themselves, or to put it another way, in its presence they become reacquainted with themselves—whether they want to or not. The final twist of this complex irony is that they not only see themselves through the agency of this face but they continually provide the curé with readings of what they see of him in it. Olivier, Dr. Laville, Chantal, the Curé de Torcy, the Sacristan all give him readings, but it is the canon in his reading who puts his finger on what is at once the curé's great strength and weakness: "The secret of your strength lies in the fact that you are unaware, or daren't realize, how different you are from the others" (162). The differ-

ence, as others, too, point out, is his innocence, his child nature—
the cause of so much of his embarrassment.

How can he turn the power of his face upon himself? The answer
is his "child's copy-book." But it must be kept so well, and with such
frankness, that he can begin to discern the contours of his other
face. In formulating this, the curé brings together the governing
conceit of the mirror with the semantic paradox of two selves:

> When I first sat down before this child's copy-book I tried to concen-
> trate, to withdraw into myself as though I were examining my con-
> science before confession. And yet my real conscience was not revealed
> by that inner light—usually so dispassionate and penetrating, passing
> over details, showing up the whole. It seemed to skim the surface of
> another consciousness, previously unknown to me, a cloudy mirror in
> which I feared that a face might suddenly appear. Whose face? Mine,
> perhaps. A forgotten, rediscovered face.... [12–13]

As the text continues, it generates more and more vividly the
impression of a co-presence: "an invisible presence which surely
could not be God—rather a friend made in my image, although
distinct from me, a separate entity" (26). At last, the text itself
appears to take on a life and power independent of even the words
themselves, so that the curé can erase and tear out pages at the
command of his surface consciousness but fail to remove them from
his "heart": "It's like a voice always speaking to me, never silent
day or night" (97). It is writing from within, the hand directed from
the other side of the page.

The whole diary is a preparation for his death-sentence: at once
the apprenticeship and martyrdom of the writer and the saint. As
he hones a more and more uncompromising prose of candor, the
face in the text grows more and more distinct, until, with the discovery of his cancer (his birth warrant?), he sees it, face to face:
"There was no old man in me. This awareness is sweet. For the
first time in years—perhaps for the first time ever—I seem to stand
before my youth and look upon it without mistrust; I have rediscovered a forgotten face. And my youth looks back at me, forgives
me" (250). In the priest's diary, Bernanos has grafted the expressive
tradition onto the Catholic salvational scheme and in the process
composed what is implicitly a reflexive diary: writing that helps move

128

the life written to a certain end, writing engaged in the life it tells. Though the whole document is saturated in the ideals of the journal of self-expression—spontaneity, informality, anti-rationalism—the textual manifestation of the self is, to labor the paradox, self-transforming. The text is not (as in the expressive tradition) merely an end in itself; it is useful. To put this in more specifically Christian terms: to express the self is to save it.

Mauriac's *Vipers' Tangle*

Vipers' Tangle antedates Bernanos's diary novel by four years. It contains considerably more retrospective material, but the reciprocal relationship between writer and text is essentially the same. The book begins as a letter of confession composed by the enormously wealthy "monster" Louis, in his sixty-ninth year, and addressed to his wife. The letter had been originally designed as an act of vengeance to be found after his death, revealing the full depth of Louis's hatred for his wife and children. As the novel proceeds, however, the letter evolves into a journal intime by the end of which Louis has discovered in his heart, not hatred, but love and the desire to confess it. Like *The Diary of a Country Priest* and so many other works in the broader tradition of the expressive journal, this novel is implicitly a portrait of the artist. More exactly, it is a portrait of the artist in spite of himself. Dry old miser that he is, Louis's nature comes from somewhere in the vicinity of the Ancient Mariner. He has "strange powers of speech" that set him apart, but in producing a reflexive diary, these powers eventually carry him beyond himself. To use the operating paradox of these two novels, they carry him beyond himself to his self.

To create in the first place his original monster self, Louis employed his verbal power as a kind of arch-antiromantic artist. His "great fluency of speech"[3] which had so impressed his schoolmasters when he was a child was harnessed and disciplined to make him one of the most feared lawyers in all France. In the process, he also mastered the *written* word, becoming an expert in the power

---

[3]François Mauriac, *Vipers' Tangle*, trans. Warre B. Wells (New York: Doubleday, 1957), 21.

of the text. In fact, by the beginning of the novel, he has a collection of texts that bind people to his will. He has texts that incriminate the provincial lawyer Bourru, making him his tool. He has a file on his errant son-in-law, Phili. He has letters from his wife that he can use to thwart any plans of a separation. He can, in short, make paper work. Not surprisingly, as he moves deeper into his diary, he is struck at certain moments by the *uses* to which these pages could be put were they to fall into the wrong hands: "I must destroy them as soon as I feel that I am getting worse. . . . " (109). Recalling the curé's problems at the start of his diary—his concern for the too-conscious control he was exerting over it—we can see in the lawyer the opposite: a kind of travesty of the classical artist. He is the writer of omniscience, master of the planned text or paper weapon. It is this "aesthetic" that has guided his thoughts about the letter to his wife, right up to the moment he takes pen in hand. An expert in the realm of material objects, he has always seen this letter whole, like a bomb or a bullet: "When I lie awake, I have always imagined it, all by itself, on the shelf of my safe—an empty safe, containing nothing else but this revenge of mine which, for nearly half a century, I have kept warm" (11).

In this conception of it his letter has existed only as a plan. In contrast, the true text begins in a kind of void of consciousness, a chaos of motives that baffles the writer. "What is this fever for writing which has seized upon me to-day, the anniversary of my birth? . . . why this sudden frenzy for writing" (13). As Bernanos would do after him, Mauriac trades in this way on the association of expressive authenticity and the diary. To put this in other words, the true artist can emerge only with the loss of control. "I read over these lines which I wrote yesterday evening in a kind of delirium. How could I have let my temper carry me away like that? This is not a letter anymore; it is a diary, interrupted, begun again. . . " (28). It has all the distinguishing marks of the organic, as opposed to the mechanic, text. One sees this even in the handwriting: "these letters all bent the same way, like pine-trees by the west wind" (13). The romantic and the Christian novelist come very close together here, both putting a high premium on what the world calls madness. Truth in this view comes only in delirium, in rhapsodic moments, and the truth teller necessarily becomes very strange to normal folk. Mauriac plays on this association of madness and saintliness when Louis's children toy with the idea of having their father committed. Hubert, who actually reads the diary, attests in an appended letter to the clear evidence of his father's madness: "He surrenders himself to a fuliginous mysticism only for the purpose of being better able to attack reasonable, moderate religion, which has always been held in honour in our family. Truth is a matter of balance ... " (195).

Hubert's final function in the novel is to provide us with an example of the bad reader. As such, he can lead us indirectly into the theme of mirrors, which is as much a part of this text as it is of Bernanos's. As in any true reflexive diary, reading and writing form a partnership, the quality of the one necessarily matched by the quality of the other. Thus, Louis grows as a reader as he grows as a writer. The experience of strangeness that he has in his "delirious" composing is matched by the defamiliarization of the self cast back by the pages. All that remains the same is the visual character of the text itself. In his meticulous way, Louis pores over it as if to verify what it communicates: "It is certainly my handwriting. I examine its characters closely, the trace of the nail of my little finger beneath the lines" (137). From time to time his reading power fails him. Then he avoids the text, sees it as incriminating, plans to destroy it. But as in the case of *The Diary of a Country Priest*, the development of his eye keeps pace with that of his pen. Together, they move him toward salvation: "It is ... when I study myself, as I have been doing for the past two months, with a curiosity which is stronger than my disgust; it is when I feel myself most fully in possession of my faculties that the Christian temptation torments me. I can no longer deny that a route exists in me which might lead me to your God" (103–104).

The conversion of the text into a mirror is embedded in a thematic field that is as studded with references to mirroring and reflection as *The Diary of a Country Priest*. From childhood, Louis has had his necessary mirrors: "One cannot preserve one's faith in himself all alone. We must have a witness of our prowess: somebody who notes the hits, who counts the points ... just as ... on prize day, when I was loaded down with books, my eyes searched for my mother in the crowd" (60). His mother is later replaced by the public at large, in whose reflecting gaze he shapes himself through the power of his words: "Shy though I was in private life, I became another man in public debate. I had followers, and I enjoyed being their leader" (25). In an irony perfectly consistent with this, the misery of his later life is sustained by his own willing collaboration with the eyes of his children, that "family pack sitting in a circle before the door and watching me" (61). In a performer/reflector relationship exactly analogous to the writer/reader relationship discussed above, the "old crocodile" (as Phili calls him) plays the old crocodile. Indeed, he plays it so well that he takes it for the truth: " 'Crocodile I am, and crocodile I shall remain. There is nothing to expect from an old crocodile, nothing—except his death' " (54).

Sustaining the mirror theme, the signal event in Louis's life that led him to become the crocodile was the discovery that a previous lover (Rodolphe) had existed in the eyes of his wife with a greater luster than he had. This is the event that he struggles to record at the start of the letter to his wife. Isa had originally been important to him because of her mirror function. She had been the only one to cast back a reflection of himself as attractive: "I saw my own reflection in another human being; and my image, thus reflected, had nothing repulsive about it" (31). "I was another man" (34). But with the revelation of Rodolphe, the mirror goes blank for him. Thus, searching for some explanation for the "frenzy" that has generated at long last a letter to his wife, he hits on her "silence." Using his old language, he says he wants to "triumph" over her silence, to "avenge" himself, that is, against the broken mirror. He will at least produce for her an image in spite of all. Ironically, as we learn later, Isa has been engaged in much the same activity. Before she dies, however, she burns her diary ("She had wanted to disappear entirely. She had effaced the least vestiges of herself" [171]). Louis digs into the heap of ashes that remains "as though it concealed the secret of my life, of our two lives" (172). He comes up with enough fragments to indicate, to his welcome surprise, how jealous she had been of his passion for their adopted son, Luc, who died in the war. Thus, something of his old self comes back into the mirror: "I rejoiced in the fact that a woman had not been indifferent to me, that I had stirred these depths in her" (173). This lifelong mutual dependency of the mirror and the mirrored, its spiritual importance *and* the critical power of the text, are emblematically combined by Mauriac when he has Louis, in the same scene, catch himself and the ashes of the burnt diary in a real mirror: "I saw, in the glass, my brow smeared with ashes" (172).

A potential difficulty of a novel so abundantly supplied with mirrors is that mirrors almost inevitably bring to mind Narcissus. The challenge for the novelist, as for the character, is to transcend the equipment of narcissism as one employs it. In Mauriac's novel, the challenge is turned into an advantage, for transcendence in this case is made possible by the metaphysical distinction between the two selves that we found operating in Bernanos's novel as well: the transient self of this world and the deservedly lovable self of the other world. Mauriac enforces this distinction by populating his novel with a variety of true narcissists. None of these is so vividly true to type than the ancient dandy, Baron Philipot, whom the Fondaudèges (Isa's family) have snared for his money, using one of their pretty daughters for bait. He was, Louis writes, "one of the most unhappy men I have ever known.... always looking for a mirror" (36). The unhappy man can see only his transient self in the mirror.

By the terms of the novel, the way out of narcissism is to love oneself. But the only way to love oneself is to see one's lovable self. This brings us back to the subject of writing, for to see that other self appears to require a rare gift. Louis has the gift. He is not only a master of a prose of candor, but he has a natural genius for narrative structure. He so unerringly composes his diary, for example, that he comes upon the memories of two children he had tried to forget—his daughter Marie and his adopted son, Luc. Both are dead. Both loved him. In both, he had reliable mirrors. As in Bernanos, in this novel too the vision of children is very important, playing a critical role in Louis's dialectic of self-awareness. The mirror relationship between Louis and these children is much more complex than that of the narcissist and his mirror (a relationship that is in fact not dialectical, but static). Louis the artist, polishing his textual mirror, finds in it the children who had found him ("there exists in me a secret chord: that which Marie set vibrating, simply by nestling in my arms; and also little Luc, on Sundays, when he came back from Mass" [104]). He finds them at the end of the first movement of his diary (the conclusion of part 1). He sees himself again as a "stranger," one in whom even his "baseness" seems, in its lack of hypocrisy, a form of holiness (105).

In his own *Journal*, writing of the Jesuit orator Louis Bourdaloue, Mauriac referred to "the double perfection of the soul and the word" ("le miracle de la purité du coeur unie à celle du langage

. . . ; la double perfection de l'âme et de la parole").[4] The formula would appear to apply precisely to his novel of 1932, and almost as precisely to Bernanos's of 1936. As in the case of the curé, Louis's Election is at one with his literary—or, I should say, literary and critical—gift. Thus, after a hundred pages of his own prose, he can reread and find himself "stupefied by the backgrounds in myself which they illuminated" (103). He is, moreover, an artist who has grown to the stature of his Election. The gift of words that he formerly used against the world is now allowed to act upon himself. This is sharply underscored in a vignette that occurs shortly after Isa's death. Louis has returned from Paris and has unaccountably fainted; on coming to, he speaks "the first words that came into my head":

> "I should have liked so much to accompany her to the end, since I was not here to say 'Good-bye' to her."
> I repeated, like an actor trying to get the right key: "Since I was not here to say 'Good-bye' to her"; and these commonplace words, intended only to save appearances, which came to me because they were a part of my role in the funeral rites, awakened in me, with sudden power, the feeling of which they were the expression.
> It was as though I had told myself something which I had not yet realized. [156]

He has gone so far in his "retraining" that he cannot help but catch the true content of his words—catch it and be altered by it. Indeed, so powerful is the reciprocal, energetic relationship between language and being that in his final hour Louis appears to have been led straight from this world to the next by his pen: "I could not find the word I sought. That which stifles me, to-night, even as I write these lines; that which makes my heart hurt as though it were going to burst; that love of which, at last, I know the name ador— —" (190).

Both of these works have received high praise and continue today to enjoy devoted constituencies. The irony of their critical reception is that when they have been attacked (often as vigorously as they have been praised), the principal charge has been contrivance. It

[4]François Mauriac, *Journal* (Paris: Bernard Grasset, 1934), 1:188, my translation.

would seem that in direct proportion as they are saturated in an aesthetic of spontaneous composition, the works themselves have been arraigned for being anything but spontaneous. Mauriac and Bernanos were both aware of this danger. From their point of view, their dairy novels suffer the curse of the "novel of Grace." What may be spontaneous in the eye of God is nearly always contrived in the eye of the reader. It is a variation of the old problem of coincidences. However commonplace they may be in life, they are unbelievable in a novel. Thus, for example, the suicide of Dr. Delbende, the professed atheist in *The Diary of a Country Priest*, has an authorially coached quality. In *Vipers' Tangle* the coincidences and providential interventions, combined with Louis's unerring comprehension of Christian doctrine, are so pronounced that many critics have found in them the author's Jansenist coercion of probability. In this light, Louis is more theoretical than real, an instance of Election whose life radiates nothing so much as its predestination.[5]

By featuring the reflexivity of these works, we offset the quality of gratuitous providentiality in the transformations of their protagonists. To stress the action of the text itself is not to eliminate the sense of authorial coercion entirely, since the way these two authors view the diary and its powers ultimately rests in a metaphysical assumption about the power texts can have and the kind of truth they can show. But by locating the page as the arena of struggle, one counterbalances the suddenness of Providence. In other words, the missing action—so psychologically essential as a preparation for Grace—can be seen as the writing of the text itself. Putting the stress on the writing, as we have done, helps to relocate these works in the more broadly orthodox Christian view of salvation as a collaboration between the soul and God. God helps those who help themselves, or, in the words of Augustine, "That man is Your best servant who is not so much concerned to hear from You what he wills as to will what he hears from You."[6] Thus the spontaneity of the text itself, its release from "rational" control, is the action of the will expressing its willingness. It is an allowing of the true self to write, the true voice to be heard, the true face

[5]Perhaps the most compact presentation of this view can be found in Martin Turnell, *The Art of French Fiction* (New York: New Directions, 1959), 344–347.

[6]*The Confessions of Saint Augustine*, trans. F. J. Sheed (New York: Sheed and Ward, 1943), 192.

to appear in the mirror. In stressing this, we do not ultimately lift the charge of stage-managing or forcing events, but we moderate it by showing the weight that is given in these books to writing as part of the action. Little wonder that Mauriac himself should, with more and more frequency during his career, stress the kind of writer *he* was: instinctive, relentless, uncalculating, capable of polishing off an entire novel in two months. As he told one interviewer, his work was "entièrement subconscient."[7]

[7]Frédéric Lefèvre, *Une heure avec* ... (Paris: Editions de la Nouvelle revue française, 1924), 1:223.

8

Toward the Textual Object:
Sartre's *Nausea*

Let Pascal say that man is a thinking reed. He is wrong; man is
a thinking erratum. Each period in life is a new edition that
corrects the preceding one and that in turn will be corrected by
the next, until publication of the definitive edition, which the
publisher donates to the worms.
— Machado de Assis, *Epitaph of a Small Winner*

By the late 1930s, the contours of a genre—"the Diary Novel"—
had emerged sufficiently to be parodied. In *Nausea (La nausée,*
1938), Sartre, whose serious artistic purposes throve on cutting
against literary clichés, cut in every way against this one. All the
conventional equipment is employed and pointedly stretched: the
room, the mirror, the implements of writing; the sensitivity, intelligence, and introversion of the diarist; his loneliness, his powerlessness, his failure in love, his endless pacing of the city streets
(*flânerie*); the arid self-consciousness of his prose, its ragged inter-
ruptedness, its continual reversion to the present. But Sartre also
wrote with a sharp eye to the subsidiary type discussed in the last
three chapters: the reflexive journal of self-discovery. And perhaps
he had no single example so vividly in mind as Mauriac's fictive
journal of salvation.

In 1939, Sartre fired a major blast in the war on Mauriac with
an essay entitled "François Mauriac and Freedom." The immediate
object of his attack was Mauriac's 1936 novel, *La fin de la nuit*, but
broadly it was Mauriac's wonted relationship to his characters and,
by extension, to his readers. Mauriac epitomized for Sartre the
absolute abolition of spontaneity. The development of plot and
character in his novels was neither organic nor free but preor-
dained. In Sartre's metaphysic, the honorific title of artist was the

last thing Mauriac deserved, since, in robbing his characters of their freedom, he sought ultimately to rob his readers as well. He practiced not art but indoctrination. "His sole aim is to make me as knowing as himself":[1]

> Why? Why hasn't this serious and earnest writer achieved his purpose? Because, I think, of the sin of pride. Like most of our writers, he has tried to ignore the fact that the theory of relativity applies in full to the universe of fiction, that there is no more place for a privileged observer in a real novel than in the world of Einstein. . . . M. Mauriac has put himself first. He has chosen divine omniscience and omnipotence. But novels are written *by* men and *for* men. In the eyes of God, Who cuts through appearances and goes beyond them, there is no novel, no art, for art thrives on appearances. God is not an artist. Neither is M. Mauriac.[2]

From this perspective, the employment of the diary mode in *Vipers' Tangle* is a compounding of literary bad faith. The author exploits the mode's illusion of spontaneity for his subversive purpose. He has his cake and eats it. Moreover, in *Vipers' Tangle* Mauriac cuts further into the freedom of his reader by giving his purpose everything but explicit utterance in an editor's note that precedes Louis's diary: "No, it was not gold that this miser cherished; it was not revenge for which this madman hungered. The real object of his love—you will know it if you have the strength and the courage to bear with this man, even to the moment of his last avowal, cut short by death. . . ." We are constrained to look to the end, to follow a secret teleology that is really no secret at all.

For the most part, then, Sartre's critique comes from within that literary tradition that includes the expressive text. He shares with that tradition, as he does with Mauriac, the watchwords of Freedom, the Unpremeditated, and the Unexpected. Thus, when he wrote his own diary novel in the year preceding his attack on Mauriac, he wrote essentially as a refiner of the tradition.[3] But in contrast

---

[1] Jean-Paul Sartre, *Literary Essays*, trans. Annette Nicholson (New York: Philosophical Library, 1957), 19.

[2] Sartre, *Literary Essays*, 23.

[3] Many commentators have noted how strongly Sartre seems to have been influenced by Rilke's diary novel, *The Notebooks of Malte Laurids Brigge (Die Aufzeichnungen des Malte Laurids Brigge*, 1910). But none to my knowledge has noted how Sartre also wrote with an eye to the diary type we have been discussing in the last three chapters.

to Mauriac, the refinement he sought was essentially a rigor that would not allow his diarist to be deflected toward an essential self, much less toward God. His diarist would not lapse into the false order that caps the journal of self-discovery. In using the form, Sartre's motive was a higher purity of disorder, an austere dedication to chaos that would allow no illusory blossomings of order. Therefore, like the protagonists we have already looked at, Roquentin is (despite Sartre's later disclaimers) a bona fide hero; and like them, too, he is a hero of insight. As in the cases of the curé and Louis, his special superiority of insight falls on him like a sickness. And though it is of the character of his affliction that the very word "hero" must lose its meaning, he stands out in contrast to the absurdly believing folk who comprise the Bouville bourgeoisie. Honest and incapable of self-deception, he is a direct, though bastard, descendant of the sentimental hero of sincerity.[4]

Correlatively, the particular strain of self-consciousness about one's literary form, endemic in journals of self-discovery, is also almost everywhere present in *Nausea*. A problem of life is, more than ever, a problem of literature. In his new condition as a man fallen outside of shaped time into a world in which all objects and all events are unlinked, gratuitous, absolutely singular, Roquentin finds that the only authentic mode of composition, and a barely authentic one at that, is the disorganized notebook—a compendium of moments keeping pace with the present, constantly imitating what Roquentin calls the "jerky, incoherent aspect" of his life.[5] Roquentin's attempts to compose a structured biography of the Marquis de Rollebon are frustrated by his discovery of the same disruption of continuity in Rollebon's life that he is experiencing in his own. The conventions of storytelling, so common in retrospective fiction and so commonly transposed to the narratives of "real life," are no longer transposable for Roquentin. Man, as he says, "tries to live his own life as if he were telling a story." But, he goes on, "you have to choose: live or tell" (39).

Traditional Aristotelians, of course, can understand that there

---

[4]Sartre has hard words for the sincere man (see particularly the chapter entitled "Bad Faith" in *Being and Nothingness*), but his critique rests on the grounds that sincerity itself, as it is understood and pursued, is necessarily a form of dishonesty.

[5]Jean-Paul Sartre, *Nausea*, trans. Lloyd Alexander (New York: New Directions, 1969), 5.

is a difference between living and telling, but they can endorse the validity of telling because they believe that causality governs human affairs. Historical causality may be different from literary causality, but it nevertheless can be instructively mimed by the end-dominated causality of the latter. The common Marxist position is quite similar:

> Whereas in life "whither?" is a consequence of "whence?", in literature "whither?" determines the content, selection and proportion of the various elements. The finished work may resemble life in observing a causal sequence; but it would be no more than an arbitrary chronicle if there were not this reversal of direction. It is the perspective, the *terminus ad quem*, that determines the significance of each element in a work of art.[6]

But when belief in life's causality dissolves, causality in mimetic art becomes invalid. Indulging in "literature," or stories, then becomes a perpetuation of the kind of fraud Sartre complained of in Mauriac:

> You seem to start at the beginning: "It was a fine autumn evening in 1922. I was a notary's clerk in Marommes." And in reality you have started at the end. It was there, invisible and present, [giving to the words] the pomp and value of a beginning.... "It was night, the street was deserted." The phrase is cast out negligently, it seems superfluous; but we do not let ourselves be caught and we put it aside: this is a piece of information whose value we shall subsequently appreciate. And we feel that the hero has lived all the details of this night like annunciations, promises, or even that he lived only those that were promises, blind and deaf to all that did not herald adventure. We forget that the future was not yet there. [39–40]

In turning to the diary as an antidote to this common weakness, Roquentin must be very careful not to be lulled by the diary's own illusion of endlessness. The treachery of the spontaneous mode is that under the guise of the artless, "literature" can be foisted in everywhere. And with literature come form and causality. For this reason, the catch phrases of the traditional expressive diarist take on a new urgency for Roquentin: "Beware of literature. I must

---

[6]Georg Lukács, *The Meaning of Contemporary Realism*, trans. John and Necke Mander (London: Merlin Press, 1962), 55.

follow the pen, without looking for words" (56). He must be especially vigilant. Like Sartre, he has grown up in the afterglow of the great age of the intimate journal. The bookstalls are cluttered with cheap imitations in which all the formulas of sincerity have long became clichés. For the disenchanted, the diary has become its opposite—a slick version of what Roquentin calls the "true story." Its function, as Paul Valéry wrote in 1930, is not to render true interior being but to provide the illusion of a life where there is in fact none:

> Authors of Confessions or Memoirs or Journaux intimes are invariably dupes of their own desire to shock; and we are dupes of these dupes. It is never one's real self that one wants to exhibit; we all know that a real person has nothing much to teach us about himself. One writes, then, the confessions of some more remarkable being, more pure, more wicked, more lively, more sensitive, even more *oneself* than one can be, because the self has its degrees. He who confesses lies and flees the real truth which is null, shapeless and generally indistinct. But the confidential remark aspires always to glory, scandal, excuse, propaganda.[7]

Consequently, at the beginning of his diary, we find Roquentin operating with excruciating care: "I must not put in strangeness where there is none. I think that is the big danger in keeping a diary: you exaggerate everything. You continually force the truth because you're always looking for something" (1). Austere standards and, as it turns out, unattainable ones. Try as he might, the formal *reductio* of his effort is present in embryo on the very first page. The danger Roquentin seeks to avoid lurks in the smallest molecular components of expression: the words themselves. What is that cardboard box—the one holding his ink bottle? "Well, it's a parallelopiped rectangle, it opens—that's stupid, there's nothing I can say about it"(1).

The book concludes with Roquentin determined to turn this problem of form to his advantage. He sets out to write a novel that will have none of the guilty pretense of mimesis that taints other novels but that will instead achieve the condition of pure story, as

[7]Paul Valéry, "Stendhal," in *Variété II* (Paris: Gallimard, 1930), 101–102, my translation.

the song he hears in the Rendezvous des Cheminots achieves the condition of pure music—form that repeats itself eternally in a sublime independence of existence. Roquentin hopes that some of the purity of form he achieves in his novel will descend on him—that he will become a legend in the minds of his readers, as the author and singer of the song he hears have acquired legendary qualities in his own mind. It is a trick ending, riddled with problems, and Sartre almost immediately turned to the creation of more satisfying versions of existential heroism. Still, the distinction between formal storytelling and the impossible ideal of a genuine mimesis of existence remained a fundamental Sartrean opposition. Since *Nausea* is clearly intended to be not a novel of the order that Roquentin sets out to write at the end but, rather, an attempt to render as closely as possible the free discontinuity of existence, it must do without story and rely instead on the static collection of moments, however treacherous the illusion, that are compiled in Roquentin's diary.[8]

So, briefly to summarize our first general point about *Nausea*, it is at once a refinement and a revolution in the journal of self-discovery; or better, it is a revolution that is the logical development of a refinement. The revolution, simply put, is that the diary discovers not something but nothing; not the self but a blank. For Sartre, the something-revealed that marks the journal of self-discovery is not revealed but imported. It takes a really great artist so to restrain his text that Nothing can finally emerge. Yet, in the process, how closely does Sartre keep his bark trimmed to the prevailing mode! Like the others, he appears to validate both the diary and the point of view of the diarist. Like them, he locates in his diarist a special, privileged view of the truth, a vision his diarist owes directly to his gift for words, which allows him to go behind art to a semblance of undigested time. As in Bernanos and Mauriac

---

[8]Just how the book ranks in terms of its own definitions is still a crux. Frank Kermode may have put it more fairly than I have: "Between [Roquentin's] experience and his fiction lies Sartre's book." For his excellent discussion of the problem of rendering contingency in literary vehicles that are inevitably formal, see *The Sense of an Ending* (London: Oxford University Press, 1966), 133–152. For a broader exploration of the relationship between Sartre's thought and the style and structure—including the diary structure—of *Nausea*, see Edith Kern, *Existential Thought and Fictional Technique: Kierkegaard, Sartre, Beckett* (New Haven: Yale University Press, 1970), 84–134.

especially, this lapse into pure time is a necessary "way down" that the diarist must travel to achieve salvation.

Looking further at these parallels, what is perhaps most striking is the blithe defiance with which Sartre takes over the Christian terminology of redemption. As in the quotation above in which he accuses Mauriac of the sin of pride, Sartre shows himself a master in employing the weaponry of the opposition. It is a mastery precisely because the language is so appropriate. Roquentin finds himself "cast out" in the present. The existent world is a world that has "fallen." Roquentin fears "what will be born and take possession of me" (5). Like his predecessors he has the "madness" that is the burden of his holy calling. At the end of the diary (near Easter), he sets out to be "saved," to be "washed . . . of the sin of existing." Moreover, through his reexamination of his past we are made to see the same paradox of conversion that we see in the others and that Sartre phrased so well in his study of Genêt: "that it spreads over years and gathers together in an instant."[9] One major effect of this is that the contrast with his predecessors, when it comes, comes sharply. In their dark nights, Mauriac's Louis and Bernanos's curé find absolute form, grasping the hand of Providence, which helps them help themselves. In the dark night of his absolute freedom, Roquentin finds the absolute absence of any form beyond that of his own making.

In the thematic arena of self-perception and self-reflection, so much a part of the diaries of self-discovery, Sartre again shows an acute awareness of his model. With an amused belligerency, he loads his book with mirrors (by my count, they appear in six separate scenes). But a mirror in *Nausea* is a "white hole in the wall," "a trap"; Roquentin's reflection is "the grey thing," something "well below the monkey, on the fringe of the vegetable world, at the level of jellyfish"—"nature without humanity." In a passing tour de force, Sartre weds the set piece of the mirror with his pirated metaphysical equipment. He has Roquentin fall asleep watching the mirror and while dreaming have a vision in which a grotesque nonshape grows and grows in the mirror: "an immense, light [pâle] halo gliding in the light" (16–18).

---

[9] Jean-Paul Sartre, *Saint Genêt*, trans. Bernard Frechtman (New York: New American Library, 1964), 61.

Finally, this text like the others is a reflexive diary. As in the other diaries, the text battles the diarist, who refines in the process his dual role as writer and reader to gain the truth beyond the text. In this quarter, Sartre's refinement, as Lessing's later, is to relocate the enemy in words themselves. As in *The Golden Notebook*, it is a devastating inversion because it renders out of the question all possibility of "purifying" the language. Words are the enemy because they are (in this semantic context) that which is not. To put a word, however modest or unpremeditated, in your notebook is to take one small step away from the truth. This puts both the author and his fictional agent in an impossible situation. It is like the old conundrum "All generalizations are false" or the man who says "I always lie." How do you move an inch in such a situation?

Sartre's solution was not to get out of the situation. The truth is left forever offstage, while the text becomes a *via negativa* in which the prize is won by default. Falsehood becomes the object, and the drama of the text becomes its self-exposure. The energy of this text takes the form of an active resistance to the writer's will to express, and the writer, in turn, releases this energy by rubbing words against his perceptions:

> This root . . . existed in such a way that I could not explain it. Knotty, inert, nameless, it fascinated me, filled my eyes, brought me back unceasingly to its own existence. In vain to repeat: "This is a root"— it didn't work any more.
>
>   . . .
>
>   Black? I felt the word deflating, emptied of meaning with extraordinary rapidity. Black? The root *was not* black, there was no black on this piece of wood—there was . . . something else: black, like the circle, did not exist.
>
>   . . .
>
> this fundamental absurdity. Absurdity: another word; I struggle against words; down there I touched the thing. [129–130]

This intimation of an infinite regress occurs at the heart of the book when Roquentin attempts to record a vision he has had in a park (which is *not* the Garden of Eden) before a tree (which is *not* the Tree of the Knowledge of Good and Evil) in an ecstasy (which is *not* the ecstasy of bliss but a "horrible ecstasy"). The vision remains *in absentia*, as Roquentin struggles to render it through the falsehood of his rendering. In this battle with his notebook, the diarist takes the "way down" that leads to the novelist who ascends in the last pages.

There are at least two other ways in which Sartre features an active reflexive relationship between diarist and diary. One is effectively the opposite of the battle just discussed and something we also found in Lessing. It is what you could call Roquentin's continual experience of the warmth of falsehood, the protection of language. From time to time Roquentin is awakened to the relief his notebook affords him from that visceral awareness of existence that he calls the Nausea: "The truth is that I can't put down my pen: I think I'm going to have the Nausea and I feel as though I'm delaying it while writing. So I write whatever comes into my mind" (173). I write whatever comes into my mind—the old diary formula but in this context a strategy for avoidance, not discovery. However random and spontaneous, words reestablish the comfort of form. They counter that perception of absolute disorder that Roquentin calls his "messy suffering."

His diary offers the same relief that the Autodidact receives from his own foolish notebook in which he writes in the hope of repeating the thought of someone great. The comfort of form is the comfort of the repeatable. It is *the* comfort of language itself, a comfort Roquentin shares with M. Achille when Doctor Rogé calls the latter a crazy loon: "He relaxes, he feels protected against himself: nothing will happen to him today. I am reassured too. A crazy old loon: so that was it, so that was all" (67). The comfort is the category—the repeatable mode of the loon. As all language is labeling, the truth is necessarily beyond it. Little wonder that Roquentin should feel "more and more need to write—in the same proportion as I grow old" (13). In this way, Sartre seeks to reverse our whole understanding of the virtues of the diary mode. That flow, that outpouring of language from the unconscious, so prized by surrealist automatic writers as a tapping of the real real and by psychiatrists as a prescription for depression ("Write something. Write anything. Just put something down"),[10] owes its power to soothe and to restore

[10]Prescribed for the writer of Wallace Stegner's diary novel, *The Spectator Bird* (Lincoln: University of Nebraska Press, 1979), 8.

not to its "connection with inner truth" or to its power to purge, or to its freedom from the distortions of convention but to its falsehood. The truth for Sartre is intolerable because it is absolutely shallow. The unpremeditated language of the diary soothes because it restores the illusion of depth.

The shallowness of truth takes part in a third way in which writing figures reflexively in Roquentin's development. Here reflexivity takes the form of a repeated short-focus on the implements of writing. The book is swamped by its technology, abounding in references to pages, and ink, handwriting and print, broken words, advertisements, book covers, notebooks, and letters. In an exemplary sequence (one to which Sartre could not resist giving emblematic embellishment), Roquentin, struggling to write of Rollebon, his subject's letters beside him, suddenly and distressingly finds the point of his focus retracting from meaning to implement:

I picked up my pen and tried to get back to work; I was up to my neck in these reflections on the past, the present, the world. I asked only one thing: to be allowed to finish my book in peace.

But as my eyes fell on the pad of white sheets, I was struck by its look and I stayed, pen raised, studying this dazzling paper: so hard and far seeing, so present. The letters I had just inscribed on it were not even dry yet and already they belonged to the past.

"Care had been taken to spread the most sinister rumours ..."

I had thought out this sentence, at first it had been a small part of myself. Now it was inscribed on the paper, it took sides against me. I didn't recognize it any more. [95]

Roquentin, without at all wanting to, undergoes a textbook example of what has come to be called the "foregrounding" of his craft. It is quite literally what Ortega y Gasset had, in the preceding decade, described as the "dehumanization of art." Moreover, the experience that Roquentin has with his own writing is repeated on the next page with the writing of someone else, someone who wrote in an epoch well before the modern. Roquentin turns to the precious letters of Rollebon that he had stolen in Moscow: "He is the one,

I said, he is the one who made these marks, one by one. He leaned on this paper, he put his hand against the sheets to prevent them from turning under his pen. Too late: these words had no more sense. Nothing existed but a bundle of yellow pages which I clasped in my hands" (96).

The truth about words is that they are as flat as everything else: violations of the whiteness of a page, disturbances of air. Thus, the experience that Mauriac's Louis has of the creative power of words, their metaphysical depth, is matched by its exact opposite in the life of Roquentin:

> I made one last attempt; I repeated the words of Mme de Genlis by which I usually evoked the Marquis: "His small, wrinkled countenance, clean and sharp, all pitted with smallpox, in which there was a singular malice which struck the eye, no matter what effort he made to dissemble it."
>
> His face appeared to me with docility, his pointed nose, his bluish cheeks, his smile. I could shape his features at will, perhaps with even greater ease than before. Only it was nothing more than an image in me, a fiction. I sighed, let myself lean back against the chair, with an intolerable sense of loss. [97]

To complete the sequence, Roquentin crucifies himself just the tiniest bit. With his pocketknife, he stabs his palm, clumsily, and then watches "with satisfaction, on the white paper, across the lines I wrote a little while ago, this tiny pool of blood which has at last stopped being me" (100).

It is now time to confront a problem that has been hovering on the periphery throughout this analysis of Sartre's diary novel, a problem quite similar to the one that would later split Lessing's diary novel. Briefly to review the discussion so far: by refining the salient features of the journal of self-discovery, and particularly the journal of salvation, in *Nausea* (not simply its external form but its mystique about spontaneity, its concern for linguistic purity, its literary self-consciousness, its metaphysical apparatus, and its reflexive kinetic agency in the life of its diarist), Sartre has sought to invert each of these features. The end of this process is to turn the entire document on its head. Sartre does not validate the form but declares its unredeemable invalidity. This is the problem. One can, of course, argue that the necessary falseness of language has also been a part of the tradition on which Sartre has drawn. Commonly, in the journal of self-discovery, both emotive and metaphysical truth stand beyond the actual words.

> I sometimes hold it half a sin
> > To put in words the grief I feel;
> > For words, like Nature, half reveal
> And half conceal the Soul within.[11]

But in replacing transcendence with its opposite—an equally ungraspable contingency—Sartre makes all that is signified, by words or by whatever, that which is not. Roquentin's diary has, therefore, a stark falseness that is nowhere accorded earlier diaries in the tradition.

So the whole book is really in the camp of the enemy. The illusion of a truer language that it borrows from the diary tradition makes it even more insidious. This contradiction is not resolved. Though we understand that Roquentin experiences the truth only offstage, as it were, Sartre uses Roquentin to make an argument onstage, an argument we are meant to attend to very seriously. Everything in the novel—set pieces, emblematic sequences, type characters, passages of intellection—works rhetorically. In other words, everything implicitly validates the language and the literary form even as it argues their invalidity. The form overwhelms the argument. It is a point that brings us back to where we started with Sartre, for precisely the charge he makes against Mauriac appears equally makeable against Sartre. As he, reading Mauriac, was unable to forget Mauriac; so we, reading Sartre, are unable to forget Sartre. Where he accuses Mauriac of only pretending to grant his characters and his readers freedom, it is hard to keep from thinking of the *quod erat demonstrandum* quality of the scene in the Bouville Portrait Gallery or of Sartre's disposal of socialist humanism through the homosexuality of the Autodidact. If Mauriac's editor's note is blatant in its determination to control our response to his novel, Sartre's editors' note to *Nausea* is perhaps more insidious in its seeming innocence. (Who is this fellow Roquentin that he should deserve editing—and by more than one editor? A legend, no doubt.)

---

[11]Alfred, Lord Tennyson, *In Memoriam*, sec. 5, ll. 1–4.

At bottom, this is the criticism of Sartre that has been leveled repeatedly by the literary generation that succeeded him in France. Alain Robbe-Grillet, who sought in his own works an honesty of pure surface, argued that Sartre, for all his attack on depth in *Nausea*, smuggled it in through his language.[12] And it is a similar "inner contradiction" in his plays, as Martin Esslin pointed out, that distinguishes his work from that of the absurdist playwrights.[13] These later writers, however, did not seek to reestablish literary good faith by abandoning language altogether nor by turning to the purity of story, as Roquentin promises to do at the end of *Nausea*. They sought to do so by effecting a revolution in the language and structure of the text itself. Where Sartre sought in *Nausea* so to refine aspects of his chosen form that they served ends opposite to the ends they served traditionally, the New Novelists sought to break and rebuild the form from within.

One is never really done with Sartre. I have made the case that in composing *Nausea* he affected his revolution within the traditional constraints of the journal of self-discovery. By staying within those constraints, he wound up in a contradiction between his form and his content. *Nausea*, from this point of view, became the end of a certain line, and it remained for his successors to break with the old form and create a new. To appropriate Beckett's description of Kafka, it remained for them to find a way to put "the consternation *in* the form."[14] I would now like to make the case that this formal revolution is, in fact, something that Sartre also experimented with in *Nausea*. If his experiment was too slight to offset the "contradiction" discussed above, it is too substantial to be written

---

[12] Alain Robbe-Grillet, *For a New Novel*, trans. Richard Howard (New York: Grove Press, 1965), 41, 64–68.

[13] "If Sartre argues that existence comes before essence and that human personality can be reduced to pure potentiality and the freedom to choose itself anew at any moment, he presents his ideas in plays based on brilliantly drawn characters who remain wholly consistent and thus reflect the old convention that each human being has a core of immutable, unchanging essence—in fact, an immortal soul. And the beautiful phrasing and argumentative brilliance of both Sartre and Camus in their relentless probing still, by implication, proclaim a tacit conviction that logical discourse can offer valid solutions, that the analysis of language will lead to the uncovering of basic concepts—Platonic ideas" (Martin Esslin, *The Theatre of the Absurd* [New York: Anchor, 1961], xx).

[14] Israel Shenker, "Moody Man of Letters," *New York Times*, May 6, 1956, sec. 2, p. 1.

off. His experiment is also significant to our study because it was an experiment with the diary mode, which points directly to a reduction of the reflexive text that is at the heart of much of what is called the *nouveau roman*.

In one of his long footnotes to *What Is Literature?* Sartre refers to a series of turn-of-the-century attempts to make "the reader contemporaneous with the action" by casting novels in the form of plays. To record the thoughts of their characters, the authors used italics and parentheses. Sartre called the form "an attempt without a future. The authors who used it had a vague feeling that new life could be put into the novel by writing it in the present. But they had not yet understood that it was not possible if one did not first give up the *explanatory attitude*."[15] As a result they produced not psychic reality but rhetoric. Roughly during the same period as these "failures," however, there were also a number of experiments in a distinct mutation of the diary novel. Notable examples are Henri Barbusse's *L'enfer* (1908) and Hugues Le Roux's *Au champs d'honneur* (1916). Like the diary, the narrative of these works is intercalated, that is, it is made up of dated or undated entries that keep pace with the chronology of events. Unlike the diary, the entries are not "written"—that is, there is no fiction of writing. Like a monologue, the entries are in the first-person present tense, but unlike the monologue, there is no necessary fiction of voicing either ("the candle is out, but someone is there. It is the maid. Obviously, she has come in to clear the room, as she has stayed. She is alone. She is very near me").[16] These, too, were motivated by a desire to make "the reader contemporaneous with the action," but unlike the other experiments, they did give up "the explanatory attitude," and, moreover, they appear to have had a direct influence on Sartre.

In my earlier discussion, I showed how Sartre refined the journal of self-discovery, a quite pointedly "written" mode. At the same

[15]Jean-Paul Sartre, *What Is Literature?* trans. Bernard Frechtman (New York: Harper, 1965), 139n.

[16]Henri Barbusse, *L'enfer* (Paris: Albin Michel, 1908), 17, my translation. See also Barbusse's *Le feu* (1916). The mode appears to have evolved out of late nineteenth-century monologue fiction by authors like Arthur Schnitzler, V. Garshin, and even Thomas Hardy ("A Tryst at an Ancient Earthwork," 1885). This is not an extinct mode. It has survived notably in Par Lagerkvist's *The Dwarf* (1945) but also in such works as Geneviève Gennari's *Journal d'une bourgeoise* (1959), Frédéric Dard's *C'est mourir un peu* (1967), and Sandrine Forge's *Lily: The Diary of a French Girl in New York* (1969).

time he also attempted, with equal self-consciousness, to marry it
with the mode of the "unwritten journal." "Married" is not exactly
the right word. In Sartre's text, the shift from one to the other is
often quite noticeable:

> I let go of the railing, turned back towards the houses and streets of
> the town and half-aloud I murmured, "It's Sunday."
> It's Sunday: behind the docks, along the seacoast, near the freight
> station, all around the city there are empty warehouses and motionless
> machines in the darkness. [40–41]

> I close the book. I'm going out for a walk.
> It was almost three o'clock when I came out of the Brasserie Vézélise;
> I felt the afternoon all through my heavy body. [50]

Could the present tense in the long passage between these two
excerpts be seen as a device, consciously adopted by Roquentin to
give us the presentness of that Sunday? Certainly possible, though
in eliminating "us" from the proposition (as we must, since Roquentin writes for himself) the strain on credibility becomes more
acute. But what about Sartre, the author behind Roquentin? He
certainly has much to gain from the communication of presentness
to "us," as it is of the very nature of existence that it is present.
Surely he can be granted this liberty to manipulate his character's
style? "The thing which was waiting was on the alert, it has pounced
on me, it flows through me, I am filled with it. It's nothing: I am
the Thing. Existence, liberated, detached, floods over me. I exist"
(98). But then, if this is granted, why not interior monologue as
well (for even greater immediacy)? "Someone takes me from behind, they force me to think from behind, therefore to be something, behind me, breathing in light bubbles of existence, he is a
bubble of fog and desire, he is pale as death in the glass, Rollebon
is dead, Antoine Roquentin is not dead, I'm fainting" (102). But
then, if this is granted, why not the third person (to communicate
the feeling of otherness)? "He goes into the Bar de la Marine, the
little mirrors of the little brothel, he is pale in the little mirrors of
the little brothel the big redhead who drops onto a bench" (102).
    The liberties add up. And though the legitimate needs for these
liberties—for this grafting of the two modes—are quite easy to
identify (as I have done in parentheses), the liberties stand out as

liberties (the word is a good one) because there is, throughout the
diary, such a pointed and continual stress on its *written* character.
It is this that makes it an uneasy text. Sartre goes out of his way
to include those little mechanical asides that maintain the true diary
status of the text ("The waiter has just awakened me and I am
writing this while half-asleep" [155]). Instead of subtly weaving the
two modes together, Sartre ensures a dissonance between them.
This dissonance itself appears to have been his object. The way out
of the "inner contradiction" was through a more profound contradiction in the form itself. This is what Sartre, gropingly, through
the long gestation of his first novel,[17] and with no clear end in sight,
seems to have worked toward. By knocking the ontological pins
out from under the book itself, he seeks to give it precisely those
qualities of inexplicableness, of dissociation from all other things,
of freedom from category and defiance of meaning that his character experiences in the world offstage. A felt impossibility.

My own reading tells me that if this was his object, he failed. The
strength of the "written" fiction overrides the "unwritten." Though
contradiction was one of Sartre's specialties, it was in the area of
intellectual and emotional contradiction that he excelled: "Fake to
the marrow of my bones and hoodwinked, I joyfully wrote about
our unhappy state. Dogmatic though I was, I doubted everything
except that I was the elect of doubt. I built with one hand what I
destroyed with the other, and I regarded anxiety as the guarantee
of my security; I was happy."[18] It is even possible to conceive Sartre's
entire literary corpus as a diary in which each entry in some way
contradicts the last. Thus, for example, the man whose fictive agent,
for compelling reasons, abandons biography in 1938 becomes a
biographer whose last project (unfinished) is 2,800 pages on the
life of Flaubert. But the kind of contradiction in the form of literary
art itself that I have just been discussing was not an area in which
Sartre broke much ground. There are minor experiments here and
there (some of the paragraphing of *The Reprieve*), but by and large
Sartre's literary approach was classical, his characters consistent,

---

[17]Charted in roughly the first third of the second volume in Simone de Beauvoir's
autobiography *The Prime of Life* (*La force de l'âge*).

[18]Jean-Paul Sartre, *The Words*, trans. Bernard Frechtman (Greenwich: Fawcett,
1964), 158.

his narrative persuasion omniscient, and his language as logical as it was elegant.

This makes the experiment in *Nausea* as important as it is singular. It may have been that Sartre was able to achieve this formal singularity because of the two traditions of diary fiction that offered themselves for synthesis. However it came into being, and however it may have misfired, the experiment looks forward to that subsequent revolution, carried on all over the text by such authors as Michel Butor, Robert Pinget, Claude Simon, and Robbe-Grillet.

Sartre may not have had a strong or direct influence on the *nouveau romanciers*, but his fictional diarist is clearly heading in their direction. The tentative mimetic corruption I have just discussed is something Claude Simon accomplishes handily when, for example, he orchestrates the text of *Les corps conducteurs* from five utterly disjoined situations. As Jonathan Culler would describe it, Simon creates a text that cannot be "naturalized."[19] With the nouveau roman we have at last got a text that is, in Roquentin's term, quite simply *there*. All surface, no depth, it begins and ends with itself. Like music, it has a pure presence, assisted by a narrative tense Robbe-Grillet called the "instantaneous present."[20] Such a text "is based on no truth that exists before it; and one may say that it expresses nothing but itself. It creates its own equilibrium and its own meaning." Correlatively, "the genuine writer has nothing to say.... He has only a way of speaking."[21] In the terms of Ortega y Gasset, this is an entirely "foregrounded" art, a true textual object.[22]

In all the reflexive diary texts I have discussed, we have observed

[19] Jonathan Culler, *Structuralist Poetics: Structuralism, Linguistics, and the Study of Literature* (Ithaca: Cornell University Press, 1975), 134–160.

[20] Alain Robbe-Grillet, "Objectivity and Subjectivity in the *Nouveau Roman*," *New Hungarian Quarterly* 7 (Summer 1966), 84.

[21] Robbe-Grillet, *For a New Novel*, 45.

[22] Where Ortega and some historians of modernism identify this as a recent development, the new novelists like some formalists (Viktor Shklovsky) and structuralists see this aesthetic "shallowness" as a universal property of literary art. The key historical change, in this latter view, has been awareness of this fact. For Derrida, ours is the first period in which we have fully realized the text's complete freedom from any "Presence" or fixed signified. Barthes's refinement on the argument was to introduce the distinction between texts that are aware of their self-referentiality—writerly texts (*scriptible*) composed by authors (*écrivains*)—and texts that are unaware of it—readable texts (*lisible*) composed by writers (*scripteurs*). Thus, historical classics in context can generally be said to be readable; but readable texts can be transformed by the enlightened reader into writerly ones.

a dialectical interplay between a character and a text. Conventionally, the character has dominated the relationship; the text has played a subsidiary role. This was even true in Doris Lessing's unresolved and unresolvable diary novel, *The Golden Notebook*. But in *Nausea* we can observe a crisis in the relationship of these terms. Their comparative power is suddenly reversed—not only reversed but put way out of balance. Roquentin, as he is enlightened to the terrible, all-generative power of language, turns and sees himself on the verge of disappearing in the mirror. The New Novelists let him go. In taking for their starting point the assumption that in their art "there is nothing but what is written,"[23] they cancel the possibility of character. Character is a consistency that stands beyond the words and that refers through its typicality to yet another beyond, the external world. In these texts, what we might take for character is really a series of verbal occasions continually and exclusively referring back to the text in which they are embedded. Thus, the whole fiction of a diary (as conceived here) is put out of the question, since there is no character to keep it. No diarist, no diary. When Sartre's successors let Roquentin evaporate, what they appeared to do, in effect, was take his place. Moreover, where Roquentin agonized, they accepted the new terms and set out thoroughly to enjoy themselves.

The evaporation of the diarist explains why there is, comparatively speaking, so little diary fiction among the works of the New Novelists. In the one outstanding case in which diary form is used, Michel Butor's *L'emploi du temps* (*Passing Time*, 1956), it is used to subvert precisely what the form encodes. The form is made to participate in the setting-at-naught of all it signifies: reference to the world, recovery of the past, expression of a self, exactitude in time, achievement of a life tale. The fiction of diarist is displaced along with the fiction of character. In its place we have Revel, a proper name wielded by his entries, one of the shifting elements in their contrapuntal project. Lorna Martens made essentially this point when, comparing Butor to Proust, she argued that *L'emploi du temps* "replaces 'involuntary memory' with 'involuntary language.' The noncharacter Revel is simply a mouthpiece whose per-

---

[23]"Claude Simon: 'Le roman se fait, je le fais, et il se [sic] fait,' " *Les lettres françaises* (Apr. 13–19, 1967), 3, my translation.

sonality has no effect on what happens to language. He is just a force to set the play of words in motion, a curtain raiser for the drama in which language is the main actor."[24] I would only purify her wording of the phrase "a force to set the play of words in motion," since it suggests, however barely, some existence apart from the words.

In the absence of a separable character, the only reflexive, kinetic relationship of interest would appear to be that between the author and his book. In the accounts given by these novelists the relationship proceeds from moment to moment, very much like that of a diarist and his diary, without plan and with a strong emphasis on its catalytic vigor (what will it generate? what will come next?). So it may be possible to argue that after a period of theoretical extinction, the author in the 1950s began making a comeback. If this is so, these *écrivains journalists* have nothing of the pretensions of their romantic forebears. Though they may put themselves (as authors) in the light again, it is a soft light. The hard light is on the language and what will be expressed in and of it.

> C.S. . . . more and more I let myself go where the writing takes me. Instead of saying to myself: "This is not in my plan" and refusing some contribution, I take what comes.
> *Comes from where?*
> C.S. I told you: from the writing. From the rhythm, from the words themselves. Each word attracts other words, calls forth other images, sends out tentacles that catch some other thing.[25]

The author is there, but barely. And though Simon elsewhere affirms the reciprocity of the arrangement—"the novel makes itself, I make it, and it makes me" ("Le roman se fait, je le fait, et il me fait")[26]—even in that formulation, the balance of power lies with the novel. Butor, who speaks of his writing as a kind of spinal column in his life, can at the same time refer to the writer as an "obstetrician," an instrument for the "bringing into the world" ("mise

---

[24]Lorna Martens, "Empty Center and Open End: The Theme of Language in Michel Butor's *L'emploi du temps*," *PMLA* 96 (Jan. 1981), 59.
[25]"Claude Simon: Il n'y a pas d'art réaliste," *La quinzaine littéraire* (Dec. 15–31, 1967), 4, my translation.
[26]"Claude Simon: Le roman se fait . . . ," 4.

au monde") of certain novels.[27] It is here with the author that Martens's description of Revel would seem to apply: "a force to set the play of words in motion." Once in motion, the novel contains the power to continue its own generation, as if the text were, in Robbe-Grillet's phrase, "secreted by the style itself."[28] Long after the author has quit, it keeps going on. To adapt the phrasing of Jean Ricardou, the text becomes a perpetual meaning-changing machine.[29]

In one of Raymond Queneau's novels, the writer heroine, calling herself "a pretended imaginary author" ("un auteur prétendu imaginaire"), pens a preface to her book in which she discusses Queneau, "a so-called real author" ("un auteur soi-disant réel").[30] The phrase nicely balances the embarrassment of both terms, "auteur" and "réel." Whatever we are referring to when we speak of the author—an open-ended system of changes, a pressure on the language—we are referring to nothing so enduring and itself as the text. The author follows the character offstage, and it is the text, if anything, that becomes the reality. This reality may in turn cast a shadow of being over its author in a distant version of Roquentin's concluding idea in *Nausea* ("Madame Bovary, c'est moi"; Flaubert's phrase has gained resonance in retrospect). But the shadow of being is faint. Once written, these texts have little to do with anything but themselves. We find in them the last twist of our mirror theme, for though they abound in mirrors, the mirrors are turned to the text. The device of internal reflection—part reflecting part reflecting part (as in Simon's *Triptique*: the shaft of a pen and the shaft of a penis, the pink body of a skinned rabbit and the pink tongue of a girl)—is perhaps more than any other their common structural principle. It is as if the light were all trapped inside such novels to be shunted endlessly back and forth on a complex ar-

---

[27] Of all the *nouveau romanciers*, Butor has worked hardest in his essays to maintain attention on both sides of the relationship: the work and the world outside it (including the author). To be fair to him, here is the full passage: "In one sense it is not the novelist who creates the novel, it is the novel that creates itself and the novelist is only the instrument of its emergence into the world, its obstetrician; one knows what science, what awareness, what patience that implies" (*Répertoire* [Paris: Editions de Minuit, 1960], 273, my translation).

[28] Robbe-Grillet, *For a New Novel*, 44.

[29] Jean Ricardou, *Pour une théorie du nouveau roman* (Paris: Editions du Seuil, 1971), 52.

[30] *Les oeuvres complètes de Sally Mara* (Paris: Gallimard, 1962), 3.

rangement of internal reflecting planes. Consistent with this is the New Novelist's revival of the *mise en abîme*, a baroque device in which the whole is reflected in one of its parts (as the Cathedral of Bleston, for example, in *L'emploi du temps* becomes a mirror inset of the verbal structure that is the book itself). In the cold beauty of these works one has arrived at a terminus—a final narcissism of the text.

9

The Writer's Laboratory: Saul
Bellow and the Return to Character

> Even the most eminent man lives only by the day, and enjoys but
> a sorry entertainment when he throws himself too much back
> upon himself, and neglects to grasp into the fullness of the external
> world, where alone he can find nourishment for his growth and
> at the same time a standard for its measurement.
>
> —Goethe, *Poetry and Truth*

We have been examining in these chapters a generally hidden
reflexive condition of first-person narrative made demonstrable by
the unique conditions of the diary strategy. Each case has been
fictional with the exception of *In Memoriam*, and there is evidence
that the demonstrable reflexivity of the latter was "fictionally" assisted
by Tennyson. Periodically I have touched on a reflexive drama behind the scenes involving the nonfictive author and his or her
artistic development. The writing of *Werther*, as Goethe noted himself in his autobiography, purged him of an authorial self and with
it a mode of writing embedded in a particular world view. *Werther*'s
reflexive effect upon him was to contribute to his maturity as a writer.
Lessing's *Golden Notebook* came roughly on the cusp of the two major
curves in her literary development. Its complex structure allowed
her to X-ray the traditional realistic novel that she had mastered
so well over the course of her first roman-fleuve, *Children of Violence*.
At the same time it points toward the explosion of the traditional
novel in the concluding volume of that series, *The Four-Gated City*.
    It is a commonplace that any genuine work of art, diary-struc-
tured or not, is for the artist a process of discovery and as such the
writing of it is reflexive in the sense in which I have been using the
term. The artist to a degree takes the lead of his or her art, but it
is no coincidence that diary novels, specifically, should come at

critical evolutionary moments in Goethe's and Lessing's canons. Diary fiction concentrates attention on the production of narrative, which explains why so many fictive diarists are writers by trade or aspiration. For the real writer, implicated behind the fictive one, diary fiction can be a writer's laboratory in which the chemical interchange between kinds of writing and kinds of being is exposed. For us, it can provide an opportunity to see how literary art participates in its own further development. The opportunity is especially clear in the careers of Saul Bellow and Samuel Beckett because of the striking, if implicit, causal relations between their diary novels and the texts that follow in their canons. In both cases, the text we shall look at initially (the diary text) is what appears to be a last text. As in Werther's letters and Anna Wulf's notebooks, it appears to be a text from which there is no meaningful recovery of craft. By examining, then, how the craft went on, we can infer something of the catalytic agency the very writing of this "last text" must have exerted upon its author. We can see how the art itself engaged in its own alteration.

Bellow has tended to refer somewhat dismissively to his diary novel, *Dangling Man* (1944), which was also his first novel. He has said that his first novel was his M.A. and his second, his Ph.D., a necessary jumping of the hurdles for the establishment before he could write the way he wanted in *Augie March*.[1] But his first novel was more important than that. If it was in a way tricked out for the *literati*, it was also an antiestablishment novel, composed in dead earnest. Bellow announced his presence in the American literary scene by importing the latest version of an ultrasophisticated, introverted, intellectual European genre, the diary novel. He adhered closely to its formal requirements. His hero diarist is an alienated, bookish, unemployed part-time flaneur, part-time room hermit, whose impotence and hermetic isolation are underscored:

> Into the silence of the house there fall accentuating sounds, the closing of a door in another room, the ticking of drops from a faucet, the rustling of the steam in the radiator, the thrum of a sewing machine upstairs. The unmade bed, the walls, are brightly striped. The maid knocks and pushes open the door. She has a cigarette in her mouth.

[1] On the Dick Cavett show, Feb. 2, 1982.

I think I am the only one before whom she dares smoke; she recognizes that I am of no importance.[2]

In adopting the genre, it is more than likely that Bellow had in mind Sartre's recent publishing sensation. Like Roquentin, Joseph is a lapsing intellectual whose old modes of thinking have failed him (both diarists are in the process of giving up biographical studies of eighteenth-century figures). Like Roquentin, Joseph takes up writing his journal intime to get to the bottom of his crisis. Similarly, he is led to a wearying perception of inner formlessness, the city takes on the aspect of disorganized junk, and the host of minor characters are revealed to be consummate—and at heart desperate—self-deceivers. In the end, both protagonists revert rather abruptly to modes of absolute form (Roquentin to the traditional novel, Joseph to the army).[3]

In appropriating the genre, Bellow appropriated much of the ontological equipment that Sartre had refined. The effect was to give Bellow's first novel the appearance of being his last, in the commonly accepted sense that "the novel" owes its identity to a conviction that the self inhabits character. Without character, there may be texts (for example, nouveaux romans), but no novels. Much more strenuously than Roquentin, Bellow's diarist fights the verdict against character. Late in the book, he records two interviews he has with his alter ego, a coy, rather pale Mephistopheles whom he calls *Tu As Raison Aussi*. In the interviews, Joseph sounds a theme that Bellow has never abandoned. He manfully denies that it is impossible to be "human" in the present. For that matter, the present, he argues, is hardly so bad as it has been made out to be. " 'It's too easy to abjure it or detest it. Too narrow. Too cowardly' " (91). As for "alienation," it is a vogue; one ought not to make a doctrine of it. The problem with Joseph's argument is that almost everything else in *Dangling Man* appears to deny the argument's validity and to support the hypothesis that the self—at least as the self was made to appear in the great literary documents of the past—is no longer

---

[2]Saul Bellow, *Dangling Man* (1941; reprint, New York: New American Library, 1965), 11.
[3]For more similarities and somewhat different slants on their significance, see John Jacob Clayton's *Saul Bellow: In Defense of Man* (Bloomington: Indiana University Press, 1968), 57–59, 120–122, and Keith Opdahl's *The Novels of Saul Bellow* (University Park: Pennsylvania State University Press, 1967), 31–49.

compatible with intelligence. Even in his imaginary interview, while Joseph is sticking up for the old-fashioned authority of self, he speaks of his yearning for an "ideal construction" or noble character type that could serve him in the present as others had been served in the past (" 'the Humanistic full man, the courtly lover, the knight, the ecclesiastic' " [93]).

As he talks, the flow of Joseph's ideas generates the reason why, for the one who thinks, a successful ideal construction is no longer possible. Character is a product of belief and is sustainable only with the conviction that it is part of an enduring reality. To see it in Sartrean terms as the arbitrary invention of one's own mind is to lose it. " 'But what of the gap between the ideal construction and the real world, the truth?' " Joseph asks (93). No answer is provided. Joseph's whole effort during the nine months in which the novel takes place falls within the tradition of his modern ancestor, the Underground Man of Dostoevsky, who, in his own notebook, yearns like Joseph for character (even that of a lazy man—then he would know who he is, what to call himself) and who is prevented from having it, like Joseph, by precisely those gifts that distinguish him from the herd. Thus, Bellow's first effort as a novelist is a book that at least implicitly tells why he cannot be a novelist. Despite Joseph's protest, the book is very much in vogue, the static nonstory of a mind in a room, a yearning for character in search of its type, a man so "alienated" that he is given to the gnostic fantasy that "his parents are pretenders; his real father is elsewhere and will some day come to claim him" (21).

When he took over the European diary novel, Bellow underscored his independence from the primitivism of the American mainstream by making his protagonist a man of thought and a reader of books, with a special interest in the Enlightenment. But since the historical waning of character is directly linked in Joseph's meditations to the waning of confidence in reason, the final effect is to undermine the special status of the man of thought. Symptomatically, Joseph has recently and somewhat inexplicably lost interest in books and given over his penchant for plans. Still, he refuses to sacrifice his reason. The late collapse of rational hopes will not drive him into the opposite camp: "What are we given reason for? To discover the blessedness of unreason? That's a very poor argument" (90). Yet without some anchor beyond himself to which confidence in reason can be secured, Joseph's dilemma is exactly that of his crisis of confidence in character. "Out of my own strength it was necessary for me to return the verdict for reason, in its partial inadequacy, and against the advantages of its surrender" (46). He holds out valiantly against the seductions of *Tu As Raison Aussi*, but in the end the case for the mind appears as hopeless as the case for character. On the last page, visiting his childhood room in his father's house, Joseph has a sudden vision of the transience both of his life as a child and of the very room itself. Shaken, he takes the experience for a forceful insight into the fundamentally gratuitous nature of all human arrangements.

> I understood it to be a revelation of the ephemeral agreements by which we live and pace ourselves. . . . Such reality, I thought, is actually very dangerous, very treacherous. It should not be trusted. And I rose rather unsteadily from the rocker, feeling that there was an element of treason to common sense in the very objects of common sense. Or that there was no trusting them, save through wide agreement, and that my separation from such agreement had brought me perilously far from the necessary trust, auxiliary to all sanity. [126]

To keep one's eye on the truth, in short, is to risk one's sanity. Reason, which seeks the truth, must back off or be destroyed. At the end of the book, Joseph asks to be inducted into the army. As he says, he has failed to use his freedom. No self, no character, no new Joseph, has flowered in the hothouse in which he has confined himself. Instead his sense of himself has become increasingly tenuous. In the process, his reason, poring over the facts of his existence, has run a parallel course. To preserve both his sense of himself and his sanity, Joseph abandons the authority of his reason for the authority of society's arbitrary "agreements." He closes his diary and joins the army.

The adoption of the diary novel allowed Bellow to announce his arrival on the American scene *against* the prevailing fashion in yet another way. Joseph declares at the start that he is going to employ the inward, self-expressive form of the diary for the overt expression of his feelings. On the first page, he clearly informs us that he is *not* going to be a part of the tight-lipped, Hemingway tradition; that he is not going to endure the "inhibitory effect" of "closemouthed straightforwardness"; that he is instead going to express his emotions and talk at length about his inner problems. At the same time, he declares that he is abandoning literary formality, the Mandarin correctness and smooth polish of craft that are very much a part of the stoic mode, and instead is adopting the European tradition of the intimate diary, a necessarily informal genre, adaptable to the spontaneous expressions of the inner self. A consciously self-indulgent writer, Joseph is almost as pugnacious as his opposition: "Most serious matters are closed to the hardboiled. They are unpracticed in introspection, and therefore badly equipped to deal with opponents whom they cannot shoot like big game or outdo in daring" (7).

If there is truth to the hypothesis that Bellow, eighteen years after the publication of *The Sun Also Rises*, was letting Robert Cohn get his revenge, Joseph, nonetheless, like the Jewish butt of Hemingway's novel, carries expressive lack of restraint to the point of violence, covers himself continually with shame, and shows anything but "grace under pressure."[4] Rejecting the stoic mode, he produces not self-expressive clarity but turbulence and smoke. His lack of success in this regard is tied to the failures observed above. Expressing the immediate, passionate contours of who he truly is, fulfilling the expressive ends of the journal intime to which he has committed himself, assumes the availability of a self, which, as we have noted, fails to materialize during his experimental confinement. Formal unconstraint, then, leads not to the searching introspection Joseph spoke of at the start, but to an irrational and increasingly explosive belligerency that he records in his diary but rarely reflects upon. His violence, culminating in a brawl with a fellow boarder, finally demoralizes him and leads him to shut down his experiment. Again, the book in this regard appears to declare its own failure. The emotional and expressive unconstraint that marked it at the start is abandoned at the end, the diary is shelved, and Joseph joins the very army with which Hemingway himself was so closely associated. Indeed, though Joseph sets out to do battle with the Hemingway mode, he recognizes, not unsympathetically, that

---

[4]"The dangling man, Joseph, might be characterized as a sensitive and intelligent Robert Cohn who did not go to Princeton" (Jonathan Baumbach, *The Landscape of Nightmare* [New York: New York University Press, 1965], 36).

the mode itself is a response to the same frightening perception of human insignificance that he strives to overcome:

> Great pressure is brought to bear to make us undervalue ourselves.... We are schooled in quietness and, if one of us takes his measure occasionally, he does so coolly, as if he were examining his fingernails, not his soul.... Who can be the earnest huntsman of himself when he knows he is in turn a quarry? Or nothing so distinctive as quarry, but one of a shoal, driven toward the weirs. [79]

The immediate background for this passage is the war, but Joseph makes it clear that the war simply brings to focus the general dilemma of human beings trying to live in a vacuum, without belief. In such a world, one adopts the code of the Hemingway hero as an "ideal construction" both to give the illusion of being and to cut short any further discussion of the subject.

Considering the outcome of his first experiment as a novelist, how did Bellow manage to pick up and carry on? And carry on so vigorously? One of the strange things about Bellow's career as a novelist is that it appears to go backward. *Dangling Man* is his most modern book. In spite of its apparent failures on all fronts, Bellow did not become "post-modern," did not make those failures the basis of his future work. Instead, the life that Joseph fails to find in himself and that his immediate successors seek, grows up in abundance everywhere in the secondary characters of these busy novels, until finally, with *Henderson the Rain King*, the vividness and clarity of being that distinguish so many of Bellow's minor figures penetrate the central figure himself. These attributes, in fact, are what give Bellow's 1959 novel a certain fraudulence, insofar as it pretends to be a *Bildungsroman*, because, for all Henderson's search for an "ideal construction" (in his mentor Dahfu's words, a "noble self-conception"), for all his despair over being a "becomer" rather that a "be-er," he is as sharply defined at the beginning of his narrative as he is at the end, equipped with an abundance of being on which his travels have little noticeable depth of effect. It is almost as if the theories of Dahfu were an appendage to the novel and that the real meaning and appeal of the work resided in the character of Henderson himself.

The principal condition of Bellow's first novel that in a sense allowed his subsequent reversion to character is the book's distinctively tentative quality. Though it appears to conclude, to end with a certain finality, Bellow in fact takes no position in its final pages. This tentativeness is of a piece with an intellectual restraint in evidence throughout. Though he was consciously adopting a European vogue, Bellow's relationship to literary tradition was, even at this early stage of his career, quite sophisticated. If he went to Europe for a form commensurate with his aspirations, he went not as a thief but as an imitator.[5] Thus, in turning to Sartre's version of the diary novel, he is at once respecting it and revaluing it. Whether he was consciously attempting to create a mid-Atlantic form, I cannot say, but certainly at the center of his revaluation of *Nausea* is the figure of Joseph himself and in particular his relationship to the bleak insight that is the philosophical core of Sartre's novel. Whereas Sartre's hero bravely shoulders the burden of nothingness, Joseph resists it right up to the end. He is a reluctant Roquentin. And though all the evidence appears to confirm the hypothesis that character, like all other form, is only the arbitrary invention of mind, Joseph leaves the case open. Roquentin sets out at the end of his book on a plan (to write a novel) that is predicated on the conviction he now has about life, but Joseph abandons his diary with few convictions and no real plans. His decision to join the army is, as he says, a "move" in a game that is still in progress. His inquiry is far from complete: "The next move was the world's."

It may well be that Bellow had the conclusion of *Nausea* in mind when he introduced the artist, John Pearl, into the collection of representative minor characters of *Dangling Man*. At the end of *Nausea*, Roquentin, listening to his favorite record for the last time, finds himself imagining the composer and the singer of the song

[5]Much like epic poets, Bellow consciously "competes" with his predecessors, adapting work to his own ends in a way that declares both respect for the model and pride in his own achievement. The relationship can be found between his next novel, *The Victim*, and Dostoevsky's *The Eternal Husband* and between his short story "The Gonzaga Manuscripts" and James's *The Aspern Papers*. More broadly it can be found between *The Adventures of Augie March* and the picaresque tradition and between *Herzog* and the epistolary tradition. Much of this "competition" is playful and consistent with his love of gentle travesty (in *Henderson*, the medieval bestiary; in *Seize the Day*, the Renaissance unities of time, place, and action). All of this in turn is part of Bellow's attempt on a number of fronts to resist American literary provincialism.

working together on the twenty-first floor of a New York skyscraper. His last entry tells us that he has followed their lead, ascending to the *second* floor of the Hotel Printania to compose a story about "something which would not exist, . . . beautiful and hard as steel."[6] Bellow situates his artist in a New York skyscraper *fifty-three* stories high and gives him an aesthetic credo that is broadly of the same type: "There is only one worthwhile sort of work, that of the imagination." It is a work that is "in the strictest sense not personal" (61). But Joseph cannot allow himself this alternative, much as it appeals to him.

> It is an attractive idea, it confers a sort of life on him, sets him off from the debased dullness of those fifty-three stories. . . . he has escaped a trap. That really is a victory to celebrate. I am fascinated by it, and a little jealous. He can maintain himself. Is it because he is an artist? I believe it is. Those acts of imagination save him. But what about me? I have no talent for that sort of thing. My talent, if I have one at all, is for being a citizen, or what is today called, most apologetically, a good man. Is there some sort of personal effort I can substitute for the imagination? [61]

His question goes unanswered. Though Pearl's and Roquentin's alternative is rejected, the fixed, unimaginative order of military discipline to which Bellow's diarist is delivered is not a matter of choice, but, for the moment, passive acceptance.

Though Joseph, as he repeatedly describes himself, is a man of plans, a throwback to eighteenth-century rationalism, who seeks a program of self-education and an ideal construction by which to identify himself as citizen and good man, there is no ideological fixity in *Dangling Man*. When it comes to reflecting on himself in his diary his thoughts are unsorted; he slips from one to the other with none of the Frenchman's ability to conclude. Compare, for example, the way Sartre and Bellow fulfill the formal requirement of the mirror scene. When Roquentin looks in the mirror, he sees the image of his own formlessness: "below the monkey, on the fringe of the vegetable world, at the level of jellyfish."[7] The ex-

---

[6]Jean-Paul Sartre, *Nausea*, trans. Lloyd Alexander (New York: New Directions, 1969), 178.

[7]Sartre, *Nausea*, 17.

perience, like so many of the other experiences of defamiliarization recorded in Roquentin's diary, leads directly to the formulation of its nature and significance that takes place later in the city park. It becomes a part of what eventually emerges as the novel's *thesis*.

Joseph's own mirror scene is by contrast pointedly restrained: "I observed new folds near my mouth and, around my eyes and the root of my nose, marks that had not been there a year before. It is not pleasant to find such changes. But, tying my tie, I shrugged them off as inevitable, the price of experience, an outlay that had better be made ungrudgingly, since it was bound in any case to be collected" (115). The passage is determinedly modest. Where Roquentin finds an idea of self (that is, of its absence), Joseph notes in passing that he has aged. Abstract discourse, itself, seems to embarrass him. The most "intellectual" parts of the work, Joseph's conversations with *Tu As Raison Aussi*, read like elliptical parodies of their Dostoevskian equivalent.

"How seriously you take this," cried *Tu As Raison Aussi*. "It's only a discussion. The boy's teeth are chattering. Do you have a chill?" He ran to get a blanket from the bed.

ꞌ I said faintly, "I'm all right." He tucked the blanket around me and, in great concern, wiped my forehead and sat by me until nightfall. [112]

Joseph's inability to develop his ideas in an orderly, systematic way and his general embarrassment about conceptual thought are, in their extremity, a reaction against his own recent experience of such thought in its most rigid and doctrinaire form. The exponent of rigidity in the novel is Comrade Jimmy Burns, with whom Joseph once had a close working relationship. Burns, when Joseph encounters him in a restaurant, refuses to recognize his backsliding former colleague. Joseph makes a scene and finally forces Burns to acknowledge his existence in what is the first of many instances in which Bellow records a basic antagonism between ideological thought and individual being. In *Dangling Man* this antagonism relates directly to the intellectual looseness of the novel itself. For all his eggheadedness, Joseph's failures of conceptual thought are what preserve him. At the end, the evidence against the self does not prevail, because no "position" is taken. There is only the recognition that a certain experiment has failed. "Perhaps," says Joseph, "I could sound creation through other means" (126). At any rate, as he enters the army, the game is still in progress. And it may not be too farfetched to see the quest of Eugene Henderson, former soldier, lover of military discipline, and travesty of Hemingway the lion hunter, as a sequel to that of Joseph the Dangler.[8]

Bellow packed away the notebook for good. One is tempted to say that what Anna Wulf embraces in the Golden Notebook, Joseph escapes; but there is an important nuance of difference here. The text of the diary in Bellow is diabolic; it betrays the diarist: first, because there is no being toward which such a text leads, only emptiness; and second, because this emptiness is not a necessary emptiness. To be able to identify this final blank with the truth would be some consolation, but the end at which this document aims is manufactured in part by the document itself. It is a theoretical blank—though no less deadly for that. Joseph saves himself by packing away the diary as he would an instrument of suicide. But Joseph is also preserved by what seems to be a constitutional inability to conclude. His mind continually fails to settle; it skips off the facts of his life as they appear to him in his text. In short, a good deal of the reflexive energy in this text remains a potential energy. The diarist refuses to collaborate with it, to go where it would lead.

This key capacity (or incapacity) of Joseph's anticipates a recurrent theme of Bellow's numerous essays and interviews. Put simply, the theme amounts to this: there is a big difference between thinking and having an idea. Thinking, according to Bellow, is vital to a novel. At its best, it is energetic, passionate, and (crucially) open. Having an idea, in contrast, is a state of closure and can be deadly.[9]

---

[8]Not a whimsical suggestion. Both men have the same problem of coping with their often destructive violence. Henderson fears that his yelling may have killed Miss Lenox, but may not Joseph have hastened the death of Mrs. Kiefer by the vehemence of his last outburst against Mr. Vanaker?

[9]Under this heading, Bellow finds little to distinguish the cerebral French writer from his primitive American counterpart. They are both too easily impressed by ideas. Though this might be obvious in the work of the European, it is equally the case even in such populists as Farrell and Steinbeck. Much as they insist on "sitting on the curb playing poker and talking about whores," they submit to the restraint of a few ideas (Sanford Pinsker, "Saul Bellow in the Classroom," College English 34

An idea in fiction must be a part of thinking, it must be at play, it cannot be allowed to dominate, to imprison the text and the life it records. Moreover, Bellow has implicitly argued that there is much in an author's craft and in the life it imitates that has very little to do with ideas at all. His best and most forceful expression of this view is still his early critique of popular New Criticism in the *New York Times Book Review* entitled "Deep Readers of the World Beware!"[10] His example in that brief essay is the bright student in the class who, reading that Achilles drags the body of Hector three times around the walls of Troy, finds in it a pattern of three rings rather than what it is—an expression of the anger of Achilles.

[1973], 976). They are didactic. Ideas weigh them down, often at great personal cost, for this is a sort of willful deracination of authors who are personally quite sophisticated: "We have developed in American fiction a strange combination of extreme naïveté in the characters and of profundity implicit in the writing, in the techniques themselves and in the language, but the language of thought itself is banned, it is considered dangerous and destructive" (Saul Bellow, "Where Do We Go From Here: The Future of Fiction," in *To the Young Writer*, ed. A. L. Baker [Ann Arbor: University of Michigan Press, 1965], 144). For his ideal in this regard, Bellow goes back to Shakespeare and Dostoevsky, who, as he says, were writers first, not philosophers. In "Where Do We Go From Here?" he singles out Dostoevsky's performance in the Grand Inquisitor sequence as an outstanding example of thinking in fiction. As an individual, Dostoevsky has a set of Christian ideas that constitute a position, but in the Grand Inquisitor scene "he has in advance all but devastated his own position." This free opposition of ideas raises his work from the level of a tract to the level of art: "The opposites must be free to range themselves against each other, and they must be passionately expressed on both sides" (Bellow, "Where Do We Go From Here," 146). If Bellow's own works do not attain the complexity of argument found in Dostoevsky, the continuing dilemma of their conclusions— their resistance to interpretation—may well be a conscious formal strategy aimed at this effect. By the way they end, they avoid a reduction to idea. Thinking, in other words, is still in progress, and this, as Bellow states, is part of the "art." Another and more fundamental part of the art is emotion. Bellow recurs to this point again and again. What thinking there is must, as he says of Dostoevsky, be "passionately expressed." "Nothing is legitimate in literature or any work of art which does not have the support of some kind of emotional conviction. The ideological conviction means almost nothing. The emotional conviction means everything" (Robert Boyers, "Literature and Culture," *Salmagundi* 30 [Summer 1975], 14). The problem with the fiction of such novelists as Camus, Sartre, Mann, or Koestler is that it is "as strong as their intellectual position—or as weak" (Saul Bellow, "The Writer as Moralist," *Atlantic Monthly*, March 1963, p. 62). Even in America, a heavy intellectuality has developed among both writers and readers, an unhealthy symbiosis, so that "books are strongly shaken to see what usable things will fall out of them to strengthen a theory or support some system of ideas," and "the poet becomes a sort of truffle hound who brings marvelous delicacies from the forest" (Saul Bellow, "A World Too Much with Us," *Critical Inquiry* 2 [Autumn 1975], 9).

[10]*New York Times Book Review*, Feb. 15, 1959; reprinted in *Herzog: Text and Criticism*, ed. Irving Howe (New York: Viking, 1976), 365–368.

Whether or not Bellow's accounting for this is correct (a keen insight, I think: the student is frightened by what he reads), an appropriate reading of *The Iliad*—at least of the scene referred to—puts the bright student and the type of critic he represents out of business. The truth is that there is *no* idea expressed here, unless one wants to say that "Achilles is angry" qualifies as an idea. What is present is not an idea but a character, Achilles, at once inventing and revealing himself through the expression of his anger.

The example of Achilles throws a good hard light on the concern that underlies both Bellow's wariness of ideas and his conviction of the emotional primacy of the text. The concern is for a freedom that in Bellow appears coextensive with the self. By dragging the body of Hector three times around the walls of Troy, Achilles is, in a frightening way, expressing his originality. In so doing, he is at the same time expressing who he is. His being requires the creative freedom to surprise us. Thus, to overlook the centrality of the character in the scene who, powered by his feelings, invents himself—to appropriate him for a purely cognitive design as the student does—is to overlook that for which the scene was created.

The student's response to Achilles is a parody of the antagonism between selfhood and theory that Bellow first expressed in the fight between Joseph and Comrade Burns. In an interview for *Salmagundi*, he took it up from another perspective in some remarks on psychoanalysis.[11] He dwelt on the case of a doctor who had written Freud about how he had lost his faith when, as a student, he had seen the body of a very beautiful old woman on the dissecting table. Freud's comment is that what the doctor had seen was "of course" his mother. Bellow's question is: "Was it not possible to experience beauty or pity without thinking of your mother, or without the Oedipus complex?" The rigidity of the theorist in this instance is a kind of intellectual fascism, for it denies the doctor his freedom to be himself. Freud does not literally presume to dominate the doctor, but he presumes to have the key to that which does.

About the theorists who crowd his fiction, Bellow is much more ambivalent. He is, to begin with, intrigued by the fertility of mind that generates theories; in addition, his own theorists generally express their originality in spite of their fondness for theory. In

---

[11] Boyers, "Literature and Culture," 18–19.

effect, they are made to fail as theorists. They are the kind of theorist that makes a genuine theorist shudder. We never see how their theories cohere, and this vital incoherence is itself an expression of the theorist's capacity to exceed his theories. Certainly the most benign example is Dahfu. His ellipticism and capacity to contradict himself are embedded in a richly expressive but often ungrammatical English. Moreover, as I have noted, Henderson is gifted with such fullness of being that he seems from the start a man basically immune to the domination of his mentor. His love and admiration for Dahfu are principally inspired not by his theories but by the dazzling man himself and rightly so, for part of the attraction of such a character as Dahfu is his ability continually to surprise us. In this sense he is always ahead of our capacity to predict his behavior, given the fragments of his theory at our disposal.

The darker aspects of the theorist emerge in such figures as Tamkin and Bummidge and most appallingly in the madman Basteshaw of *The Adventures of Augie March*.[12] Basteshaw claims to have created life itself, and his plan for the future is a utopia, imposed (like all utopias) on humankind for its own good. His lineage goes back to *Frankenstein*, and he is produced with much the same cautionary intent. Adrift in the Atlantic on a lifeboat, Basteshaw literally ties Augie up. The episode is about as close to allegory as Bellow ever gets.

Bellow's resistance to theoretical fixity first jelled in his diary novel. That early novel, so markedly designed as a repudiation of prevailing American models, generated over the course of its composition a counterrepudiation of its Sartrean model. In the years since, Sartre has come to occupy much the same status for Bellow as Freud did for Nabokov, and for almost identical reasons. He is one of those "masterminds whose ideas ('class-struggle,' 'Oedipus complex,' 'identity crisis') come down over us like butterfly nets."[13] As in Nabokov's view of Freud, Sartre for Bellow is a kind of

[12]For a good differentiation between the intellection of Bummidge and Herzog see Ronald Weber, "Bellow's Thinkers," *Western Humanities Review* 22 (1968), 305–313.
[13]This and the following quotations come from ten pages Bellow devotes to Sartre in *To Jerusalem and Back* (New York: Knopf, 1976), 118–128. For more on Sartre see *Writers at Work: The Paris Review Interviews* 3d series (New York: Viking, 1968), 194–195, and "A World Too Much with Us," 4–5.

threatening clown, a figure of fun who is not all that funny: a figure of fun, because he is like "the Swiftian philosopher extracting sunshine from cucumbers and getting spiders to manufacture silks"; but not all that funny, because in his rigid commitment to the "Larousse Syndrome" he is willing to sacrifice both his humanity and the humanness of others on the altar of concept. There is in Sartre a readiness to tell people who they are, and, on more than one occasion, he has not only told the Jews who they are but has gone on to tell them how they should therefore behave as Jews. Bellow's anxiety on this score is as acute as it is when critics attempt to classify him as a Jewish novelist. His repudiation of labels is similar to Geronimo's refusal to have his picture taken. The fixity of the classification, like that of the photograph, obscures the originality that is so essential to Bellow's own sense of self.

One consequence of Bellow's sensitivity to the destructive power of fixed categories is that in his work after *Dangling Man*, he has drawn a rather large circle around the self and posted it. He has declared it a preserve not only from the depredations of ideologues and other theorists but even from his own reverential intrusion as a fictionist. Bellow's 1951 short story "Looking for Mr. Green" can be read as a parable of Bellow's own relation to his characters. As such, it makes an illuminating companion piece to *Dangling Man*. The later story concerns a social worker whose attempts to deliver a relief check to Mr. Green are subjected to a potentially infinite series of impediments. Late in the day, when Grebe believes he has at last ferreted out his prey, what emerges slowly into view down a stairway is not Mr. Green but a black woman whose name Grebe never learns. "She was entirely naked, climbing down while she talked to herself, a heavy woman, naked and drunk. She blundered into him. The contact of her breasts, though they touched only his coat, made him go back against the door with a blind shock. See what he had tracked down, in his hunting game!"[14] In mixed de-

---

[14]Saul Bellow, *Mosby's Memoirs and Other Stories* (Greenwich: Fawcett, 1968), 106. Bellow provides a gentle roasting of the "Larousse Syndrome" through one of the people Grebe does find. Mr. Field will not accept his check until he has proven to Grebe who he is. He does this by laying all his papers of identification out in a circle: "Social Security card, relief certification, letters from the state hospital in Manteno, and a naval discharge dated San Diego, 1920.... 'There's everything I done and been. Just the death certificate and they can close book on me' " (100).

spair and relief, Grebe lets her sign for the check. "Whoever she was, the woman stood for Green" (107–108).

Nine years earlier, when he began writing his first novel, Bellow did not appear to have had the clear perception with which "Mr. Green" concludes. Even so, *Dangling Man* evolved into a cautionary tale with essentially the same burden. The difference, and it is an important one, is that the object of the search in *Dangling Man* is the searcher's own self, as if Green were to seek Green. Looking into the "craters of the spirit," Joseph discovers nothing so distinguished as a self. He finds instead his double, Mr. Vanaker.[15] Vanaker is at once everything and nothing: a "werewolf," who, like Mr. Knott, the nonbeing in Beckett's novel *Watt*, is never the same thing twice. All we learn of Vanaker are tedious fragments of information as, for example, "that he is engaged to marry a lady of sixty who insists that he be converted to the Catholic faith" (21–22), that he receives "large quantities of mail from the Masonic Scottish Rite" (22), that he moves his bed at 2:00 in the morning. He is, in short, that shabby disintegration of character that Joseph, brooding over his diary in the room next door, feels taking place in himself. Obviously, the anger that Vanaker arouses in Joseph is directly proportional to the intensity with which Joseph feels his devolution toward the state Vanaker represents. In his climactic fight with his double, Joseph exhibits the same noisy vulgarity for which he is fighting him. Joseph, keeping his own case open, will not allow that Vanaker is the truth about his interior self, but the fight precipitates the next move in his life, his volunteering for the army. In the context of Bellow's canon, Joseph is correct: Vanaker is not the final word, but the lesson of Vanaker is, in its essentials, the same as that of "Looking for Mr. Green": the self will not tolerate a frontal attack. Joseph's experiment has something of the moral quality of certain works in the hermetic/demonic tradition. Confined to his cell, he calls up out of his own power a sort of monster (parodied at one point when Vanaker actually starts a fire in his room—from which he finally emerges, singed, red-eyed, coughing).

If the novel and the later short story express the same conviction, it is necessary also to note that there is a big difference between

---

[15]The evidence for doubling here is almost needlessly elaborated. Bellow even has Vanaker steal Joseph's socks—not the finest apparel.

the eroticism and sharp-tongued vitality of Mr. Green's surrogate and the ghostly, doglike shabbiness of Mr. Vanaker. For where the naked lady is a vibrant and exotic emblem of a self preserved, Vanaker is a transatlantic idea of a self dissolved. The difference suggests an additional caution in the novel: that what Joseph seeks cannot exist in captivity. This applies to the literary document he is employing, too. However formless and spontaneous the nonart of his diary, its words will never accommodate what Joseph seeks. The apprentice novelist had the same revelation about what would happen to his craft if pursued further in the same direction. Vanaker, in his characterlessness, is necessarily the devolution of the novel as well as of Joseph. As I have suggested, that Bellow did not go any further in this direction makes *Dangling Man* his most "modern" novel. Like Joseph, he abandons the experiment, packs away his diary, and returns to the world of tradition and form. He does not take that next step that many in the European tradition following Sartre took: into an antinovelistic mode predicated on the nonexistence of character.

Does this mean, then, that Bellow sacrificed the truth to save his craft? As Joseph says, "What of the gap between the ideal construction and the real world?" Did Bellow take on the arbitrary conventions of the novel in the same way that Joseph opts for the arbitrary conventions of the army or that Anna Wulf appears to have done in composing *Free Women*? Is the novel a form of belief, necessary for the preservation of sanity but basically a lie? Again, by way of a partial answer, I must stress the fundamentally skeptical nature of Bellow's conception of his craft: its necessary freedom from any ideological commitment, including convictions as to the absolute absence of self. If Joseph's quest can be said to lead to the destruction of his self, it does not follow that the nonexistence of his self was a reality that antedated the quest. To put this another way, the degeneration of self that Joseph glimpses might not be a discovery he is led to but a product of the quest he pursues. It is as if Bellow were to say that Sartrean "existence" is not a fact but the creation of Roquentin. Bellow's subsequent return to character in fiction, to the limitations of type, was a way of making the case for the reality of the self—a self inseparable from its own freedom and inviolability—but he did not proceed in the manner of the nineteenth-century novelist who accepts character with no question as to its reality. Character instead became the subject, that which is under observation.

One can see the beginnings of this dwelling on character, too, in *Dangling Man*—not in Joseph or his faceless wife, Iva, but in the diversity of vivid characters on the periphery (his in-laws the Almstadts, his successful brother Amos, Alf Steidler the operator) who make up the city outside the diarist's room. Mary McCarthy came close to describing the appeal character has for Bellow when she isolated the special distinction of what she called "comic character": "A comic character, contrary to accepted belief, is likely to be more complicated and enigmatic than a hero or a heroine, fuller of surprises and turnabouts; Mr. Micawber, for instance, can find the most unexpected ways of being himself; so can Mr. Woodhouse or the Master of the Marshalsea. It is a sort of resourcefulness."[16] One of the accepted beliefs that McCarthy is contradicting is the Bergsonian one that the laugh aroused by the comic character is a laugh at its mechanical predictability, its machinelike and therefore inhuman quality. Such a laugh is necessarily tinged with contempt. We laugh to separate ourselves from the object of mirth.

Yet there is no real contradiction here, rather two fundamentally different kinds of character, for neither of which need one exclusively appropriate the designation "comic." Indeed, there are many examples of the Bergsonian fixed character at which one does not laugh at all, demonic characters who would impose their own machinelike predictability on others (especially fascinating to Bellow), or simply boring ones like those wholly predictable products of their needs and background whom late nineteenth-century novelists often found as necessary as furniture. The difference between free and fixed characters is Bellow's major subject in the work of his maturity.

The most focused study of the difference is Bellow's 1968 short story "Mosby's Memoirs." It is another good story to put beside *Dangling Man* because, like the earlier work, it features an autobiographer at work on the job of defining who he is. But where Joseph, a backsliding intellectual at the beginning of his career,

[16]Mary McCarthy, *The Humanist in the Bathtub* (New York: New American Library, 1964), 211–212.

seeks to discover himself in the formless mode of the diary, Mosby, a "fanatic about ideas" near the end of his career, is coldly embalming his public image in a highly formal mode patterned on the memoirs of Adams, Nicholson, Santayana, and Russell. The irony on which the story turns is that the "life" Mosby records is actually that of a dead man. The fantasy he has that he had already died years before in an automobile accident turns out to be more than a fantasy. At the end of the story, visiting a Zapotec temple reserved for human sacrifice and observing the mathematical precision with which it had been constructed, Mosby finds in it an image of the tomb he has constructed for himself and called his life. "A finished product, standing under the sun on large blocks of stone, on the stairs descending into this pit, he was complete. He had completed himself in this cogitating, unlaughing, stone, iron, nonsensical form."[17] Though he is not a comic character, Mosby epitomizes the abandonment of human freedom. The type is combined here with the type of the man of ideas, made especially treacherous in Mosby's instance because, at first look, he appears so independent, so free of party. Light years separate his cool sophistication and the sublety of his thought from, say, *Dangling Man*'s Jimmy Burns and the political clichés in which the latter finds his "life." Yet they are brothers under the skin, for the motive behind their adopted rigidity is the same: a fear of the unpredictable. That which is beyond control appalls them, but in opposing it, they oppose that seminal freedom that, as I have argued, Bellow identifies with genuine selfhood. To Mosby, "Liveliness, beauty, seemed very dangerous. Mortal danger" (151). He prefers to die by his own hand than to run the risks of being alive.

A second irony of "Mosby's Memoirs" is that a minor character in the memoirs becomes a hero of the story. With cold premeditation, Mosby selects Hymen Lustgarten to serve as a comic diversion, "to relieve the rigor of this account of his mental wars" (156). What the story gradually reveals is that there is more than diversion involved here. Mosby must reduce Lustgarten by laughter because Lustgarten (the name is perhaps too emphatically suggestive) represents exactly the condition that it has been Mosby's lifetime effort to avoid. Lustgarten "didn't have to happen." As he is inexplicable,

[17]Bellow, *Mosby's Memoirs*, 176.

so he must be laughable. Still speaking of himself (as Adams) in the third person, Mosby stumbles momentarily over this tendency of his to reduce by laughter:

> At this time, Mosby had been making fun of people.
> "Why?"
> "Because he had needed to."
> "Why?"
> "Because!" [175]

Because if he were to take Lustgarten seriously his own fundamental lack of seriousness, the absurdity of his own life, would become apparent. Mosby flatly reverses Bergsonian theory ("Lustgarten didn't have to happen. And so he *was* funny" [175]) and in so doing preserves in himself the sterile elegance he later sees mirrored in the temple. Converting Lustgarten into mere comic relief is thus an act of aggression against Lustgarten. It continues into the memoirs the concealed aggression that Mosby had engaged in when he had first known Lustgarten. Back then, Mosby had destroyed Lustgarten's marriage by teaching his wife (with whom Mosby slept) to laugh at her husband as Mosby did (a fact that goes *un*recorded in the memoirs).

What Lustgarten demonstrates is that there is a kind of freedom other than the drab and "terrible" freedom that Joseph created in *Dangling Man*. His self-expressive acts are as vivid and surprising as they are typical (in Paris, for example, sleeping at night in the Cadillac he has imported but cannot sell). At the end, this power is linked with suggestions of his fertility as we are surprised once again by Lustgarten, ascending on the wrong elevator. He tells of his new life—married again, children, running a laundromat in Algiers. "For Plato," notes Mosby, "this child-breeding is the lowest level of creativity" (172). In spite of his contempt, Mosby provides a lens through which we can see the radiant contours of a free character. Lustgarten is the kind of "comic character" McCarthy distinguished from heroes and heroines—*seen from the outside* and thus preserved as an enigma. He is different from other sorts of character as well precisely because of the internal resourcefulness implied by the twists of his story. To Mosby, the artificer and man of exquisite form, this story appears to be a chaos of amusing but gratuitous accidents. "A man like Lustgarten," he thinks, "would never, except with supernatural aid, exist in a suitable form" (168). What Mosby reveals is a basic misunderstanding of form. In all his surprising acts, Lustgarten is "in character"; we recognize him, repeatable, familiar, at the very same time as we laugh with surprise. Like Achilles circling the walls of Troy, he invents himself through a collaboration with the discipline of his type.

Perhaps the most striking example of Bellow's movement outward to character from the gray interiority of Joseph's journal is the novel that superficially most resembles it. *Herzog* has all the appearances of a very "modern" book in its excessive subjectivity, its rambling, inconclusive interior argument. Unlike "Mosby," in which Lustgarten is tracked by a kind of peripheral vision, *Herzog* takes place largely in the mind of its protagonist. His mental correspondence, which consists mainly of fragments of letters, seems in its very plenitude far more hopelessly disjunctive than Joseph's diary and has led at least one critic to see the book as yet another improvisation on the same journal form Bellow began with in *Dangling Man*.[18]

But the mere fact of a work's "interiority" is not in itself evidence for the dissolution of either character, the self, or the novel. For all its steamy subjectivity, the interiority of *Herzog* is embedded in a sequence of actions in the external world. The book has plot—a comic variant of the revenge plot. Furthermore, plot and character mesh in precisely the symbiotic way James approved in "The Art of Fiction." Thus, *Dangling Man's* airless, plotless luxury of onto-logical freedom is replaced in *Herzog* by the immediate pressure of emotions that in turn arise from an action in progress. Herzog's revenge trip to Chicago, for example, is motivated directly by the things he sees and hears in the New York City courthouse. The trial for a brutal child murder augments his fears for his daughter, while a host of grim details arouse his own nihilistic thoughts and suggest that anything (even murder) is permitted. Herzog himself reflects upon himself as he would upon a character. Thus, as confined as the book is to the interior Herzog, the mind we hear is

[18]Earl Rovit, *Saul Bellow* (Minneapolis: University of Minnesota Press, 1967), 24–25.

continually engaged in trying to gain knowledge of itself by reading the acts it has commanded. Herzog has to pick up the gun, load it, go to Madeleine's house and sight Gersbach through the window before he knows for certain that he will not shoot him. As always, the act (or nonact) is "in character," fitting, and as always it comes as a surprise. As he notes: "It was worth the trip."[19]

The self-destruction of form that occurred when Bellow set his intellectual *journaliste* on his quest in *Dangling Man* also leads directly to the kind of "intellectualism" one finds in works like *Herzog*. Bellow has been called both an intellectual novelist and an antiintellectual novelist, a crisis of labeling directly attributable to the crisis of his first novel. Since then, the intellection of his intellectual novels has performed basically a negative job of work. In his *Paris Review* interview, Bellow described Herzog as a man who "comes to realize that what he considered his intellectual 'privilege' has proved to be another form of bondage."[20] Though Herzog is often motivated by ideas, much of his cogitation is a process of dealing "with ideas in negative fashion. He needs to dismiss a great mass of irrelevancy and nonsense in order to survive." In so describing his work, Bellow interestingly (and with a certain ironic relish) appropriated the term *Bildungsroman*: "Any *Bildungsroman*—and *Herzog* is, to use that heavy German term, a *Bildungsroman*—concludes with the first step. The first *real* step. Any man who has rid

---

[19]The stroke of genius in this particular scene is the vision of Gersbach, which is the catalyst to Herzog's nonrevenge. With the force of a revelation, Herzog sees in the man washing his (Herzog's) child the same qualities of freedom, inviolability, and enigma that he is continually rediscovering in himself. Gersbach, who up to now has been a caricature of the fixed, Bergsonian type, is for a moment converted into the kind of free character we have been discussing. Recognizing him as such, Herzog can no more impose his will on him than he can allow his various "realityinstructors" to tell him (Herzog) who he is. The physical act of dominating another by one's will (here, murder) is equated with the mental act of categorizing another according to one's ideology. As Herzog knows, the latter is a forerunner, a necessary preliminary, of the former. Conversely, the recognition of inner mystery is a possible stay against the violence of authoritarianism. "Even that Gersbach, call him any name you like, charlatan, psychopath, with his hot phony eyes and his clumsy cheeks, with the folds. He was unknowable. And I myself, the same. But hard ruthless action taken against a man is the assertion by evildoers that he is fully knowable. They put me down, ergo they claimed final knowledge of Herzog. They *knew* me! And I hold with Spinoza (I hope he won't mind) that to demand what is impossible for any human being, to exercise power where it can't be exercised, is tyranny. Excuse me, therefore, sir and madam, but I reject your definitions of me" (*Herzog: Text and Criticism*, 299).

[20]This and the following quotations are from *Writers at Work*, 3d series, 193–195.

himself of superfluous ideas in order to take that step has done something significant." But a glance at the tradition that extends from *Wilhelm Meister* to *The Magic Mountain* is sufficient to show that Bellow's stress in describing his work as a Bildungsroman is skewed to meet the specifications of his own mid-Atlantic variant of the form. It is a form adapted to the needs of an author under siege, who feels in a narrower, more acute way than his nineteenth-century European predecessors a threat to the self, a threat that derives from a perverse relationship to ideas. For this reason, most of the secondary figures in the book, for all their superficial differences, represent the same basic illness. Epitomized by Herzog's mad ex-wife Madeleine, their intellection is shown to have little to do with thought and much to do with an obsession with ideas, which they take on in the manner of religious converts. All of them are possessed by reigning ideas that they impose on reality. All of them stake a claim on Herzog, defining him according to these ideas.

Thus Bellow, whose apprenticeship and continuing effort as a novelist have been fed by a healthy opposition to the narrowness of American fiction, has made his own distinctive contribution to that same narrowness. Even in its "mid-Atlantic" aspect, the bias of his work is basically American. Call *Herzog* a Bildungsroman; but X-rayed, it shows essentially the same bone structure as *Huckleberry Finn*. Like its "primitive" American forerunner, it is preeminently a novel of *un*learning, a process of divesting ideas in order to reach essential internal knowledge. Twain in his stress on the internal authority of the self was a blood relation of his Transcendentalist contemporaries. In Bellow there is, I think, no diminishment of the tradition, simply an increasing sense of urgency. Herzog's victory at the end, however precarious, is to have found his way back to what he is. In his country cabin, like Thoreau before him, he finds his end in his own Being: *"pretty well satisfied to be, to be just as it is willed, and for as long as I may remain in occupancy"* (340).

Joseph reads Goethe's autobiography and comments on it in his diary. This is fitting. The document he keeps is a direct descendent of Werther's letters, and Bellow's experience of it is a direct parallel of Goethe's experience of his surrogate's letters. The big difference between the tales is that whereas Goethe's agent endorses his own writing and follows it to his death, Bellow's puts his diary away and saves himself from extinction. But the reflexive relation of author and fiction would appear to be the same. As Goethe did, Bellow inherited as his literary birthright the latest European version of intimate discourse. Where Werther adopted the fashionable narcissistic mode of the passionate effusion, Joseph adopted what Béatrice Didier called *the* twentieth-century mode of the private diary: not "the confidence of a man, but the elaboration of a text."[21] In Bellow's treatment, especially, the tendency of such a diary is toward the extinction of the self in a residue of words. By resisting this powerful magnetic influence through his agent Joseph, Bellow in his succeeding work moves outward to track the self from the outside, that is, as character. What dissolves close up, becomes visible from a distance.

This was not an easy reversion to character. Bellow is not "conservative" in reverting to character, for he is not reverting to nineteenth-century practice. After Joseph's typically "modern" experience, an innocence has been lost. Character can no longer be a comfortable assumption for the novelist. It becomes, rather, *the* problem, at once vexing and enchanting.

Bellow's development throws light on the whole subject of "the death of character." I mean particularly the subject's insistence. Like its corollary, the death of the novel, what is striking is how frequently it has been reannounced. It is not only Robbe-Grillet who has argued that "the novel of characters belongs entirely to the past."[22] Nor has it been necessary for the structuralist to argue that the individual is really "a space in which forces and events meet rather than an individuated essence."[23] With or without an accompanying theoretical explanation, the death of character appears to have seeped into the bloodstream of criticism itself. And it continues to *insist*. In a conference celebrating the tenth anniversary of the journal *Novel*, one of the panels was significantly

[21]Béatrice Didier, *Le journal intime* (Paris: Presses universitaires de France, 1976), 46, my translation.
[22]Alain Robbe-Grillet, *For a New Novel*, trans. Richard Howard (New York: Grove Press, 1965), 28. In his Nobel lecture, Bellow replied to Robbe-Grillet with some rancor: "There is no reason why a novelist should not drop 'character' if the strategy stimulates him. But it is nonsense to do it on the theoretical ground that the period which marked the apogee of the individual etc., is ended. We must not make bosses of our intellectuals" (Stockholm: U.S. Information Service, 1977), 10.
[23]Jonathan Culler, *Structuralist Poetics: Structuralism, Linguistics, and the Study of Literature* (Ithaca: Cornell University Press, 1975), 230.

entitled "Character as a Lost Cause."[24] Though the panel included a couple of voices struggling against the current, the whole transcript has an elegiac quality, as if the panelists were attempting to cope with life after the passing of the only one who had made life worth living.

What I have just been saying about Bellow, together with what I have been calling this *insistence* on the death of character, may put the whole theme in a different perspective. It suggests that what is distinctively modern about character is neither its trivialization, conversion into words, death, or diminishment, but the concern for it that would lead to a panel on the topic. In this view, what has changed—in the novel, as in meetings of humanists to discuss it—is that character has become a subject. We can no longer take character for granted. Our attention does not dwell easily on characters; it does not rest on them in order to follow them in their adventures; it continually seeks to look through them, for they express individually the general mystery of the self.[25]

[24]*Novel, a Forum on Fiction* 11 (Spring 1978), 197–217.
[25]One can trace this shift of focus back to Conrad, and particularly back to *Lord Jim* and *Heart of Darkness*. In these books, character is no longer clear, but precisely because of that, character has become the subject of Conrad's meditation, sustained through his fictive agent, Marlow. One can find the same narrowing and deepening in Faulkner's *Absalom, Absalom!* If we are constrained not to cast our generalizations too broadly, we can at least note that this is a line that leads directly to Bellow.

10

The Writer's Laboratory: Samuel Beckett and the Death of the Book

Derrida is doing no more than revive an old old tradition ... a pedagogy which teaches the pupil that there is nothing outside the text, but that in it, in its gaps, its blanks and its silences, there reigns the reserve of the origin; that it is therefore unnecessary to search elsewhere, but that here, not in the words, certainly, but in the words under erasure, in their *grid*, the "sense of being" is said.
> —Foucault, "My Body, This Paper, This Fire"

The experience of my reader shall be between the phrases, in the silence, communicated by the intervals, not the terms, of the statement. ... his experience shall be the menace, the miracle, the memory of an unspeakable trajectory.
> —Beckett, *Dream of Fair to Middling Women*

Asked what he thought of Samuel Beckett as a writer, Bellow remarked: "I can't speak for him. He's too mysterious to be spoken for."[1] But if Bellow could not speak *for* Beckett, he found that he could, and quite aptly, speak *of* him. In the same interview, when the subject of his recent meeting with Beckett arose, Bellow set off immediately by sketching the character from the bare evidence he had:

He shows the physical tension of having removed himself inwardly to some deeper location inside. He's physically an old man, worth looking at, worth studying. There's an odd twist to him. The color of the eyes is like nothing I've ever seen. Even the growth of the hair expresses some kind of torsion—there's a twist of sorts to his constitution. It's very appealing, most attractive. His constitution has its own sort of grain.

[1] William Kennedy, "If Saul Bellow Doesn't Have a True Word to Say, He Keeps His Mouth Shut," *Esquire* 97 (Feb. 1982), 54.

This is what Bellow delivers: something "worth looking at, worth studying." He provides a collection of externally observed indicators—bright, expressive evidence of something out of sight, of some vital energy that resides at "some deeper location inside."

It would be very hard to imagine Beckett providing a cameo of this sort for Bellow. As Bellow says: "He's an extraordinary writer," but "not my sort. I'm not his sort either." Indeed, they are as different as writers can conceivably be. They have proceeded in opposite directions: Bellow backing off from the text to gain a perspective on character, Beckett pressing relentlessly through the text into a kind of dimensionless internal space. But there is a significant similarity in their attitude toward "ideas" and their correlative regard for the free unnameability of the self. It is a metaphysical openness that is at the same time a literary openness: a refusal to "close" whose austerity makes both of these authors exceptionally alive to the possibilities of their craft.

Beckett, especially, has continued to be perhaps the most consistently inventive writer of his generation. To concentrate on one particular passage of his career, as we shall do, is not to deny that Beckett, at almost eighty years of age, continues to produce works of such vigorous originality that they succeed each other with the force of revelations. What makes his diary novel, *Malone Dies* (composed in 1948), such a critical stretch in this series of works is that in it Beckett openly wrestled for the last time with the thematic and metaphorical difficulties of written language and the paged book. Like *Dangling Man*, with its vivid foregrounding of text production, *Malone Dies* was Beckett's writing laboratory. Like Bellow's, the experiment Beckett conducted blew up the lab, and the result was a fundamental shift in his art the signs of which are still turning up in his work today. The key divide, then, in Beckett's career opens in the gap two-thirds of the way through the trilogy that falls between *Malone Dies* and *The Unnamable*. At the time of composition, it covered roughly three months from October 1948 to January 1949, time enough to accommodate the writing of *Godot*. The gap marks the end of Beckett's major fictions of writing, his abandonment of the page. From here on, with few exceptions (*Enough*, the mimes), Beckett's work would be, in the phrase from *The Unnamable*, "entirely a matter of voices." What carried him across the gap was a momentum gained from writing *Malone*.

Whereas Bellow's reflexive relations with his diary text most strongly resemble those of Goethe with *Werther*, Beckett's resemble those of Lessing with *The Golden Notebook*. As did Lessing, Beckett brought into focus not just a type of writing but writing itself. Like Lessing, he X-rayed his métier. Unlike her, he did not do it by combining notebooks with a contrasting "traditional novel"; instead, he took the available genre of the diary novel and reduced it to its skeletal parts. The violence he did to the form is an extreme version of that inflicted on the diary novel by Sartre and Bellow. But in breaking down the genre, he was self-consciously undoing the book itself through its most primitive representative.[2]

So extreme is Beckett's reduction of the diary novel that one is tempted to call it a travesty or grotesque satire. Never has there been so doomed a diarist (from the very first line, "I shall soon be quite dead at last in spite of all").[3] Never has there been so oppressive a room (being moribund, Malone's confinement is absolute: the room, a relentless presence that swells and changes shades). Nor has there ever been so separating a window (through which Malone, straining to see, catches a glimpse of strange goings on, and in the process, his own perfect strangeness), nor so complete an alienation (his only visitor—an undertaker?—raps him on the head and sits watching him for seven hours; no communication takes place), nor such a failure in love (relived, perhaps, in the courtship of Moll and Macmann; "I do not expect to see my sex again, with my naked eye, not that I wish to, we've stared at each other long enough, in the eye"[235]). But *Malone Dies* is not satire. It is, rather, a continuation of the diary novel in much the same spirit as its earlier practitioners. If we concentrate on a few of the conventions of the diary novel as they appear in *Malone*, we can show not only how Beckett penetrated to the function they served but also how, by pushing these conventions so far into the foreground, he revealed perplexities that are at the root of written narrative. We shall concentrate on three conventions in particular:

[2]Frank Kermode speculates that the diary may well have been the first version of the codex, which in turn was the precursor of the book. See Chapter 2, note 6.

[3]Samuel Beckett, *Three Novels* (New York: Grove Press, 1965), 179; unless otherwise indicated, page references for *Molloy, Malone Dies,* and *The Unnamable* are to this edition.

the threatened manuscript, the temporal conflation of discourse and action, and the blank entry.

   The topos of the threatened manuscript bears directly on the crucial documentary character of diary fiction discussed in Chapter 1. It reflects the traditional importance to the novel itself of the text as a material object or empirical certainty: that instability at the heart of the form that Jean Rousset called the "exigence anti-ro-manesque" ("the obligation to present, not a fiction, but documents, direct evidence of reality. In the eighteenth century the novelist had a bad conscience; the novel always pretended not to be a novel").[4] Studies of the eighteenth-century novel have generally located this importance of the document in its appeal to a conception of reality biased (by science and the expanding middle-class) toward the material and the measurable. Thus an art form came of age disguised as a form of nonart. It pretended not only to tell "true" stories in the words of "real" people (as opposed to professional authors), but also to provide the objective evidence of these stories in the form of letters or diaries that often comprised in themselves the whole of the narration.

   But if this emphasis on the physical text had its roots in a bourgeois or vulgarly scientific fixation on the visible and the material, one of its major consistent functions was to give testimony to the invisible and nonmaterial. Paradoxically, the text's degree of materiality and visible exactitude constituted its credentials as a testimony of the spirit. This was particularly true of novels like those we discussed in Chapter 5, which came out of a Puritan or sentimental frame of mind. When Pamela asks permission to rewrite one of her letters before turning it over to Mr. B, he protests that she must leave it exactly as it is, "because," he tells her, "they are your true sentiments at *the time*, and because they were *not* written for my perusal."[5] The letters are an archaeological record of precisely how what we cannot see in Pamela—that is, what is really important about Pamela—moved at the time. And as we read them,

---

   [4]Jean Rousset, *Forme et signification: Essais sur les structures littéraires de Corneille à Claudel* (Paris: Librairie José Corti, 1964), 75, my translation.
   [5]Samuel Richardson, *Pamela, or Virtue Rewarded*, ed. William M. Sale, Jr. (New York: Norton, 1958), 292.

our invisible natures are moved too. Not to be so moved is to miss their significance—that is, to be hopelessly materialistic.

So what is curious is the combination. A material artifact is required as evidence of a particular spirit. The spirit cannot be taken for granted. And correlatively, a story cannot just be a story. We have already had occasion to note how, as the time of her certain departure from this world draws near, Clarissa takes great pains to ensure the perpetuation of her letters—the literary evidence of her existence—in their exact form. When one thinks about it, the urgency of her concern can appear an odd element in the story of her life, considering her avowed confidence in the universe, how it is constituted, by Whom and to what end. So it is possible that her concern for the texts of her letters in this material world expresses her—and no doubt her author's—submerged uncertainty about the invisible world.

Readers shared Clarissa's anxiety about the physical preservation of the manuscript, and for this reason threats to the existence of the document became standard equipment of the evolving genre of the diary novel. Manuscripts have been scorched and water-soaked, rescued from fire, mildewed, eaten by worms, stuffed in boxes, lost, buried, bottled and floated upon the sea. When Pechorin's diaries are flung upon the ground in anger, one after the other, it goes to the heart. The drama of the survival of the text has become a part of the drama of the tale. Frequently augmenting this drama is the fact that the diarist or letter writer is dead by the time we read the evidence of his or her life. The text is all that remains. Moreover, a good many of them are not only dead but doomed or dying even as they write.[6]

This is the tradition that Malone dies into. In the context of Beckett's literary career, Malone's diary comes at that point when Beckett, moving closer and closer to the page, suddenly brings the document itself into focus before plunging on through it into the "Where now? Who now? When now?" of the monologue that follows. At the point of focus, Beckett brings the diary novel into focus at the same time–but seen now so close up that it appears a gro-

---

[6]Clarissa, Werther, Jacopo Ortiz, Pechorin, Hugo's Condemned Man, Turgenev's Superfluous Man, Poe's author of the "MS Found in a Bottle," Bernanos's Curé, Mauriac's Louis, Gustafsson's Beekeeper.

tesque caricature. Never has there been so wasted a moribund. Never has the room in which he writes been so throughly an enclosure, so thoroughly an expression of his isolation, and never has the document itself been so continually at risk. Its existence depends, not on a pen but on a pencil—and one so used that its life expectancy barely equals that of the writer. Sharpened at both ends, it is reduced by the last pages to a small piece of lead. As for the exercise book, it gets lost, falls on the floor, at one point is "harpooned" by Malone with his stick.

By such means does Beckett augment the metaphysical anxiety—for so long a part of the mode—that drives reader and writer alike to want to hold fast to the material document. Like Pamela secreting her letters in the pockets of her dress, Malone hides his notebook under the bedcovers when the undertaker comes. This anxiety is also rather brilliantly augmented by Beckett's inclusion of a distinct remnant of the novel's middle-class origins: the inventory of his goods and chattels that Malone is so concerned to make. In evoking this annual rite of shopkeepers, here hopelessly botched, Beckett goes beyond satire to the heart of the businessman's very human ailment. You cannot take it with you. Moreover, once he is fully launched on his enterprise, Malone finds that by his definition (those things are his he can lay hold of) "nothing is mine anymore, . . . except my exercise-book, my lead and the French pencil, assuming it really exists" (255). Now the French pencil, he cannot lay his hands on. And the lead is doomed. This leaves only one possession, as he has anticipated: "No, nothing of all that is mine. But the exercise-book is mine, I can't explain" (247). Malone's text is his only thing.

In *Malone Dies*, the whole business of possessions and inventories, of the entire material universe, draws to a point. Malone, at the end of this history, resigns himself to the suppressed intuition that led Clarissa to expend so much energy on the fate of her letters. "This exercise-book is my life," he says at last, "this child's exercise-book, it has taken me a long time to resign myself to that" (274). But in resigning himself, Malone at the same time relinquishes both the book and the "life." In coalescing words with things, Beckett puts them on one side of a gulf, on the other side of which Malone maintains his allegiance, however reluctantly, to the wordless and immaterial. In this, Malone shows a deeper conviction of the invisible than Clarissa, and a deeper commitment to it, just as his creator exposes the book and its words as a snare and a delusion—not the right vehicle after all. Malone's skewered notebook brings to an end the tradition of meticulous fictional editing that began with Richardson.

The same terminal point is latent in another convention of the diary novel, one that serves another of the temporal functions we discussed in Chapter 1. This is the tendency to close the gap between the time of the narrating and the time of the narrated, between discourse and story. To put this in other words, the narrative aspires to the warmest possible relationship with time. Again, as in the case of the threatened manuscript, it is a convention that serves a deeper need of the culture. If I am not mistaken, early intimations of this can be seen in Milton's expansion of the conventional epic invocation of the muse to a periodic reunion with time in which he expatiates on what Malone would call his "present state." This aesthetic merging with time is essentially what Beckett focused on in his valuation of Proust as a romantic. The classical artist, by contrast, "raises himself artificially out of Time in order to give relief to his chronology and causality to his development."[7] From this point of view, the dying Malone, whose time finally runs out, is the ultimate romantic artist; and his exercise book, the final collapse of art into time.

What is missing in Malone and what is essential to many of his romantic predecessors is a belief that form and time are compatible: morever, that genuine form (as opposed to artificial, classical form) can be tapped by merging with time. This idea is inseparable from the theory of spontaneous artistic creation. It resides in a faith that the origins of form are internal and invisible. The faith is latent in Edward Young and it guides Werther in his effusions. Later, Coleridge, as noted previously, drew on the ideas of Schlegel and called such form "organic," opposing it to "mechanic," or imposed, form. One could say that Coleridge, in his conversation poems, sought to submit himself to the vital, invisible forming agency by submitting himself to time. Tennyson sought the same thing in *In Memoriam*. As Tennyson points out in the poem itself, it was only

<hr>

[7]Samuel Beckett, *Proust* (New York: Grove Press, 1957), 62.

through his submission to time that he achieved the form of *In Memoriam*, a form in the shape of a curve extending from grief to rejoicing. But to repeat, the difference between Malone and his romantic predecessors is that for Malone form and time are completely at odds. This dissociation, of course, is not new with Malone. One can find it implicitly or explicitly in many of the French and Scandinavian diary novels inspired by the intimate journals of Amiel. These novels in turn lead to that baldest, most explicit expression of the dissociation of form and time developed by Sartre in *Nausea*.

Here, too, there is a difference between Malone and especially this latest representative of the tradition. Malone maintains attention on the Invisible, both as a mystery and as a kind of presence. Though one of his terms for the Invisible is now "formlessness," he carries over from his romantic precursors their awed regard for it. He cannot just accept the text. He cannot *play*. Instead, he is continually drawn by this nontextual presence. It is the source of seriousness and gravity. If it is the opposite of Milton's informing spirit, Malone employs a very Miltonic intensity, echoing the fall of Satan, in expressing his devotion to "earnestness, to home, to him waiting for me always, who needed me and whom I needed, who took me in his arms and told me to stay with him always, who gave me his place and watched over me, who suffered every time I left him, whom I have often made suffer and seldom contented, whom I have never seen" (195).

So, again, as he did with the convention of the threatened manuscript, Beckett maintains our attention on the absent subject by accentuating a traditional element of the diary novel. He compounds the collapse of mechanic form by having Malone aspire hopelessly to the condition of the omniscient and omnipotent artist. Malone draws on what remains of the left lobe of his brain to fulfill the requirements of a plan ("four stories, each one on a different theme"), a plan which, as we know, begins to fall into ruin the moment it is formulated. His stories are swamped by his present state; time lies heavily on the notebook. It does so because Malone cannot help but keep faith, even more so than his romantic forebears, with the invisible power, shrouded in darkness, which is the source of his mordant vitality—"the nourishing murk," as he calls it, "that is killing me" (193).

The final convention I wish to consider is what could be called the blank entry. It is a more infrequent element than the two I have discussed already, one strictly limited to the diary strain of intercalated narrative. The blank entry is the entry in which nothing is recorded. One finds the date, followed by a blank, or a question mark, or at most, some verbal formula for blankness: "Nothing at all to report today." Its close relative is the boring entry, which could be any such desultory noncomment as "Ate at 7:00, fell asleep shortly thereafter." Such entries are what can make the reading of real diaries such a low-yield, searingly tedious activity. Curiously, if it is doubled, a blank entry can take on interest: a cipher for tedium with its own rhythmical pleasure:

> July 19. Hot as time. nothing particular today.
> July 20. Hot as time. nothing particular today.[8]

Georges Duhamel parodied both devices, the boring and the blank, in *Salavin's Journal* when he had Salavin decide to become a saint. Salavin buys a new journal, which he begins with great anticipation:

> On with the new life! Would that I were older by one year, to be able to re-read this journal and weep with joy! I am ready. I'm waiting. I'm off to meet myself.
> January 8—Nothing to report.
> January 9—Nothing to report.
> January 10—Nothing.
> January 11—Nothing that has to do with the situation in any way.
> January 12—Nothing.
> January 13—Nothing. It's snowing, but that's of no importance. (to be struck out if I copy this journal.)
> January 14—Nothing.
> January 15—Nothing to report.
> January 16—Nothing.
> January 17—Nothing.
> January 18—Nothing.
> January 19—Nothing—still.
> January 20—Nothing.

[8]Henry A. Shute, *The Real Diary of a Real Boy* (Boston: Everett Press, 1903), 108.

January 21—Nothing. I have a bad cold. I accept it with serenity, I
might almost say with joy. It's not even worth noting.
January 22—Nothing.
January 23—Nothing.
January 24—I think there is something. No, it is not important enough.
January 25—Nothing.
January 26—Nothing.
January 27—Nothing. While I'm waiting I think I'd better make a few
more explanations. The thing that strikes me . . .[9]

In *Nausea*, Sartre parodied the same device when he had Roquentin
make the entry, "Nothing. Existed,"[10] which was especially coy,
since Roquentin had just achieved insights into the linked nature
of Nothingness and Existence.

In fictional diaries, the blank or boring entry is an obvious lia-
bility, one that is rarely indulged in with any frequency. Its principal
function is documentary realism. Like the conventions discussed
early in Chapter 1, it can be classed with those devices Ian Watt
collected under the heading Formal Realism. It is a way of saying,
This is not art (assuming the logic that if this were art, there would
not be this kind of wasted space). It increases the documentary
illusion. Yet here, too, as with the other two conventions we examined, there is an ambivalence of motive. If the blank or boring
entry increases the documentary illusion, it does not do so inno-
cently. Inevitably we cannot help knowing that this *is* art and therefore necessarily concentrated, full of import. So the blank or boring
entry is also a way of saying, Watch out, something must be pre-

---

[9]Georges Duhamel, *Salavin*, trans. Gladys Billings (London: Dent, 1936), 92.
Twain notes the same propensity in his childhood journal:
Monday—Got up, washed, went to bed.
Tuesday—Got up, washed, went to bed.
Wednesday—Got up, washed, went to bed.
Thursday—Got up, washed, went to bed.
Friday—Got up, washed, went to bed.
Next Friday—Got up, washed, went to bed.
Friday fortnight—Got up, washed, went to bed.
Following month—Got up, washed, went to bed.
"That journal," Twain comments, "finished me. I never had the nerve to keep one
since" (Mark Twain, *The Innocents Abroad, or the New Pilgrims' Progress* [Hartford:
American Publishing Co., 1970], 637).
[10]Sartre, *Nausea*, 140. For more fun with the device see Stanislaw Lem's *The
Futurological Congress*, trans. Michael Kandel (New York: Avon, 1976), 64.

paring itself. The ratio of these two opposed functions would appear to depend on just how firmly we believe that despite the nonretrospective appearance of the document, there is a secret teleology at work. Roquentin's comment about the traditional fat of the retrospective story is apt even for the nonretrospective document: "It was night. The street was deserted."[11] As he says, we do not let these words pass unnoticed. We read them as annunciations of adventure, endowed with meaning by a future that preexists them. Nonretrospective structure can at once increase the legitimacy of such dullness as it increases the excitement.

Malone Dies is, in effect, an extension of the principle of the boring entry to the entire novel. It is one of the few books in which the teleological illusion Roquentin writes of, which redeems an entry of its tedium, is absent from the start. The only conclusion, a foregone one, is the writer's death, which, in the case of Malone, is basically a matter of being "quite dead at last." It is an arbitrary, radically unclimactic terminus for the words he writes. Its onset is marked by one of the blankest of blank entries:

> never anything

> there

> any more

The only thing blanker is the blankness of the page that one may project from the last word to eternity.

Still, the actual blankness of the page is, in fact, something that plays a significant role in the body of this novel. It pierces the text at points throughout—a whiteness separating blocks of prose. And it figures as the ultimate logical development, not only of the device of the blank entry, but of the diary novel and, indeed, of textual representation itself. It expresses in its blankness the same double quality we have found behind the other conventions, for it implies at once nothing and something that exceeds the importance of the text it sets off. If one can find texts that give this paradox thematic development, one can find only a few that in the manner of *Malone*

---

[11]Sartre, *Nausea*, 58.

Dies actually incorporate the total blank as a recurring element in the text—an element that operates, if you will, as a signifier.[12]

"My notes," writes Malone, "have a curious tendency . . . to annihilate all they purport to record" (259). But in the blanks "the noises begin again, . . . those whose turn it is" (206). In one forty-eight-hour blank, he claims that the whole "unutterable" business of Malone and "of the other" was brought to a "solution and conclusion" (222). These blanks are, in effect, the ultimate means of humbling the text. They are where the action is. They signify a presence not completely unlike that for which Derrida took Rousseau to task. It is another, final, and quite understandable paradox that in the very violence Beckett exerts against the text, here in the last outpost of the novel, he preserves not only the idea but the urgency of the text's referential function.

He preserves this function as, in another sense, he says goodbye to it. Beckett's reflexive engagement with this text led him beyond the fiction of texts altogether. For the most part, there would be no more imitation of writing, no more documentary illusion. There is real anticipatory exasperation here: frustration and bitterness in coming to what was originally foreseen as the end of the line (a pair of books, not a trilogy). One can guess what depth of feeling there must have been in saying goodbye to what was, up to then, the "art and craft." "Moll," Malone writes in a murderous mood, faced with the hopeless accumulation of fictive junk piling up under his pen, "I'm going to kill her" (264). One can hear the authorial echo: "Malone. I'm going to kill him." The whole typographical setup of the last blank entry, with its relentlessly increasing ratio of white to black, stresses the death of the text as well as that of the writer. Having fictionally set out to sea moments before, Beckett confounds the sea and the page so that they become a mutual surface below which sink Malone, his stick, and his pencil. The next thing we know we are in a place so strange it is like being submerged in another element, listening to a voice that murmurs, "Where now? Who now? When now?"

[12]By this, of course, I mean a contrived blank, one that artificially calls attention to itself as a blank. Perhaps the most recent example is the fifty-two character space perforating the epistles in Jacques Derrida's *La carte postale de Socrate à Freud et au-delà* (1980), but as I imply further on, there is a critical difference between a blank in Derrida and a blank in Beckett.

Much has transpired between *Malone* and the present. In what follows I do not wish to slight the energetic originality of Beckett's art—the fact that every new work is a new departure and a new surprise. But in concentrating on the exceptional difference of *The Unnamable*, we can see the critical result of *Malone Dies*. Beckett was, in effect, drawn by his writing to a point beyond writing. He did not literally give up writing (though the fear that he would have to do so appears to have been quite genuine). He continued to produce texts, but the stress passed from their written to their aural character. With the drowning of Malone, Beckett passed from a fiction of writing to a fiction of voices. As he did so, the vigor of Beckett's originality passed from the narrative to the voice. The meaning of this shift lay not in a change of subject but in an increase of concentration on that subject—a tightening of the screws.

One of the things that happened when Beckett was led by his text to abandon the text was that he markedly altered the nature of his own literary "depth." It corresponds to the difference between a book in which something happens and a book in which nothing happens. The first two books of the trilogy, however disastrous they may be, have nonetheless the depth that accompanies both narrative and the nameable, mobile elements of narrative. In *Molloy*, to alter Vivian Mercier's inspired description of *Godot*, something happens twice. As a consequence, what *Molloy* and *Malone Dies* have is promise. Alterations take place, limbs stiffen, toes disappear, death comes. All this reasonably coherent detail allows us to respond to these narratives as if they were both literal and symbolic journeys. By virtue of this, they have dramatic power; they suggest further developments and deeper awarenesses. Thus Moran's farewells to the structures that give his life order—his garden, his maid, his chrome fixtures—are elegiac. And the sudden, fierce pain that first strikes his knee as he prepares to depart is highly dramatic—we have already seen Molloy and can guess what is in store. All this is moving, cathartic. With Malone's diary the pace slows as it approaches an absolute present, yet we still look forward. When Malone finally sinks beneath the page all the figurative, expressive *business* of narrative comes to an end. If there is any single function of the next book's inordinate length, it is to put beyond all doubt that there are no further developments.

The bottom eliminates depth. *The Unnamable* is not "deep" in the

same sense as *Molloy* and *Malone*, because it has little equipment
left with which to intimate something hidden, yet to be found,
despite the fact that its whole ostensible subject is out of sight. By
contrast part of Moran's depth is Molloy. Moran "resonates"—to
use the critical commonplace—with Molloy, just as Molloy in his
gradual decomposition and increasing confusion resonates with
Malone. There is little depth or resonance in *The Unnamable* because
there is nothing nameable (and therefore nothing symbolic) any
more. Images have become invalid, and those that develop—a seated
figure, his beard saturated with tears; a hard undented ball resting
on one of its "numberless poles"; Mahood crutching in spirals or
festering in a jar—are clearly spurious, meant to emphasize the
distance between them and what the voice seeks. Starting as we do
in this volume at the bottom, looking up at these creatures, their
effect on us is quite different from the effect of Molloy, Moran,
and Malone. Mahood and Worm are neither mysterious nor important. Beckett parodies himself in these fictions. They liven the
pages for a while but are inevitably disposed of.

One watches their departure with a certain regret, for it is difficult to read what takes their place for more than twenty pages at
a stretch. One is asked to concentrate so hard on the same enduring
absence: something whose commonest pronominal replacement is
"I." We call it the self, understandably, for language abhors a vacuum. The speaker of *The Unnamable* shares our weakness, producing names for itself though it knows it has no name, creating
the words we read though it knows it does not exist in words. Its
confusion is so profound that it is not sure if the "it" that speaks
is the same "it" that is sought. Something seeks to give birth to
something wordless in words. It is the same subject as that of *Malone*,
but now triangulated grammatically: an immediate evocation *by
voice* of being elsewhere.

Beckett trained for this project by writing *Waiting for Godot*. I do
not mean necessarily that he trained consciously but that leaving
Malone Dies and then working in one continuous endeavor from
October 1948 to January 1949 on the kind of dialogue he perfected
for the play had a direct effect on *The Unnamable*, to which he
turned next. Listen to the following monologue:

> So here he is again, is he? Yes, I'm glad to see him back, I thought
> he was gone forever, he too, no doubt. Together again at last, we'll

have to celebrate. But how? we'll embrace, no, not now, not now, but where did he spend the night? In a ditch, there's a ditch, where they beat him, I suppose, the same lot as usual, the same or another, I don't know, when I think of it, all these years, but for me, where would he be? Nothing more than a little heap of bones at the present minute, no doubt about it. And what of it?

It is not uncharacteristic of *The Unnamable* to stage a reunion of this sort with one of its surrogates. The pacing is that of *The Unnamable*. Yet the passage, with certain alterations and the format changed, comes from the opening lines of *Waiting for Godot*.[13] Here is another example,

> All the dead voices, . . . they all speak at once, each one to itself, rather they whisper, . . . what do they say, they talk about their lives, to have lived is not enough for them, they have to talk about it, to be dead is not enough for them, it is not sufficient,

> that's why they always repeat the same thing, the same old litany, the one they know by heart, to try and think of something different, of how to say something different from the same old thing, always the same wrong thing said always wrong.

The first half of this quotation is ten lines of dialogue adapted from *Godot* (40); the second half is from *The Unnamable* (374). The comparison shows, at least, how the kind of stichomythia Beckett polished in *Godot* allowed him to perfect a short phrasal unit that could be used as a structural base in a hundred pages of solid monologue, each phrase building on the last as a response or amplification. There is nothing "written" about these lines. They are fluid, vocal, unceasing. Compared with Malone's written pages, they are at once more tenuous and more indomitable: more tenuous because not written down, not fixed in lead; more indomitable because not subject to loss or harpooning. The documentary illusion is replaced by that of words continually welling out of nowhere. In the process, Beckett's release from the text allowed him an entirely new approach to depth. His power of invention poured into the voice, and he did things to monologue that had never been done before.

[13]Samuel Beckett, *Waiting for Godot* (New York: Grove Press, 1954), 7.

To help see this, imagine a stage—so faintly lit that all we can see is an outline, say, of a head and shoulders facing forward. Let it say, "I've always been here, here there was never anyone but me, me." Now add two figures exactly like the first and slightly behind it. Call the original figure A and the two new Figures A1 and A2, and let the dialogue go like this:

> A: I've always been here, here there was never anyone but me.
> A1: Never.
> A2: Always.
> A: Me.
> A1: No one.
> A2: Old slush to be churned everlastingly.

A1 and A2 provide a choral emphasis, slightly out of sync because A1, despairing more out of loneliness, is perhaps more nervous and excitable and responds more quickly to his cue. A2, despairing more out of boredom, his voice perhaps lower, is barely up to responding.

Now bring in two more figures, giving them somewhat sardonic voices, and name them B and B1. Situate them as a separate group off to the right, but instead of having them face us, have them face the other group, observing them.

> A: I've always been here, here there was never anyone but me.
> A1: Never.
> A2: Always.
> A: Me.
> A1: No one.
> A2: Old slush to be churned everlastingly.
> B: Now its slush, a minute ago it was dust.
> B1: It must have rained.

And now, once more, with yet two more figures. Station them still farther to the right and have them, like the first group, face forward. For good measure let's make them blind, give them smoked glasses. We can call them C and C1.

> A: I've always been here, here there was never anyone but me.
> A1: Never.

A2: Always.

 A: Me.

A1: No one.

A2: Old slush to be churned everlastingly.

 B: Now it's slush, a minute ago it was dust.

B1: It must have rained.

 C: He must have travelled.

C1: He whose voice it is.

 C: He must have seen.

C1: With his eyes.

 C: A man or two.

C1: A thing or two.

 C: Been aloft, in the light.

C1: Or else heard tales, travellers found him and told him tales.

 A: That proves my innocence.

 C: Who says, That proves my innocence?

 B: He says it.

B1: Or they say it.

 B: Yes, they who reason, they who believe.

 C: No, in the singular, he who lived, or saw some who had.

 A: He speaks of me.

A1: As if I were he.

A2: As if I were not he.

 A: Both.

I do not know how many letters of the alphabet we would run through were we to develop the entire piece as if it were to be staged. But in this passage we have certainly three of the main participants: A, who talks like an experiencing subject; his amplifiers, qualifiers, afterthinkers or whatever we wish to call them, A1 and A2, the one lonely, the other bored; B and his amplifier, who mock A's presumption, who can never forget that his belief in his existence is ill-founded; and C and his amplifier, who resist B's cynicism, yearn to believe in the authenticity of A, to locate him in some kind of setting or tale, perhaps even give him a name, like Mahood, or Worm.

The actual format for this "dialogue" is paragraphless monologue:

I've always been here, here there was never anyone but me, never, always, me, no one, old slush to be churned everlastingly, now it's slush, a minute ago it was dust, it must have rained. He must have

travelled, he whose voice it is, he must have seen with his eyes, a man
or two, a thing or two, been aloft in the light, or else heard tales,
travellers found him and told him tales, that proves my innocence,
who says, That proves my innocence, he says it, or they say it, yes,
they who reason, they who believe, no, in the singular, he who lived,
or saw some who had, he speaks of me, as if I were he, as if I were
not he, both. [403][14]

Read thus, the effect is different (the difference is important and
we shall return to it), but breaking it down into dialogue is inform-
ative because it shows that though *The Unnamable* appears to be a
monologue, it is more accurately a dialogue, or more accurately
still a colloquium, cast in the form of a monologue: a *symposion
monologikon*, if you want to be elegant; "entirely a matter of voices,"
if you want to call it what it calls itself.

A: Well I prefer that, I must say I prefer that.
C: That what?
A: Oh you know.
C: Who you?
A: Oh I suppose the audience.
B: Well well, so there's an audience.
B1: It's a public show, you buy your seat and you wait. [381]

In vocal, as opposed to textual, fiction we are allowed only one
fact, and that is the "noise." It constitutes half the subject of this
text, the other being the "I," and by separating them, putting the
relationship between them in doubt, the author, Beckett, was led
to create this colloquium for one voice.

I and this noise, on the subject of which, inverting the natural order,
we would seem to know for certain, among other things, what follows,
namely, on the one hand, with regard to the noise, that it has not
been possible up to date to determine with certainty, or even ap-
proximately, what it is, in the way of noise, or how it comes to me, or
by what organ it is emitted, or by what perceived, or by what intelligence apprehended, in its main drift, and on the other, that is to say

[14]The Grove Press text concludes "as if I were not he, as if I were not he, both."
On the basis of the French text, I have assumed the first "not" to be a misprint
and have eliminated it.

with regard to me, this is going to take a little longer, with regard to me, nice time we're going to have now, with regard to me, that it has not yet been our good fortune to establish with any degree of accuracy what I am, where I am, whether I am words among words, or silence in the midst of silence, to recall only two of the hypotheses launched in this connexion. [388]

But, though *Godot* provided a training that allowed Beckett stylistically to express a dilemma like this, *The Unnamable* in its intended monologue format is different in its effect from the dialogue of *Godot*. By casting these voices in the shape of a monologue, Beckett encourages us to seek a consistent point of view, even though none exists. We are listening to a noise that is at once voice and auditor or, more precisely, a voice and the voice of an auditor of that voice or, more precisely still, a voice responding to a voice that is the same voice making the same response, and so forth. It is an auditory Morton Salt box. When the voice says, "It is they who dictate this torrent of balls, they who stuffed me full of these groans that choke me," "they," of course, is a fiction, alternately "he," Basil, Mahood, "the bright boy of the class," "the everlasting third party." Yet whatever it is, it is also not "I," though it says "I. Unbelieving."

He thinks he's caught me, he feels me in him, then he says I, as if I were he, or in another, let us be just, then he says Murphy, or Molloy, I forget, as if I were Malone, but their day is done, he wants none but himself, for me, he thinks it's his last chance, he thinks that, they taught him thinking, it's always he who speaks, Mercier never spoke, Moran never spoke, I never spoke, I seem to speak, that's because he says I as if he were I, I nearly believed him, do you hear him, as if he were I, I who am far, who can't move, can't be found, but neither can he, he can only talk, if that much, perhaps it's not he, perhaps it's a multitude, one after another, what confusion. [403]

I think I have quoted enough, finally, to say that this is no more dialogue than it is monologue. It is both. Beckett clearly intended it that way, and as such it departs from the dramatic effect of *Godot* with the play's clear and distinct voices and what you could rightly call its social interest:

I seem to speak, that's because he says I as if he were I.

In this phrase "I" is "he," and "he" is "I." If I am not mistaken, Beckett is the first to have employed a grammatical effect of this sort—certainly the first to use it as a principle of sustained composition. The more you bear down on the phrase above, the more rapidly does the word "I" pulsate between two ways in which the sentence wants it: as an objective other ("the I seems to speak, that's because he says I as if he were the I") and as a subjective self ("*I* seem to speak, that's because he says I as if he were *I*"). Thwarted thus, it is difficult to impose order through our improvised characters: A, A1, A2, B, B1, C, C1, and so on. They are all the same voice denying each other.

> The Unnamable: I seem to speak, that's because he says I as if he were I, I nearly believed him,
> The Unnamable: do you hear him, as if he were I, I who am far, who can't move, can't be found.

Time and again we are forced to float, as it were, momentarily while our minds adjust to these sudden inversions of subject and object. It is a grammatical version of the effect one has viewing some of the etchings of Escher in which people seem to be inhabiting different gravitational fields in the same visual space (for example, walking up the underside of a staircase). One's mind keeps flashing between two incompatible gestalts, as if there were some third it could finally rest in that would reconcile all the contradictions. Beckett produces the same effect with his multitude of voices, all cohabiting in the same long sentences. He keeps alive the possibilities in that hidden space—of something lurking there, waiting to be discovered in the split second one travels through it, from subject to object, from object to subject, over and over again.

So we do have, after all, something like depth after *Malone*, though it is not so much deep as it is indefinitely offstage. I have isolated a principal means of intimation, which differs from symbol and allusion in that it provides neither visual nor conceptual prefiguring, neither shaggy moving shape nor philosophical abstract of self nor even the whiteness of the page. It does not point, but carries us beyond sight and sound, indeed quite beyond thought, toward whatever it is, or they are, that drives the words and listens to them.

Over thirty years after the death of Malone, the voice in *Ill Seen Ill Said* rummages in a coffer (the construction is exact, the voice rummages): "Empty after long nocturnal search. Nothing. Save in the end in a cranny of dust a scrap of paper. Jagged along one edge as if torn from a diary. On its yellowed face in barely legible ink two letters followed by a number. Tu 17. Or Th. Tu or Th 17. Otherwise blank. Otherwise empty."[15] I cannot pretend that my own study does not throw a brighter light on this passage with its fragment of a diary than Beckett intended, but almost always in Beckett what comes up in the present was sedimented long ago in the history of his art. So it is not forcing this scrap of text about a scrap of text to see in it an evocation of the late faint hope of texts. The term "minimal art" has rarely been so appropriate: an ancient blank entry in ink so "barely legible" as to render it a kind of absolute minimum in the history of problematic texts: "Tu or Th."

The major shift in literary procedure from an art of texts to an art of voices explains the general bias of the art since *Malone* toward a concentration of both script and focus. It is a concentration that can be called poetic in the demand that it makes upon the reader, especially on the reader's ear. The achieved effect is that continually recurring frisson of bewilderment that I have described as a sensation of floating. By the agency of vocal signifiers we are momentarily carried beyond them to what they cannot signify, nor we imagine. At times, as in his recent work *Company*, Beckett uses precisely the grammatical innovation he invented for *The Unnamable*: "Use of the second person marks the voice. That of the third that cankerous other. Could he speak to and of whom the voice speaks there would be a first. But he cannot. He shall not. You cannot. You shall not."[16]

In a way strikingly like Bellow's experience of *Dangling Man*, the major shift in Beckett's art that we have examined came about through the paradoxical combination of a pursuit of his subject and a determination to preserve that subject from his own predation. Like Bellow, Beckett must therefore be kept distinct from those who would begin to limn the features of a metaphysical presence beyond words and from those who would either abandon that

[15]Samuel Beckett, "Ill Seen Ill Said," *New Yorker*, Oct. 5, 1981, p. 54.
[16]Samuel Beckett, *Company* (New York: Grove Press, 1980), 8.

presence as an artistic occasion or deny it altogether. As Beckett has more frequently been associated with the latter than the former, one should stress the significance of that one consistent feature of his public remarks on his art: the *despair* of bridging art and its occasion. This is no act. Unlike the *nouveaux romanciers*, Beckett cannot accept this disjunction. Like Malone, he cannot play (which is to deny neither the amusement nor the beauty of his work). As he told Lawrence Harvey, the ways in which form continually distorts being are "unbearable."[17] The spirit in which he writes is, therefore, at an opposite remove from most current versions of *fröhliche Wissenschaft*—as, for example, the Barthesian spirit that rejoices in "the infinite deferral of the signified": "the signifiers' *infinitude* does not refer back to some idea of the ineffable (of an unnameable signified) but to the idea of *play*. The engendering of the perpetual signifier within the field of the text should not be identified with an organic process of deepening, but rather with a serial movement of dislocation, overlappings, and variations."[18]

Barthes's is only one of a number of ways that has been used to describe, in Eric Levy's phrase, the "postmetaphysical" Beckett. Levy's own recent study is more allegorical than Barthesian, less playful, but aims to show how Beckett boldly expresses "the experience of Nothing."[19] Michel Foucault, for a third, would have us drop the whole tiresome question of being and stick to the answerable ones of science. In one essay, inspired by Beckett, he looks forward to the day when we are long past bothering with the question Who is speaking? and instead hear only the "anonymity of a murmur" and ask only such questions as "what are the modes of existence of this discourse?"[20]

---

[17]*Samuel Beckett: Poet and Critic* (Princeton: Princeton University Press, 1970), 435. In the same series of interviews (1961–1962), Beckett went so far as to maintain that Being "must have its form. ... Someone will find it someday. Perhaps I won't, but someone will. It is a form that has been abandoned, left behind, a proxy in its place" (249).

[18]Roland Barthes, "From Work to Text," in *Textual Strategies*, ed. Josué V. Harari (Ithaca: Cornell University Press, 1979), 76.

[19]Eric Levy, *Beckett and the Voice of Species* (Totowa, N.J.: Barnes and Noble, 1980), 4.

[20]Michel Foucault, "What Is an Author?" in *Language, Counter-Memory, Practice: Selected Essays and Interviews*, ed. Donald F. Bouchard, trans. Bouchard and Sherry Simon (Ithaca: Cornell University Press, 1977), 138. See also his appropriation of *Molloy* in "The Discourse on Language" in his *The Archaeology of Knowledge*, trans. A. M. Sheridan Smith (New York: Harper, 1972), 215.

Edward Said has written of the structuralists that they have particular difficulty accounting for "force."[21] This may be precisely the appropriate term. Foucault's version of Beckett's text seeks to finesse both the force that brings it into being and the force to which it is devoted. While the structuralist and, by and large, the poststructuralist have endeavored (like Robbe-Grillet and Simon) with ever sharper, keener, more disciplined intelligence to remain on the surface and to avoid any illusion of depth, Beckett has devoted his art—its entire surface—to the enigma of what is behind, or below, or beyond it. What the postmetaphysical view denies is Beckett's deepest need for his art, a need that is nothing if not metaphysical. Yet as soon as we use the term "metaphysical" we must rein in hard. The conceptual bareness of our metaphysical condition is the other side of Beckett's skepticism. Criticism of Beckett is past the early embarrassment of Christian interpretation, but these things go in cycles, so it is worth stressing that Beckett's resistance to closure applies to the embrace as to the denial. It will not accept anything that goes by the name of belief. By extension, his fictions are governed by no blind metaphysics of presence nor any illusion that being can be recovered in the text. Rather they assert at every line being's unrecoverable reality. This is what has made failure the single most important repetition in Beckett's canon. Each failure is a *mise en abîme* of the general failure of transcription. At the same time, each failure pays homage to a metaphysical presence of which the text is a distant commotion in the world of signs.

The death of the book in *Malone Dies* is the critical moment in Beckett's continual undoing of the forms of belief in the forms of art. This willful murder, more, I think, than any of his other acts of literary violence, throws into sharp relief Beckett's passionate fidelity to that metaphysical pressure that binds him to his art. He needs this art, needs it precisely because of the reflexive

---

[21]"The moving force of life and behavior, the *forma informans*, intention, has been, in their work, totally domesticated by system" (Said, *Beginnings: Intention and Method* [New York: Basic Books, 1975], 319). Later, he writes: "the gravest problem that structuralism has yet to deal with wholeheartedly is how seriously to account for change and force, how to assimilate the powerful and sometimes wasteful behavioral activity of man—what Blackmur calls the Moha—to the numinous order of structure" (335).

relations by which he and it jointly advance. Their mutual fidelity to that unvoiceable freedom which is at once their source and object commands the continual originality of their mutual enterprise.

A Bibliography of
Diary Fiction

The following two lists (the second a chronological restatement of the first) are meant to be helpful, not definitive. In compiling them, I have profited from the work of Lyn Barstis, Juliet Kincaid, Lorna Martens, and Valerie Raoul. I have stuck to the territory I know best and have consequently left out of account the rich development of the diary mode in Japan, which antedates the Western development by half a millennium and goes on vigorously today (a good introduction to the subject can be found in Earl Miner's *Japanese Poetic Diaries*). Having also imposed upon myself the condition of personally checking the credentials of a work before entering it, I have omitted some promising candidates because I was unable to find copies for verification.

Entries listed include both fiction cast strictly in the diary format and epistolary fiction of the single letter-writer variety. I have included the latter on the grounds that the diary effect depends less on the absence of an addressee than on our confinement to the text of a single periodic writer (see Preface). To assist those who may wish to honor the distinction between letters and a diary I have marked epistolary works with an asterisk (*). Finally, I have imposed certain constraints in the way of defining the features of "diary fiction" itself, without which the bibliography would have lost much of its focus and meaningfulness.

Prose. Despite what appears to be a still gathering wave of poetic diaries, there has not been a correspondingly rich development in fictional poetry. Lamartine's *Jocelyn* (1836) would be the outstanding example. Of dramatic diaries, the only instance that appears to qualify is Beckett's *Krapp's Last Tape*.

A fiction of writing. By this I mean some clear indication that the words of the text are composed by some fictive personage. This excludes a variety of twentieth-century experimentation in inter-calated structure: third-person present (Malraux's *Les conquérants*), first-person monologue (Lagerkvist's *The Dwarf*), mental letters (Carolyn Blackwood's *The Stepdaughter*). It also excludes a favorite of bibliographers of the mode, the early anonymous *Nachtwachen des Bonaventura* (1804), a series of sixteen monologues delivered on sixteen separate nightwatches. Still, there were curiosities that a more austere bibliographer would have dropped but that I could not bring myself to exclude: Zamyatin's *We* (not written, but taped), Claire Goll's stories (written, but by animals).

Density. A good many of the entries are "impure" in the sense that they include stretches of text by hands other than that of a single diarist or letter writer. At what level is the impurity great enough to exclude a work from the list? In other words, when is a work not diary fiction but fiction that includes a diary? For fictive journals, 50 percent of the whole seemed a minimum standard that not only applied in a strictly logical sense but also gave a sufficient proportional feeling of immersion. Thus, a work like Paul Bourget's *Le fantôme* (1901), a diary sandwich of which 159 pages out of 345 are diary, lacks the density of typical diary fiction.

Because letters are a more sociable form and tend to be inter-spersed with replies, my requirements for the single letter-writer mode were more strict. As a minimum ratio of letters to replies I took for a standard Mme Cottin's *Claire d'Albe* in which it stands at thirty-six to ten. This easily qualified the first volume of *Pamela*, four-fifths of which is a letter journal composed by Pamela for her parents, but disqualified the sequel, a genuine correspondence novel in which the ratio falls just short of three to one. Anyone reading these two volumes in sequence will, I think, be struck by the dif-ference of effect caused by these two different ratios.

Intercalated chronology of events. Entries had to be what in English criticism is imperfectly called "nonretrospective." Since there is a good deal of recalling of the past in any diary, discriminations here involved much in the way of judgment calls. I sought to limit my exclusions to those works that intercalated only the narration, keeping the story entirely in the past. Thus, Gorky's "Karamora" includes sufficient present activity to qualify, but Hauptmann's *Phantom* does not.

Fiction. Judgment calls again: Sénancour's *Obermann* qualified; Sainte-Beuve's *Joseph Delorme* did not. Certain convicted frauds, like *The Story of Opal*, were included.

It is impossible ever to cut this fine enough. Though my chief interest all along has been the inward psychological attention enabled by the mode, the logic of my instruments has forced me to include representatives of the centrifugal, outward, social and satiric deployment stretching from Marana's *L'espion turc* and Fontenelle's *Lettres galants* through Goldsmith and Twain. These are generally in the genre of the letters by a foreign visiter. My rule of density has applied here as well, eliminating such well-known works as Montesquieu's *Lettres persanes* and José Cadalso's *Cartas marruecas*, which include replies and cross-correspondences.

I

Adam, Paul. "L'inéluctable" (1893) ["The Ineluctable"].
——. *Robes rouges* (1891) [Red robes].
Aldiss, Brian W. *The Brightfount Diaries* (1955).
Andreyev, Leonid. *Dnevnik Satany* (1919) [*Satan's Diary*].
——. *Igo voĭny* (1916) [trans. as *Confessions of a Little Man during Great Days*].
——. *Krasnyĭ smekh* (1904) [*The Red Laugh*; fragments of a retrospective narrative that evolve past the middle into a diary].
Anonymous. *The Butler's Diary, or the History of Miss Eggerton* (1792).
——. *Go Ask Alice* (1971).
*——. *Hermione, or the Orphan Sisters* (1791).
*——. *Letters Writ by a Turkish Spy* (1691–1694) [seven-volume sequel to Marana's original *L'espion turc*].
*——. *Pamela in High Life, or Virtue Rewarded* (1741).
Barbé-Marbois, François. *Lettres de madame la Marquise de Pompadour depuis 1746 jusqu'à 1762* (1771) [trans. as *Letters of the Marchioness of Pompadour from 1753 to 1762 Inclusive*; attributed by some to Crébillon fils].
Beauvoir, Simone de. *La femme rompue* (1967) [*The Woman Destroyed*; third novella in a volume of the same title].
Beckett, Samuel. *Malone meurt* (1951) [*Malone Dies*].
Bellow, Saul. *Dangling Man* (1944).
Bermant, Chaim. *Diary of an Old Man* (1966).

Bibliography

Bernanos, Georges. *Journal d'un curé de campagne* (1936) [*Diary of a Country Priest*].

Bessette, Gérard. *Le libraire* (1968) [The bookseller].

Blicher, Steen Steenson. "En landsbydegns dagbog" (1824) ["Journal of a Parish Clerk"].

——. "Praesten i Vejlbye" (1829) ["The Parson at Vejlbye"].

Blond, Georges. *Journal d'un imprudent* (1936) [Diary of an imprudent man].

Böhme, Margarite. *Tagebuch einer Verlorenen von einer Tote* (1905) [trans. as *Diary of a Lost One*].

Bowles, Paul. "If I Should Open My Mouth" (1967).

Boyle, Kay. *Primer for Combat* (1942).

Bremer, Frederike. *En dagbok* (1843) [*A Diary*].

——. "Den ensamma" (1828) ["The Solitary"].

Brod, Max. *Ausflüge ins Dunkelrote* (1909) [Excursion into the deep red; published with *Die Erziehung zur Hetäre*].

Brower, Brock. *The Late Great Creature* (1972).

Bryant, Dorothy. *Ella Price's Journal* (1972).

Bury, Lady Charlotte. *Diary Illustrative of the Times of George the Fourth* (1838).

Butor, Michel. *L'emploi du temps* (1956) [trans. as *Passing Time*].

Byron, (Miss) Medora. *The Bachelor's Journal* (1815).

——. *The Spinster's Journal* (1816).

Carossa, Hans. *Doktor Bürgers Ende* (1913) [republished as *Die Schicksale Doktor Bürgers*].

Cèspedes, Alba de. *Il quaderno proibito* (1952) [trans. as *The Secret*].

Chagall, David. *Diary of a Deaf-Mute* (1933).

Charbonnière, Ramond de. *Chant de Schwarzbourg, ou les aventures du Jeune d'Olban* (1777) [Song of Schwarzburg, or the adventures of the young d'Olban].

Chardonne, Jacques. *Eva, ou le journal interrompu* (1930) [Eva, or the interrupted journal].

Charles, Elizabeth Rundle. *The Diary of Brother Bartholomew, a Monk of the Abbey of the Marienthal, in the Odenwald, in the Twelfth Century* (1865).

——. *The Diary of Kitty Trevylyan* (1865).

*Charrière, Isabella A. de (Zélide). *Lettres de Mistriss Henley* (1784) [largely retrospective].

*——. *Lettres écrites de Lausanne* (1785) [Letters written from Lausanne].

*——. *Lettres neuchâteloises* (1784).

Chitty, Susan. *Diary of a Fashion Model* (1958).

Clark, Eleanor. "A Summer in Puerto Rico" (1941).

Coetzee, J. M. *In the Heart of the Country* (1977).

Conan, Laure (Marie-Louise-Felicité Angers). *Angéline de Montbrun* (1882).

Connell, Evan S. *The Diary of a Rapist* (1966).

*Constant de Rebeque, Samuel de. *Le mari sentimental, ou le marriage comme il y en a quelques-uns* (1783) [The sentimental husband, or marriage as it sometimes is].

*Cottin, (Mme) Marie. *Claire d'Albe* (1798).

*Crébillon, Claude Prosper Jolyot de (Crébillon fils). *Lettres de la Duchesse de *** au Duc de **** (1768).

*———. *Lettres de la Marquise de M *** au Comte de R**** (1732).

*Damours, Louis. *Lettres de Ninon de Lenclos au Marquis de Sévigné* (1750) [attributed by some to Crébillon fils].

Daninos, Pierre. *Les carnets du bon Dieu* (1947) [The notebooks of the good lord].

Davis, Clyde Brion. *"The Great American Novel ... "* (1938).

Delafield, E. M. (Elizabeth Monica Dashwood). *Diary of a Provincial Lady* (1930).

Dostoevsky, Fyodor. "Belyi nochi" (1848) ["White Nights"].

———. *Igrok* (1866) [*The Gambler*].

Drieu La Rochelle, Pierre. "Journal d'un homme trompé" (1934) [Diary of a deceived man].

Dubois la Chartre, André. *Journal intime d'Hercule* (1957) [Hercules' private diary].

Du Camp, Maxime. *Mémoires d'un suicidé* (1855) [Memoirs of a suicide].

Duhamel, Georges. *Journal de Salavin* (1927) [*Salavin's Journal*].

Durrell, Lawrence. *The Black Book* (1938) [mixed form: diary and novel in progress].

*Elliott, George P. "The NRACP" (1949).

Elman, Richard M. *Lilo's Diary* (1968).

Feuillet, Octave. *Le journal d'une femme* (1878) [A woman's diary].

*———. *La petite comtesse* (1857) [The little countess].

*Fontenelle, Bernard le Bovier de. *Lettres galantes du Chevalier d'Her ...* (1683-1687).

*Foscolo, Ugo. *Le ultime lettere di Jacopo Ortis* (1802) [*The Last Letters of Jacopo Ortis*].

Fowles, John. *The Collector* (1963).

France, Anatole. *Le crime de Sylvestre Bonnard* (1881) [*The Crime of Sylvestre Bonnard*].

Frisch, Max. *Stiller* (1954) [trans. as *I'm Not Stiller*].

Garborg, Arne. *Traete maend* (1891) [Tired souls].

Garshin, Vsevolod. "Trus" (1879) ["The Coward"].

Gautier, Jean-Jacques. *Cher Untel* (1974) [Dear So-and-so].

*Gautier, Théophile. *Mademoiselle de Maupin* (1835–1836).

Geijerstam, Gustaf af. *Medusas hufvud* (1895) [The head of the medusa; barely half in diary form].

Gide, André. *Les cahiers d'André Walter* (1891) [*The Notebooks of André Walter*].

———. *L'école des femmes* (1929) [*The School for Wives*].

———. *Paludes* (1895).

———. *La symphonie pastorale* (1919) [*Pastoral Symphony*].

Gilman, Charlotte Perkins. "The Yellow Wallpaper" (1892).

Gissing, George. *The Private Papers of Henry Ryecroft* (1903).

Godbout, Jacques. *Salut Galarneau!* (1967) [Hail, Galarneau!].

Bibliography

Goebbels, Joseph. *Michael: Ein deutsches Schicksal in Tagebuchblättern* (1929) [Michael: a German fate in diary form].

*Goering, Reinhard. *Jung Schuk* (1913) [*Young Schuk*; mixed form: letters, novel in progress].

Goetel, Ferdynand. *Z dnia na dzien* (1926) [*From Day to Day*].

*Goethe, Johann Wolfgang von. *Die Leiden des Jungen Werthers* (1774) [*The Sorrows of Young Werther*].

Gogol, Nikolai. "Zapiski cumashedshego" (1835) ["The Diary of a Madman"].

*Goldsmith, Oliver. *The Citizen of the World* (1762).

Goll, Claire. "Confessions d'un moineau du siècle" (1919) [Confessions of a worldly sparrow].

——. "Journal d'un cheval" (1919) [Diary of a horse].

Gore, Catherine Grace Francis. *Diary of a Desennuyé* (1836).

Gorky, Maxim. "Karamora" (1924) [borderline: retrospective in diary form].

Gracq, Julien (Louis Poirier). *Un beau ténébreux* (1945) [trans. as *A Dark Stranger*].

Graffigny, (Mme) Françoise de. *Lettres d'une Péruvienne* (1747) [trans. as *Letters of a Peruvian Princess*].

Graves, Wallace. *Trixie* (1969).

Grossmith, George and Weedon. *The Diary of a Nobody* (1892).

*Guilleragues, Gabriel-Joseph de Lavergne de. *Lettres portugaises* (1669) [trans. as *Letters of a Portuguese Nun*].

Gustafsson, Lars. *En biodlares dod* (1978) [*The Death of a Beekeeper*].

*Hailey, Elizabeth Forsythe. *A Woman of Independent Means* (1978).

Hansen, Martin A. *Lögneren* (1950) [*The Liar*].

Hardy, Thomas. "Alicia's Diary" (1887).

Haydn, Richard. *The Journal of Edwin Carp* (1954).

Hazzard, Mary. *Sheltered Lives* (1980).

*Helprin, Mark. "The Letters of the *Samantha*" (1977).

Herlihy, James Leo. *The Season of the Witch* (1971).

Hersey, John. *The Wall* (1950).

Hesse, Hermann. "tagebuch 1900" (1901) [notebook 1900; published under the pseudonym Hermann Lauscher].

*Heyking, Elizabeth von. *Briefe, die ihn nicht erreichten* (1903) [trans. as *The Letters Which Never Reached Him*].

*Hofland, (Mrs.) Barbara. *The Young Cadet* (1921).

Horwitz, Julius. *The Diary of A. N.* (1970).

Hugo, Victor. *Le dernier jour d'un condamné* (1828) [*Last Day of a Condemned Man*].

Huxley, Elspeth. *The Red Rock Wilderness* (1957).

James, Henry. "The Diary of a Man of Fifty" (1879).

——. "The Impressions of a Cousin" (1883).

Jameson, (Mrs.) Anna Brownell. *Diary of an Ennuyée* (1826).

Jameson, Storm. *The Journal of Mary Hervey Russell* (1945).

Johnson, Eyvind. *Drommar om rosor och eld* (1949) [Dreams of roses and fire].

*Jouffroy, Alain. *Le mur de la vie privée* (1960) [The wall of the private life].

Kaufman, Sue. *Diary of a Mad Housewife* (1967).

Keyes, Daniel. *Flowers for Algernon* (1966).

Kierkegaard, Sören Aabye. *Forförens dagbog* (1843) [*Diary of a Seducer*; part of the volume *Enten/Eller (Either/Or)*].

——. *"Skyldig?"—"Ikke-Skyldig?"* ("Dagbog") (1845) [*Guilty—Not Guilty* ("Quidam's Diary")].

King-Hall, Magdalen. *The Diary of a Young Lady of Fashion in the Year 1764–1765* (1925).

Kraf, Elaine. *The Princess of 72nd Street* (1979).

*Krüdener (Mme de), Barbara Juliane von. *Valérie, ou lettres de Gustave de Linar à Ernest de G ...* (1804).

Krusenstjerna, Agnes von. *Ninas dagbog* (1917) [Nina's diary].

*Lamarche, Courmont Ignace Hugary de. *Lettres d'Aza ou d'un Péruvien, conclusion des lettres péruviennes* (1749) [Aza's letters, conclusion of the Peruvian letters; attributed by some to Mme Graffigny].

Larbaud, Valéry. *A. O. Barnabooth, ses oeuvres complètes: C'est-à-dire un conte, ses poésies et son journal intime* (1913) [A. O. Barnabooth, his complete works: that is, a story, his poetry and his private diary].

Lem, Stanislaw. *Ze wspomnien Ljona Tichego: Kongres futurologiczny* (1971) [trans. as *The Futurological Congress*].

Lermontov, Mikhail. *Geroi nashego vremeni* (1840) [A Hero of Our Time].

Le Roux, Hugues. *Gladys, ou l'amour moderne* (1893) [Gladys, or modern love].

Lessing, Doris. *The Golden Notebook* (1962).

*Livijn, Clas. *Spader dame: en berätteise i bref funne pa Daniken* (1824) [Queen of spades: a report from Denmark in letter form; letter journal].

Loos, Anita. *Gentlemen Prefer Blondes* (1925).

Lorrain, Jean (Paul Duval). *Monsieur de Phocas* (1901).

Lowry, Malcolm. "Through the Panama" (1961).

Lurie, Alison. *Real People* (1969).

Machado de Assis, Joaquin Maria. *Memorial de Ayres* (1908) [trans. as *Counselor Ayres' Memorial*].

Manning, Anne. *Deborah's Diary* (1859) [sequel to *Mary Powell*].

——. *The Maiden and Married Life of Mary Powell, Afterwards Mistress Milton* (1855).

*Marana, Giovanni Paolo. *L'espion du grand seigneur* (commonly, *L'espion turc*; 1684–1686) [*The Turkish Spy*].

*Marat, Jean-Paul. *Lettres polonoises* (1770) [*Polish Letters*].

Maupassant, Guy de. "Un fou" (1885) ["A Madman"].

——. "Le horla" (1886).

——. "Mes vingt-cinq jours" (1885) [My twenty-five days].

Mauriac, François. *Le noeud de vipères* (1932) [trans. as *Vipers' Tangle*].

Merrill, James. *The (Diblos) Notebook* (1965).

Michaelis, Karin. *Den farlige alder* (1910) [*The Dangerous Age*].

Mirbeau, Octave. *Le journal d'une femme de chambre* (1900) [The diary of a chamber maid].

Bibliography

——. *La 628-E8* (1907).

——. *Les vingt et un jours d'un neurasthénique* (1902) [The twenty-one days of a neurasthenic].

Moravia, Alberto. *L'attenzione* (1965) [trans. as *The Lie*].

Muller, Robert. *After All, This Is England* (1965) [orig. title: *The Lost Diaries of Albert Smith*].

Mumford, Edwin. *Diary of a Paranoic: Being a Series of Fictional Associations on the Subject of Fear* (1964).

Nansen, Peter. *Julies dagbog* (1898) [Julie's diary].

Nathan, Robert. *The Mallot Diaries* (1965).

Nemerov, Howard. *Journal of the Fictive Life* (1965).

*Nodier, Charles. *Adèle* (1820).

——. *Le peintre de Saltzbourg: Journal des émotions d'un coeur souffrant* (1803) [The painter of Salzburg: diary of the emotions of a suffering heart].

Obstfelder, Sigbjorn. *En praests dagbog* (1900) [Diary of a priest].

Ognev, N. (Mikhail Rozanov). *Dnevnik Kosti Riabtseva* (1923–1924) [The diary of Kostya Ryabtsev; appeared in two parts, commonly trans. as *The Diary of a Communist Schoolboy* and *The Diary of a Communist Undergraduate*].

Patchen, Kenneth. *The Journal of Albion Moonlight* (1941).

Phelps, Elizabeth Stuart. *The Gates Ajar* (1868).

Poe, Edgar Allan. "The Journal of Julius Rodman" (1840).

——. "MS Found in a Bottle" (1831).

Prokosch, Frederic. *The Missolonghi Manuscript* (1968).

Queffélec, Henri. *La culbute* (1946) [The somersault].

——. *Journal d'un salaud* (1944) [Diary of a swine].

Queneau, Raymond. *Les oeuvres complètes de Sally Mara* (1962) [The complete works of Sally Mara; first half is Sally's journal intime].

Rathbone, Hannah Mary. *So Much of the Diary of Lady Willoughby as Relates to her Domestic History, and to the Eventful Period of the Reign of Charles the First* (1844).

——. *Some Further Portions of the Diary of Lady Willoughby* (1847).

*Restif de la Bretonne, Nicolas Edme. *Le pornographe, ou idées d'un honnête-homme sur un projet de réglement pour les prostituées* (1770) [The pornographer, or ideas of a respectable man on a plan for the regulation of prostitutes].

*Riccoboni, (Mme) Marie Jeane. *Lettres d'Adélaïde de Dammartin, Comtesse de Sancerre à M. le Comte de Nanci* (1767).

*——. *Lettres d'Elisabeth-Sophie de Vallière à Louise Hortense de Canteleu* (1772).

*——. *Lettres de Milady Juliette Catesby à Milady Henriette Campley* (1759).

*——. *Lettres de Mistress Fanni Butlerd à Milord Charles Alfred de Caitombridge* (1757).

*——. *Lettres de Mylord Rivers à Sir Charles Cardigan* (1777).

*Richardson, Samuel. *Pamela, or Virtue Rewarded* (1740) [part 1 only; four-fifths a letter journal].

Rilke, Rainer Maria. *Die Aufzeichnungen des Malte Laurids Brigge* (1910) [*The Notebooks of Malte Laurids Brigge*].

Rinehart, Mary Roberts. *The Red Lamp* (1925).

Rod, Edouard. *La course à la mort* (1885) [The race to death].

——. *Le sens de la vie* (1889) [The meaning of life].

Rolland, Romain. *Colas Breugnon* (1914).

Romains, Jules. *La douceur de la vie* (1939) [trans. as *The Sweets of Life*; vol. 18 of *Les hommes de bonne volonté* (*Men of Good Will*)].

Ross, Sinclair. *As for Me and My House* (1941).

Sagan, Françoise (Françoise Quoirez). *Des bleus à l'ame* (1972) [trans. as *Scars on the Soul*].

Salm, Constance de. *Vingt-quatre heures d'une femme sensible, ou une grande leçon* (1824) [Twenty-four hours in the life of a sensitive woman, or a good lesson]

Sand, George. *La Daniella* (1856).

——. *Isadora* (1846).

Sartre, Jean-Paul. *La nausée* (1938) [*Nausea*].

*Schiller, Friederich. *Der geisterscher* (1786–1789) [The ghost-seer; barely half in letters; unfinished].

Schnitzler, Arthur. "Der Andere: Aus dem Tagebuch eines Hinterbliebenen" (1889) [The other: from the diary of a survivor].

——. "Blumen" (1894) [Flowers].

——. "Die Frau des Weisen" (1897) [The sage's wife].

——. "Der Sohn" (1892) [The son].

Second, Albéric. "Le journal d'une jeune femme" (1857) [The diary of a young wife].

Selinko, Annemarie. *Désirée* (1951).

Sénancour, Etienne Pivert de. *Obermann* (1804).

*Sheridan, (Mrs.) Francis. *Memoirs of Miss Sidney Biddulph* (1761) [first two-thirds a letter journal].

*Shklovsky, Viktor. *Zoo, ili pis 'ma ne o liubri* (1923) [*Zoo, or Letters Not about Love*; letters interspersed with eight brief replies].

Shute, Henry A. *The Real Diary of a Real Boy* (1902) [presumed fictive].

——. *"Sequil," or Things Whitch Ain't Finished in the First* (1904) [presumed fictive].

*Sinclair, Upton. *Another Pamela, or Virtue Still Rewarded* (1950).

——. *The Journal of Arthur Stirling* (1903).

Singer, Christiane. *Les cahiers d'une hypocrite* (1965) [Notes of a hypocrite].

Smith, Stevie. *Novel on Yellow Paper* (1936).

Söderberg, Hjalmar. *Doktor Glas* (1905).

Soubiran, André. *Journal d'une femme en blanc* (1963) [Diary of a woman doctor].

*Sousa Botelho, Adelaide de (Mme Sousa). *Adèle de Sénange, ou lettres de Lord Sydenham* (1794) [Adèle de Sénange, or letters from Lord Sydenham].

——. *Charles et Marie* (1801).

——. *Eugène de Rothelin* (1808).

Stegner, Wallace. *The Spectator Bird* (1976).

Stevenson, Dorothy E. *Mrs. Tim Carries On* (1941).

Bibliography

Swados, Harvey. *Celebration* (1975).

Sylvan, Urbanus (Henry Charles Beeching). *Pages from a Private Diary* (1896–1898).

Taine, Hippolyte. *Vie et opinions de M. Frédéric-Thomas Graindorge* (1867) [Life and opinions of M. Frédéric-Thomas Graindorge].

Thackeray, William Makepeace. *The Diary of C. Jeames de la Pluche, Esq.* (1845–1846).

Tieck, Ludwig. *Ein Tagebuch* (1789) [A notebook].

Towne, Anthony. *Exerpts from the Diaries of the Late God* (1968).

Turgenev, Ivan. "Dnevnik lisniago cheloveka" (1850) ["The Diary of a Superfluous Man"].

*——. " 'Faust' " (1855).

Twain, Mark (Samuel Clemens). "Eve's Diary" (1905).

——. "Extracts from Adam's Diary" (1893).

Updike, John. *A Month of Sundays* (1975).

Verga, Giovanni. *Storia di una capinera* (1869) [Story of a blackcap].

Vidal, Gore. *Myra Breckinridge* (1968) [interspersed with seven brief tapes by Buck Loner].

——. *Myron* (1974) [alternating entries by two personalities of, technically, one diarist].

——. "Pages from an Abandoned Journal" (1956).

Vining, Elizabeth Gray. *I, Roberta* (1967).

Vulliamy, Colwyn Edward. *Doctor Philligo* (1944) [sequel to *The Polderoy Papers*].

——. *The Polderoy Papers* (1943).

Walker, Alice. *The Color Purple* (1982)

Wall, Bengt V. *Vannen Patrik, eller den sallsamma resan* (1948) [trans. as *Our Friend Patrick*].

Walser, Robert. *Jacob von Gunten* (1905).

*Webster, Jean. *Daddy-Long-Legs* (1912).

*——. *Dear Enemy* (1915) [sequel to *Daddy-Long-Legs*].

Weisser, Adolph. *Hinterlassene Papiere eines geistlichen Selbstmorders* (1841) [Literary remains of a spiritual suicide].

Whiteley, Opal. *The Story of Opal: The Journal of an Understanding Heart* (1920) [published as nonfiction; shown to be fraudulent].

Whittier, John Greenleaf. *Margaret Smith's Journal* (1848).

Wilson, Colin. *The Sex Diary of Gerard Sorme* (1963) [original title: *Man without a Shadow*].

Wohmann, Gabriele. *Ernste Absicht* (1970) [Serious intent].

Yonge, Charlotte Mary. *Journal of Lady Beatrix Graham, Sister of the Marquis of Montrose* (1871).

Zamyatin, Yevgeni Ivanovich, *My* (1924) [*We*; tapes].

Zola, Emile. "La confession de Claude" (1865) [Claude's confession].

II

1669   *Lettres portugaises* (Guilleragues)

1683–1687	*Lettres galantes (Fontenelle)
1684–1686	*L'espion du grand seigneur (Marana)
1691–1694	*Letters Writ by a Turkish Spy (Anon.)
1732	*Lettres de la Marquise (Crébillon fils)
1740	*Pamela (Richardson)
1741	*Pamela in High Life (Anon.)
1747	*Lettres d'une Péruvienne (Graffigny)
1749	*Lettres d'Aza (Lamarche)
1750	*Lettres de Ninon (Damours)
1757	*Lettres de Mistress Fanni Butlerd (Riccoboni)
1759	*Lettres de Milady Juliette Catesby (Riccoboni)
1761	*Memoirs of Miss Sidney Biddulph (Sheridan)
1762	*The Citizen of the World (Goldsmith)
1767	*Lettres d'Adélaïde de Dammartin (Riccoboni)
1768	*Lettres de la Duchesse (Crébillon fils)
1770	*Lettres polonoises (Marat)
	*Le pornographe (Restif de la Bretonne)
1771	*Lettres de madame la Marquise de Pompadour (Barbé-Marbois)
1772	*Lettres d'Elisabeth-Sophie de Vallière (Riccoboni)
1774	*Die Leiden des Jungen Werthers (Goethe)
1777	Chant de Schwarzbourg (Charbonnière)
	*Lettres de Mylord Rivers (Riccoboni)
1783	*Le mari sentimental (Constant de Rebeque)
1784	*Lettres de Mistriss Henley (Charrière)
	*Lettres neuchâteloises (Charrière)
1785	*Lettres écrites de Lausanne (Charrière)
1786–1789	*Der Geisterscher (Schiller)
1789	Ein Tagebuch (Tieck)
1791	*Hermione (Anon.)
1792	The Butler's Diary (Anon.)
1794	*Adèle de Sénange (Sousa Botelho)
1798	*Claire d'Albe (Cottin)
1801	Charles et Marie (Sousa Botelho)
1802	*Le ultime lettere di Jacopo Ortis (Foscolo)
1803	Le peintre de Saltzbourg (Nodier)
1804	*Valérie (Krüdener)
	Obermann (Sénancour)
1808	Eugène de Rothelin (Sousa Botelho)
1815	The Bachelor's Journal (Byron)
1816	The Spinster's Journal (Byron)
1820	*Adèle (Nodier)
1824	"En landsbydegns dagbog" (Blicher)
	*Spader dame (Livijn)
	*Vingt-quatre heures d'une femme sensible (Salm)
1826	Diary of an Ennuyée (Jameson)
	"Den ensamma" (Bremmer)
1828	Le dernier jour d'un condamné (Hugo)

Bibliography

1829	"Praesteni Vejlbye" (Blicher)
1831	"MS Found in a Bottle" (Poe)
1835	"Zapiski cumashedshego" (Gogol)
1835–1836	*Mademoiselle de Maupin (Gautier)
1836	Diary of a Desennuyé (Gore)
1838	Diary Illustrative of the Times of George the Fourth (Bury)
1840	Geroi nashego vremeni (Lermontov)
	"The Journal of Julius Rodman" (Poe)
1841	Hinterlassene Papiere (Weisser)
1843	En dagbok (Bremer)
	Forförens dagbog (Kierkegaard)
1844	Diary of Lady Willoughby (Rathbone)
1845	"Skyldig?"—"Ikke-Skyldig?" ("Dagbog") (Kierkegaard)
1845–1846	The Diary of C. Jeames de la Pluche, Esq. (Thackeray)
1846	Isadora (Sand)
1847	Some Further Portions of the Diary of Lady Willoughby (Rathbone)
1848	"Belyi nochi" (Dostoevsky)
	Margaret Smith's Journal (Whittier)
1850	"Dnevnik lisniago cheloveka" (Turgenev)
1855	Mémoires d'un suicidé (Du Camp)
	Mary Powell (Manning)
	*" 'Faust' " (Turgenev)
1856	La Daniella (Sand)
1857	*La petite comtesse (Feuillet)
	"Le journal d'une jeune femme" (Second)
1859	Deborah's Diary (Manning)
1865	The Diary of Brother Bartholomew (Charles)
	The Diary of Kitty Trevylyan (Charles)
	"La confession de Claude" (Zola)
1866	Igrok (Dostoevsky)
1867	Vie et opinions (Taine)
1868	The Gates Ajar (Phelps)
1869	Storia di una capinera (Verga)
1871	Journal of Lady Beatrix Graham (Yonge)
1878	Le journal d'une femme (Feuillet)
1879	"Trus" (Garshin)
	"The Diary of a Man of Fifty" (James)
1881	Le crime de Sylvestre Bonnard (France)
1882	Angéline de Montbrun (Conan)
1883	"The Impressions of a Cousin" (James)
1885	"Un fou" (Maupassant)
	"Mes vingt-cinq jours" (Maupassant)
	La course à la mort (Rod)
1886	"Le horla" (Maupassant)
1887	"Alicia's Diary" (Hardy)
1889	Le sens de la vie (Rod)
	"Der Andere" (Schnitzler)

1891	*Robes rouges* (Adam)
	Traete maend (Garborg)
	Les cahiers d'André Walter (Gide)
1892	"The Yellow Wallpaper" (Gilman)
	The Diary of a Nobody (Grossmith)
	"Der Sohn" (Schnitzler)
1893	"L'inéluctable" (Adam)
	Gladys (Le Roux)
	"Extracts from Adam's Diary" (Twain)
1894	"Blumen" (Schnitzler)
1895	*Medusas hufvud* (Geijerstam)
	Paludes (Gide)
1896–1898	*Pages from a Private Diary* (Sylvan)
1897	"Die Frau des Weisen" (Schnitzler)
1898	*Julies dagbog* (Nansen)
1900	*Le journal d'une femme de chambre* (Mirbeau)
	En praests dagbog (Obstfelder)
1901	"tagebuch 1900" (Hesse)
	Monsieur de Phocas (Lorrain)
1902	*Les vingt et un jours* (Mirbeau)
	The Real Diary of a Real Boy (Shute)
1903	*The Private Papers of Henry Ryecroft* (Gissing)
	Briefe, die ihn nicht erreichten (Heyking)
	The Journal of Arthur Stirling (Sinclair)
1904	*Krasnyĭ smekh* (Andreyev)
	"Sequil" (Shute)
1905	*Tagebuch einer Verlorenen* (Böhme)
	Doktor Glas (Söderberg)
	"Eve's Diary" (Twain)
	Jacob von Gunten (Walser)
1907	*La 628-E8* (Mirbeau)
1908	*Memorial de Ayres* (Machado de Assis)
1909	*Ausflüge ins Dunkelrote* (Brod)
1910	*Den farlige alder* (Michaelis)
	Die Aufzeichnungen des Malte Laurids Brigge (Rilke)
1912	*Daddy-Long-Legs* (Webster)
1913	*Doktor Bürgers Ende* (Carossa)
	Jung Schuk (Goering)
	A. O. Barnabooth (Larbaud)
1914	*Colas Breugnon* (Rolland)
1915	*Dear Enemy* (Webster)
1916	*Igo voĭny* (Andreyev)
1917	*Ninas dagbog* (Krusenstjerna)
1919	*Dnevnik Satany* (Andreyev)
	La symphonie pastorale (Gide)
	"Confessions d'un moineau du siècle" (Goll)
	"Journal d'un cheval" (Goll)

Bibliography

1920	*The Story of Opal* (Whiteley)
1921	**The Young Cadet* (Hofland)
1923	**Zoo* (Shklovsky)
1923–1924	*Dnevnik Kosti Riabtseva* (Ognev)
1924	"Karamora" (Gorky)
	My (Zamyatin)
1925	*The Diary of a Young Lady of Fashion* (King-Hall)
	Gentlemen Prefer Blondes (Loos)
	The Red Lamp (Rinehart)
1926	*Z dnia na dzien* (Goetel)
1927	*Journal de Salavin* (Duhamel)
1929	*L'école des femmes* (Gide)
	Michael: Ein deutsches Schicksal in Tagebuchblättern (Goebbels)
1930	*Eva* (Chardonne)
	Diary of a Provincial Lady (Delafield)
1932	*Le noeud de vipères* (Mauriac)
1933	*Diary of a Deaf-Mute* (Chagall)
1934	"Journal d'un homme trompé" (Drieu La Rochelle)
1936	*Journal d'un curé de campagne* (Bernanos)
	Journal d'un imprudent (Blond)
	Novel on Yellow Paper (Smith)
1938	"The Great American Novel . . ." (Davis)
	The Black Book (Durrell)
	La nausée (Sartre)
1939	*La douceur de la vie* (Romains)
1941	"A Summer in Puerto Rico" (Clark)
	The Journal of Albion Moonlight (Patchen)
	As for Me and My House (Ross)
	Mrs. Tim Carries On (Stevenson)
1942	*Primer for Combat* (Boyle)
1943	*The Polderoy Papers* (Vulliamy)
1944	*Dangling Man* (Bellow)
	Journal d'un salaud (Queffélec)
	Doctor Philligo (Vulliamy)
1945	*Un beau ténébreux* (Gracq)
	The Journal of Mary Hervey Russell (Jameson)
1946	*La culbute* (Queffélec)
1947	*Les carnets du bon Dieu* (Daninos)
1948	*Vannen Patrik* (Wall)
1949	**"The NRACP"* (Elliott)
	Drömmar om rosor och eld (Johnson)
1950	*Lögneren* (Hansen)
	The Wall (Hersey)
	*Another Pamela (Sinclair)
1951	*Malone meurt* (Beckett)
	Désirée (Selinko)

1952	*Il quaderno proibito* (Cèspedes)
1954	*Stiller* (Frisch)
	The Journal of Edwin Carp (Haydn)
1955	*The Brightfount Diaries* (Aldiss)
1956	*L'emploi du temps* (Butor)
	"Pages from an Abandoned Journal" (Vidal)
1957	*Journal intime d'Hercule* (Dubois la Chartre)
	The Red Rock Wilderness (Huxley)
1958	*Diary of a Fashion Model* (Chitty)
1960	**Le mur de la vie privée* (Jouffroy)
1961	"Through the Panama" (Lowry)
1962	*The Golden Notebook* (Lessing)
	Les oeuvres complètes de Sally Mara (Queneau)
1963	*The Collector* (Fowles)
	Journal d'une femme en blanc (Soubiran)
	The Sex Diary of Gerard Sorme (Wilson)
1964	*Diary of a Paranoic* (Mumford)
1965	*The (Diblos) Notebook* (Merrill)
	L'attenzione (Moravia)
	After All, This Is England (Muller)
	The Mallot Diaries (Nathan)
	Journal of the Fictive Life (Nemerov)
	Les cahiers d'une hypocrite (Singer)
1966	*Diary of an Old Man* (Bermant)
	The Diary of a Rapist (Connell)
	Flowers for Algernon (Keyes)
1967	*La femme rompue* (Beauvoir)
	"If I Should Open My Mouth" (Bowles)
	Salut Galarneau (Godbout)
	Diary of a Mad Housewife (Kaufman)
	I, Roberta (Vining)
1968	*Le libraire* (Bessette)
	Lilo's Diary (Elman)
	The Missolonghi Manuscript (Prokosch)
	Excerpts from the Diaries of the Late God (Towne)
	Myra Breckinridge (Vidal)
1969	*Trixie* (Graves)
	Real People (Lurie)
1970	*The Diary of A. N.* (Horwitz)
	Ernste Absicht (Wohmann)
1971	*Go Ask Alice* (Anon.)
	The Season of the Witch (Herlihy)
	Ze wspomnien Ljona Tichego (Lem)
1972	*The Late Great Creature* (Brower)
	Ella Price's Journal (Bryant)
	Des bleus à l'ame (Sagan)

Bibliography

1974	*Cher Untel* (Gautier)
	Myron (Vidal)
1975	*Celebration* (Swados)
	A Month of Sundays (Updike)
1976	*The Spectator Bird* (Stegner)
1977	*In the Heart of the Country* (Coetzee)
	"The Letters of the Samantha" (Helprin)
1978	*En biodlares dod* (Gustafsson)
	A Woman of Independent Means (Hailey)
1979	*The Princess of 72nd Street* (Kraf)
1980	*Sheltered Lives* (Hazzard)
1982	*The Color Purple* (Walker)

Index

Alter, Robert, 38n
Altman, Janet Gurkin, 17n, 91n
Amiel, Henri, 35, 83, 190
Amiel novel, 35-36, 83
Arnold, Matthew, 34
Atkins, Stuart, 59n
Aubignac, Abbé d': Le roman de lettres, 79n
Augustine, 135
Authenticity. See Sincerity
Autobiography, 56-57; Puritan spiritual autobiography, 87, 89, 90
Automatic writing, 84, 145

Barbellion, W.N.P., 26
Barbusse, Henri: L'enfer, 42n, 150; Le feu, 150n
Barstis, Lyn, 16n, 25n, 207
Barthes, Roland, 153n, 204
Baumbach, Jonathan, 163n
Beauvoir, Simone de, 25; La femme rompue (The Woman Destroyed), 25-26, 109, 110; La force de l'âge (The Prime of Life), 36n, 152n
Becker, Ernest, 122
Beckett, Samuel, 17, 53, 109, 149, 183-206; Company, 203; Enough, 184; Ill Seen Ill Said, 203; Krapp's Last Tape, 208; Malone Dies, 184-194, 195, 196, 202, 203, 204, 205; Molloy, 20n, 195-196, 204n; The Unnamable, 184, 195-202, 203; Waiting for Godot, 184, 195, 196-197, 201; Watt, 173
Bellow, Saul, 17, 25, 53, 109, 159-182,

203; on Beckett, 183-184; response to Sartre, 160-161, 165-168, 169n, 171-172; The Adventures of Augie March, 159, 165n, 171; Dangling Man, 159-168, 172-181, 184, 203; "The Gonzaga Manuscripts," 165n; Henderson the Rain King, 164, 165n, 168, 171; Herzog, 165n, 178-180; "Looking for Mr. Green," 172-174; "Mosby's Memoirs," 175-178; Seize the Day, 165n; To Jerusalem and Back, 171-172; The Victim, 165n
Bergson, Henri: theory of laughter, 175, 177, 179n
Bernanos, Georges, 25; Journal d'un curé de campagne (Diary of a Country Priest), 125, 126-129, 130, 134-135, 142-143, 187
Bildungsroman: Bellow's approach to, 164, 179-180
Blackwood, Caroline: The Stepdaughter, 42n, 208
Blanchot, Maurice, 17n
Bourget, Paul: Le fantôme, 208
Boursault, Edme: Lettres de Babet, 78-80
Bowles, Paul: "If I Should Open My Mouth," 22n
Boyd, Michael, 39n
Bradbury, Malcolm, 39n
Brang, Peter, 17n
Breton, André, 84
Brontë, Charlotte, 51

Index

Butor, Michel, 153, 155-156; *L'emploi du temps* (*Passing Time*), 154-155
Byron, Lord, 64n, 65, 66; *Childe Harold's Pilgrimage*, 63-64, 94; *Don Juan*, 64n

Cadalso, José: *Cartas marruecas*, 209
Cambridge Apostles, 99-100
Camus, Albert, 149n, 169n
Capacchione, Lucia, 109
Character in fiction, 32-36; in Bellow, 160-182; in the nouveau roman, 154-156
Charbonnière, Ramond de: *Chant de Schwarzbourg*, 18
Clayton, John Jacob, 160n
Cohn, Dorrit, 17n
Coleridge, Samuel Taylor, 95-99, 100, 101, 102, 105n, 106, 189; "The Eolian Harp," 98; "Frost at Midnight," 98, 105; "This Lime-tree Bower my Prison," 96-98
Conrad, Joseph, 182n
Correspondence fiction. *See* Epistolary fiction
Crébillon fils, 18, 34, 80; *Lettres de la Marquise*, 55-56
Culler, Jonathan, 153, 181

Dard, Frédéric: *C'est mourir un peu*, 150n
Davis, Clyde Brion: "The Great American Novel," 54n
Defoe, Daniel: *Robinson Crusoe*, 24, 86-88, 90, 94
Delany, Paul, 80n
Deloffre, F., 73, 78
Derrida, Jacques, 56, 153n, 194; *La carte postale*, 194n
Diary (nonfictional), 26, 43-44, 46-47; Catholic diaries, 125n; dream journals, 84; as popular therapy, 107-109; Puritan diaries, 85-86, 87, 88, 89, 94, 109; the "unwritten journal," 150-153. *See also* Journal intime
Diary novel, 80; distinguished from diary fiction, 15-18, 37; female version, 16; male version, 15-17; and Beckett's *Malone Dies*, 185-194; and Bellow's *Dangling Man*, 159-160; and Sartre's *Nausea*, 137, 160
Didier, Béatrice, 181

Dostoevsky, Fyodor, 167, 169n; *The Eternal Husband*, 165n; *Notes from Underground*, 122, 161
Dronke, E. P., 78
Duhamel, Georges: *Journal de Salavin* (*Salavin's Journal*), 86n, 191-192
Durrell, Lawrence: *Alexandria Quartet*, 54; *The Black Book*, 27, 54n

Elliott, George P.: "The NRACP," 25
Epistolary fiction, 18, 28; correspondence mode, 10-11, 24, 79-80, 91, 94; and diary fiction, 9-11; early history of, 79-80; in Goethe's *Werther*, 57-59; Guilleragues's contribution, 73, 79-82; in Richardson's novels, 88-94; single letter-writer mode, 9-11, 39, 73, 79-81, 207, 208
Esslin, Martin, 149
Expressive text, 55-64, 70-71, 81-82, 83-84; Bellow's *Dangling Man* as, 162-163; Bernanos's *Diary of a Country Priest* as, 126-129; Mauriac's *Viper's Tangle* as, 130; and Rousseau, 56-57; and Sartre, 138, 140-141

Farrell, James T., 168n
Fatalism and literary form, 34-36, 55-56, 57, 60, 62-63, 68-69, 81-82
Faulkner, William: *Absalom, Absalom!*, 41, 182n
Fingal, 60
Fletcher, John, 39n
Fontenelle, Bernard de: *Lettres galantes*, 209
Ford, Ford Madox: *The Good Soldier*, 41
Forge, Sandrine: *Lily: The Diary of a French Girl in New York*, 150n
Foscolo, Ugo, 34; *Le ultime lettere di Jacopo Ortis* (*The Last Letters of Jacopo Ortis*), 62-63, 187
Fothergill, Robert, 47
Foucault, Michel, 204-205
Freud, Sigmund, 170, 171
Frisch, Max: *Stiller* (*I'm Not Stiller*), 20, 21, 24, 27

Garborg, Arne, 35, 83
Garshin, V., 150n
Gautier, Jean-Jacques: *Cher Untel*, 54n
Genette, Gérard, 17n, 29-30

Gennari, Geneviève: *Journal d'une bourgeoise*, 150n
Gide, André, 17, 25; *Les cahiers d'André Walter* (*Notebooks of André Walter*), 35, 83-84; *L'école des femmes* (*School for Wives*), 19, 21; *Les faux monnayeurs* (*The Counterfeiters*), 47, 54
Gilman, Charlotte Perkins: "The Yellow Wallpaper," 22n
Girard, Alain, 47n, 96
Giraud, Yves, 79n
Gissing, George: *The Private Papers of Henry Ryecroft*, 37n, 54n
Goering, Reinhard: *Jung Schuk*, 54n
Goetel, Ferdynand: *Z dnia na dzien* (*From Day to Day*), 54n
Goethe, Johann Wolfgang von, 53; *Dichtung und Wahrheit* (*Poetry and Truth*), 57-60, 158, 180; *Die Leiden des Jungen Werthers* (*The Sorrows of Young Werther*), 31, 32-33, 57-63, 64, 70-71, 79, 80, 81-82, 83, 84, 94, 113, 158, 159, 180-181, 185, 187, 189; *Wilhelm Meister*, 180
Gogol, Nikolai: "Zapiski cumashedshego" ("The Diary of a Madman"), 22
Gorky, Maxim: "Karamora," 20, 24, 209
Gracq, Julien: *Un beau ténébreux*, 54n
Graffigny, Mme, 80; *Lettres d'une Péruvienne*, 81
Green, Julian, 26, 85
Guilleragues, Gabriel-Josephe de: *Lettres portugaises* (*Portuguese Letters*), 34, 44n, 72-82
Gustafsson, Lars, 80; *En biodlares dod* (*The Death of a Beekeeper*), 110n, 187n

Hallam, Arthur, 99-100
Haller, William, 85n
Hansen, Martin A.: *Lögneren* (*The Liar*), 23, 24
Hardy, Thomas: "A Tryst at an Ancient Earthwork," 150n
Harvey, Lawrence, 204
Hauptmann, Gerhart: *Phantom*, 209
Hemingway, Ernest, 162-164, 168; *The Sun Also Rises*, 163
Hemmer, Jarl: *En man och hans samvete* (*A Man and His Conscience*), 24
Highman, David E., 78

Hogg, James: *Confessions of a Justified Sinner*, 86n
Homer: *The Iliad*, 169-170
Hugo, Victor: *Le dernier jour d'un condamné* (*Last Day of a Condemned Man*), 24, 31, 187
Hunter, J. Paul, 85n, 86, 88
Huxley, Elspeth: *The Red Rock Wilderness*, 20, 32

Interior monologue, 19, 39, 42, 151

James, Henry, 43, 178; *The Aspern Papers*, 165n; "The Diary of a Man of Fifty," 29, 33; "The Impressions of a Cousin," 21, 27
Johnson, Samuel, 49
Joubert, Joseph, 85
Journal intime, 25, 35, 43, 64, 83, 96; compared to the Puritan diary, 85; Valéry on, 141. *See also* Diary (nonfictional)
Joyce, James, 107
Jung, Carl, 108, 110

Kany, Charles E., 72
Kawin, Bruce F., 39n
Keats, John: "Ode to a Nightingale," 96n
Kellman, Steven G., 39n
Kermode, Frank, 44n, 142n
Kern, Edith, 17n, 142n
Kierkegaard, Sören: "Dagbog" ("Quidam's Diary"), 22-23
Kincaid, Juliet, 16n, 207
Koestler, Arthur, 169n
Kraf, Elaine: *The Princess of 72nd Street*, 22n

Laclos, Choderlos de: *Les liaisons dangereuses*, 91
Lagerkvist, Par: *Dvärgen* (*The Dwarf*), 42n, 150n, 208
Lamartine, Alphonse de: *Jocelyn*, 208
La Rochefoucauld, François de, 77
Lem, Stanislaw: *Ze wspomnien Ljona Tichego* (*The Futurological Congress*), 192n
Lermontov, Mikhail: *Geroi nashego vremeni* (*A Hero of Our Time*), 20, 63-70, 94, 187
Le Roux, Hugues, 35; *Au champs d'honneur*, 150; *Gladys*, 125n

Index

Lessing, Doris, 53; *Children of Violence*, 158; *The Four-Gated City*, 121, 158; *The Golden Notebook*, 109, 110-124, 125, 144, 145, 147, 154, 158, 159, 168, 174, 185; *The Grass Is Singing*, 118; *The Summer before the Dark*, 118-119

Letter fiction. *See* Epistolary fiction

Levy, Eric, 204

Lorrain, Jean, 35

Lowry, Malcolm: "Through the Panama," 54n

Lukács, Georg, 140

Lurie, Alison: *Real People*, 40-43, 45-48, 50-53, 61, 70, 94; *The War between the Tates*, 53

Malraux, André: *Les conquérants*, 42n, 208

Mann, Thomas, 169n; *Doktor Faustus*, 41; *Der Zauberberg (The Magic Mountain)*, 180

Marana, Giovanni: *L'espion turc*, 209

Martens, Lorna, 16n, 32-33, 35, 87, 154-155, 156, 207

Mattes, Eleanor B., 101n

Matthews, William, 44n, 47n

Maupassant, Guy de: "Un fou" ("A Madman"), 22n; "Le horla," 22n, 32

Mauriac, François, 25; Sartre's attack on, 137-139, 148; *La fin de la nuit*, 137; *Le noeud de vipères (Viper's Tangle)*, 125, 129-136, 138, 142-143, 147, 187

McCarthy, Mary, 175, 177

Mercier, Vivian, 195

Merrill, James: *The (Diblos) Notebook*, 54n

Mersereau, John, Jr., 68n

Metafiction, 38n. *See also* Reflexivity in literary texts

Milner, Marion, 107

Milton, John, 189, 190

Miner, Earl, 207

Mirrors and mirror scenes, 15, 25-26, 68-69, 84, 127, 131-133, 143, 156-157, 166-167

Montaigne, Michel de: *Essais*, 37n

Montesquieu, Charles Louis de: *Lettres persanes*, 209

Moravia, Alberto: *L'attenzione (The Lie)*, 27, 52-53

Murdoch, K., 85n

Nabokov, Vladimir, 171; *Despair*, 43-44; *Lolita*, 22

Nachtwachen des Bonaventura, 208

Nemerov, Howard: *Journal of the Fictive Life*, 54n

Neubert, Fritz, 17n

Niermeier, Stuart F. C., 101n

Nin, Anaïs, 107-108

Nodier, Charles, 34, 44; *Le peintre de Saltzbourg (The Painter of Salzburg)*, 62

Nouveau roman, 149, 150, 153-157, 160, 204; compared to Lessing's *Golden Notebook*, 119

O'Brien, Kate, 47n

Opdahl, Keith, 160n

Ortega y Gasset, José, 54, 146, 153

Ovid: *Heroides*, 73, 79n

Pepys, Samuel, 26

Pinget, Robert, 153

Plot in fiction, 32-36, 41-45, 82, 89-90, 92, 178

Poe, Edgar Allan: "MS Found in a Bottle," 28-29, 31-32, 187

Ponsonby, Arthur, 47n

Portuguese Letters. See Guilleragues, Gabriel-Joseph de

Prince, Gerald, 16n

Progoff, Ira, 108-109

Pusack, James P., 17n

Queneau, Raymond: *Les oeuvres complètes de Sally Mara*, 54n, 156

Rainer, Tristine, 107

Raoul, Valerie, 16n, 207

Realism and the diary strategy, 18-23, 186-189, 192-193

Reflexivity in literary texts: and the artistic development of writers, 50-53, 57-63, 158-206; contrasted with "expressive" writing, 57-63, 81-82, 83-84; general studies of, 38n; in the nouveau roman, 153-157; in Sartre's *Nausea*, 137-153; as self-concealment, 55-71; as self-discovery, 94-

136; as self-preservation, 72-82; writing as action, 38-54. *See also* Mirrors and mirror scenes

Ricardou, Jean, 156

Riccoboni, Mme, 18, 34, 80

Richardson, Samuel, 33, 99, 189; "writing to the moment," 29, 88n, 91, 96; *Clarissa*, 19, 88, 89-94, 187, 188-189; *Pamela*, 18, 18n, 30, 32, 34, 88-90, 91, 186, 188, 208

Ricoeur, Paul, 49-50

Rilke, Rainer Maria, 25; *Die Aufzeichnungen des Malte Laurids Brigge* (*The Notebooks of Malte Laurids Brigge*), 27, 54n, 78, 138n

Rinehart, Mary Roberts: *The Red Lamp*, 32

Robbe-Grillet, Alain, 149, 153, 156, 181, 205

Rod, Edouard, 35, 83; *La course à la mort*, 44

Romberg, Bertil, 17n

Rousseau, Jean-Jacques, 194; *Confessions*, 20, 56-57, 64, 70, 85

Rousset, Jean, 17n, 18, 29-30, 186

Rovit, Earl, 178

Sagan, Françoise: *Des bleus à l'âme*, 54n

Said, Edward, 205

Sainte-Beuve, Charles-Augustin: *Joseph Delorme*, 209

Sand, George, 44

Sartre, Jean-Paul, 17, 25, 28, 53, 169n, 171-172, 174, 185; attack on Mauriac, 137-138, 140, 148; *L'être et le néant* (*Being and Nothingness*), 139n; *Les mots* (*The Words*), 152; *La nausée* (*Nausea*), 26, 36, 48, 54n, 109, 115, 137-153, 154, 156, 160-161, 165-168, 190, 192, 193; *Qu'est-ce que la littérature?* (*What Is Literature?*), 150; *Saint Genêt*, 143; *Le sursis* (*The Reprieve*), 152

Schiller, Friederich: *Der Geisterscher*, 30

Schlegel, A. W., 95, 189

Schnitzler, Arthur, 150n

Scholes, Robert E., 39n

Self-conscious texts, 38n. *See also* Reflexivity in literary texts

Sénancour, Etienne Pivert de, 44; *Obermann*, 19, 37n, 209

Sendry, Joseph, 101n

Shelley, Percy Bysshe: "Mont Blanc," 96n

Sheridan, Mrs. Frances, 80; *Memoirs of Miss Sidney Biddulph*, 18n

Shklovsky, Viktor, 153n

Simon, Claude, 153, 154, 155, 205; *Les corps conducteurs*, 153; *Triptique*, 156

Sincerity, 47, 55, 57, 141; and authenticity, 21-23, 52-53, 70-71, 80-82; Sartre and, 139

Sinclair, Upton: *The Journal of Arthur Stirling*, 54n

Söderberg, Hjalmar, 44, 83; *Doktor Glas*, 26, 35-36

Spitzer, Leo, 78

Starr, G. A., 85n

Stegner, Wallace: *The Spectator Bird*, 145-146

Steinbeck, John, 168n

Stoker, Bram: *Dracula*, 32

Stream of consciousness. *See* Interior monologue

Surrealism, 84

Tennyson, Alfred, Lord, 53; *In Memoriam*, 94, 99, 100-106, 107, 108, 148, 158, 189-190

Todorov, Tzvetan, 91n

Trilling, Lionel, 21, 71, 80

Turgenev, Ivan, 25; "Dnevnik lisniago cheloveka" ("Diary of a Superfluous Man"), 187

Turnell, Martin, 135n

Twain, Mark, 209; *Huckleberry Finn*, 180; *The Innocents Abroad*, 192n

Untermeyer, Louis, 47

Updike, John, 25; *A Month of Sundays*, 20, 24, 46-47, 48

Valéry, Paul, 141

Verne, Jules: *Voyage au centre de la terre* (*A Journey to the Center of the Earth*), 27-28, 30-31

Watt, Ian, 18, 33n, 99, 192

Weber, Ronald, 171n

Werther novel, 32-36, 62-63

Whiteley, Opal: *The Story of Opal*, 209

Wolff, Cynthia Griffin, 88-89, 90n

Wordsworth, William, 100, 102; *The Prelude*, 96n; "Tintern Abbey," 96n

Writing as action. *See* Reflexivity in literary texts
Writing to the moment. *See* Richardson, Samuel

Young, Edward: *Conjectures on Original Composition*, 95, 189

Zamyatin, Yevgeni, 25; *My (We)*, 54n, 208
Zimmerman, Everett, 86

LIBRARY OF CONGRESS CATALOGING IN PUBLICATION DATA

Abbott, H. Porter.
  Diary fiction.

  Bibliography. p.
  Includes index.
    1. Fiction, Autobiographic—History and criticism. 2. Diaries—History and
criticism. 3. Epistolary fiction—History and criticism. I. Title.
PN3448.A8A2 1984   809.3   84-7111
ISBN 0-8014-1713-9 (alk. paper)